MY BRIDGE TO AMERICA

SAM KUSUMOTO with Edmund P. Murray

MY BRIDGE TO AMERICA

Discovering the New World for Minolta

E. P. DUTTON　　NEW YORK

Published in the United States by E. P. Dutton,
a division of Penguin Books USA Inc.,
2 Park Avenue, New York, N.Y. 10016.

Published simultaneously in Canada
by Fitzhenry and Whiteside, Limited, Toronto.

Library of Congress Cataloging-in-Publication Data

Kusumoto, Sam, 1928–
My bridge to America : discovering the new world for Minolta / Sam
Kusumoto with Edmund P. Murray.
p.   cm.
Includes index.
ISBN 0-525-24787-4
1. Kusumoto, Sam, 1928–   .   2. Businessmen—Japan—Biography.
3. Camera industry—Japan—History—20th century.   4. Camera
industry—United States—History—20th century.   5. Minolta camera—
Marketing.   6. Minolta Corporation—History.   I. Murray, Edmund P.
II. Title.
HD9708.5.C352K87   1989
338.7'681418—dc20

[B]   89-32253
                                                           CIP

Designed by Steven N. Stathakis

1   3   5   7   9   10   8   6   4   2

First Edition

*To the generous,
bighearted,
open-minded people
of America*

Acknowledgments

Many people—and one Minolta word processor—have played important roles in the inspiration, genesis, research, editing, proofreading, and production of our manuscript. Among the most helpful have been Mayumi Moriyama, Masahiro Tano, Jesse Wilkes, Jim de Merlier, John Vacca, Jim Sparks, Al Shapiro, Andy Armstrong, Kathy Lynch, Diane Allen, Debbie Turchiarelli, and Dean Reonieri. They deserve our thanks as do many others, mentioned in the pages that follow, who created the world our book seeks to describe. Without them, this book truly could not have been written. Among many mentors and sources of inspiration there are two who must be given special mention: Kuniko Kusumoto and the late Kazuo Tashima.

Contents

IV: THE GOLDEN YEARS 1958–1969

V: DRAWN TO THE MAGNET 1969–1989

Photo sections follow pages 118 and 246.

I

MY HERITAGE

1928–1945

1

"The Henry Ford
of Korea"

Two important events in my life occurred in 1928. I was born. So was Minolta. Under the name Nichi-Doku Shashinki Shoten, Minolta was born in Osaka, Japan. Under the name Sadahei Kusumoto, I was born in Seoul, the cold and remote capital of what was then the Japanese colony of Korea.

My grandfather's adventurous spirit, which first brought our clan to Korea, marched in lockstep with Japan's military and economic expansionism of that era. Japan, an insular, isolated, and rather backward feudal empire, had been "opened" to foreign ideas and trade during the latter half of the nineteenth century. Heavy pressure from Western nations, particularly the United States and Great Britain, propelled Japan into a more active role in world affairs. Within a few decades Japan became an eager player on the international stage.

My grandfather, Kichitaro, saw great economic opportunity in Korea. He had been a soldier in the Imperial Japanese Army, serving in both Korea and Manchuria, areas that Japan saw as buffers against the rival imperialism of Russia. After Japan startled the world by winning its war with Russia in 1904–05 and driving the Russians from Korea and Manchuria, my grandfather returned to his home in

Tanabe, a port city in Wakayama prefecture about eighty miles south of Osaka. Like many young veterans of war, he was restless and ambitious. As a younger son, he had limited economic prospects at home, and so he returned to Korea to seek his fortune.

He tried many ventures, and, throughout his life, dabbled as an inventor. My grandmother, Yuki, called his inventions "silly stuff," including his dream of creating a perpetual motion machine. But my grandfather never gave up trying to follow in the footsteps of his father. My great-grandfather, whose name, like mine, was Sadahei Kusumoto, was perhaps best known for a surveying instrument he invented in the nineteenth century for measuring distances and setting boundaries. As far I know, none of my grandfather's inventions amounted to anything, but he did develop a successful business in Korea distributing an irrigation pump.

As early as 1910, he became interested in a Ford dealership. He started handling Fords, primarily trucks, and by the mid-1920s knew he had the opportunity to build a truly prosperous Ford dealership. By 1929 he had become the exclusive Ford dealer for all of Korea.

But he had a major handicap. He spoke no English. The American representatives of Ford spoke no Japanese. My grandfather had no sons, but he did have a daughter, Fumie, of marriageable age. He began looking for a suitable son-in-law. Qualifications: well educated and of good family; no prospects of inheritance; capable of taking over the business and a knowledge of English. Through friends, he found a promising candidate, Enichiro Ohara.

The proper arrangements were made and, soon after the marriage, my grandfather formally adopted my father. In time, my father could inherit the business. Until postwar changes were made in inheritance laws, such arrangements were necessary when the head of a company wanted to pass the firm on to his son-in-law.

My father and grandfather were completely opposite types. My grandfather was a distinguished-looking man, so handsome that people often said he should have been a Kabuki actor. He enjoyed life, liked to drink and party and make the people around him happy. I can remember him coming home in a rickshaw from the teahouse, happy with drink, sometimes bringing a geisha girl or two with him. My grandmother did not seem to mind and, as far as I know, there were no particular romances involved.

In selecting my father as son-in-law, adopted son, business partner, and successor, my grandfather had chosen well. My father was a more serious-minded, sobersided man. I suspect my father was a better businessman, but I have fonder memories of my grandfather.

From family conversations, I know that Benjamin Copf, who was then Ford's representative based in Japan, was a visitor to our family home and the dealership. But I have no recollection of meeting him. My earliest memories, primed by old photographs, date from the 1930s. By then, my grandfather's Ford dealership was a thriving business, and my father played a major role in day-to-day operations.

My grandfather's joyous love of life and the extent to which the Ford dealership was integrated into the way the family lived were perhaps the strongest influences on my early childhood. The Ford showroom and offices were at street level and our living quarters were on the second floor of our spacious main building. By the mid-1930s the flourishing dealership in Seoul and the suburban assembly plant for truck bodies employed about five hundred people. We usually had several employees, both Japanese and Korean, living with us. It was a teeming household. With family members, six or seven maids, plus ten or more employees, we usually totaled about thirty people.

I had my own exclusive maid, as did my brother, Koji, and in many respects our lives were sheltered. Our maids were fiercely protective of us. I remember one family argument started by Koji's maid. She was upset because I was always given new clothes while Koji, younger than I, often inherited what I had outgrown. My mother tried to explain that this was only natural, but to keep peace with the maid she had to buy at least some brand-new things for Koji.

Everyone spoiled us, but as my grandfather's favorite, I was more spoiled than Koji. My grandfather went to Japan every year and of the many presents he brought back the finest were always for me. My favorite was a miniature electric car that was very unusual in those days. The mechanics in our Ford service department fitted it out with directional signals that popped out from the sides and rice straw curtains for the windows. They even made tiny tire skirts, like those on larger vehicles, that protected pedestrians from mud splashes, which were common on the mostly unpaved roads of Korea. My customized little car caused a great sensation whenever I was allowed to play with it outdoors. My grandfather gave me so many wonderful presents, I can't remember them all. On the other hand, I don't remember any presents that my father ever gave me.

Rather than bring me gifts when he traveled, it was more my father's style to take me with him, both on trips to the north and to Japan. Though I didn't live in Japan until I was seventeen, those frequent trips and close family ties left no doubt in my mind that I was Japanese. That lesson was reinforced in Korea. It was part of our privileged life that, as a family of prosperous and important Japanese, we never had to learn to speak Korean. It was up to the Koreans to learn Japanese. But this was not just a family matter. Under a policy of assimilation that went into effect in 1937, Japanese became the only language used in schools throughout Korea. At that time, Japan sought to integrate Koreans into Japanese society.

Korea was then a poor and economically backward country. Japan thought that the way for Koreans to become more prosperous was to become fully Japanese, and they were expected to adapt to our language and culture. The brightest went to the best Japanese schools and were groomed for leadership. Intermarriage was encouraged. But what the Japanese saw as a progressive path to integration, many Koreans saw as an effort to destroy their rich cultural heritage and to deny their long history as an independent people. Japanese often pay tribute to China as the mother of our culture. We use Chinese characters in our language. Brush strokes that evolved from calligraphy to painting in the Chinese classical style influenced our art. But we ignore the fact that, with the exception of language, China's cultural influence came through a Korean civilization more advanced in many ways than Japan's had been in earlier centuries. The teachings of Confucius are reflected in our moral philosophy, and our music carries echoes from China, but Korea was the medium through which those influences reached Japan. Buddhism, though it originated in India, also came to Japan through Korea, and more direct cultural influences include pottery and other crafts which the Koreans taught us. Yet we tend to ignore all we have learned from Korea and scorn it as a primitive culture.

Today I can see why Koreans resented Japan's effort to integrate them into our way of life. And clearly, not all Japanese policies toward Koreans were well intentioned. Particularly during the war years, many Koreans were recruited, sometimes with little or no choice, to work for Japanese industries both in Korea and in Japan and even into the Japanese military. But then, living in a household with so many Japanese-speaking Koreans, I truly believed we were all one family. Of course, I was very young.

During the 1930s, Japan's relations with the United States began to deteriorate. Japan's liberal "Taisho democracy," which had evolved since 1913, had run its course by 1932. Civilian government collapsed as the military became first the *de facto* executors of foreign policy and then the dominant force in domestic politics. The occupation of Manchuria in 1931 was the first in a series of events that put Japan at odds with the United States. At the height of the Taisho democracy, during the 1920s, urban Japan experienced an era of prosperity and Westernization that left rural Japan relatively untouched. Japan has always lacked natural energy resources, and as industrialization accelerated, oil imports soaked up the country's limited supply of foreign currency. By the mid-1930s, an anti-Western backlash, set off in part by the worldwide depression that affected both cities and countryside, soon affected all aspects of life. Western cultural influences and imported products were discouraged. Even in Korea, these changes could be felt. With American dollars in short supply, the government began to curtail import licenses.

My father decided to reduce the dollar cost of his imported trucks by starting an assembly plant in Ruyzan, a suburb of Seoul about fifteen miles south of our home. He imported the chassis and engines from America, then built the bodies and assembled the trucks in Ruyzan. Our drivers had to chauffeur the bodiless chassis from the port of Pusan to the assembly plant at Ruyzan, about two hundred miles. Because the roads of Korea were so rough, the open chassis were difficult to control, and dangerous. I was always trying to get one of the drivers to give me a ride. All were wise enough to refuse.

The body shop in Ruyzan became our favorite playground. Huge piles of tires wrapped in brown gauze provided the setting for our games of hiding as Koji and I chased each other, climbing the pillars of tires. That shop had a very special smell, compounded of rubber, grease, oil, motor fuel, paint, upholstery—a mixture that I identified as a very American smell. *Smell* has a special meaning in Japanese; it is not just an odor, but also the essence of something. When we say something has "the American smell," we mean something that has characteristics we think of as typical of America. I was beginning to catch that American smell, and to dream of that land that so fascinated my father and grandfather.

As a playground, the body shop was probably dangerous. But my father insisted that we avoid the rough games played by children outdoors, thus confining us to the playground of towering tires and sharp, metal auto parts. I don't recall any serious accidents, but to this day I blame my father for my lack of ability and interest in any form of athletics or exercise. Though exposed to sports, including martial arts in school, we were too well guarded as children to develop the basic skills and physical instincts of the competitive athlete.

Our family had a new Ford four-door passenger car every year. Nearly all of our sales were to the government, but most were trucks, private cars being rare. My father's license plate always bore the number 5. Number 1 was the license plate of General Jiro Minami, the Japanese governor-general of Korea; number 2 went to the highest-ranking army general; numbers 3 and 4 went to other high-ranking police and military officials. One of my games was to slip into my father's car, turn on the ignition, and pretend I was taking Koji for a drive. Fortunately, my legs were too short for me to take my game any further. Even more fortunately, my father never caught me.

It was one of my father's fantasies that everyone in America led a refined, cultured life. Among the treasured possessions in our family were Victrolas, the old Victor phonograph players, first the windup variety with a big, hornlike loudspeaker, and then an electric model that my father played each evening at dinnertime. His favorites were twelve-inch, seventy-eight rpm classical records with red labels. The popular music, which I preferred, had black labels. Schubert's symphonies were a particular favorite with my father, if not with the rest of the family. When I came to America many years later I expected to hear Schubert played at every dinner table.

The record player was also used to accompany the promotional slide presentations provided by Ford. The recordings were in English, so no one but my father understood them. The same was true of the brochures, posters, and other printed material. I couldn't read them, but they had that American smell and were impressive to look at with images that set my mind dreaming of the idealized America they represented.

My favorite form of entertainment—and of wonderful misinformation about America—was the movies. The local movie theater was across the road from our Ford showroom and home. Many of the movies were American, and I was there as often as possible. The musical comedies, which I took as literal depictions of life in the United States, were my favorites. But I was an uncritical sponge, soaking up whatever images flickered on the screen. Japanese and German movies were also shown, and I enjoyed the popular American fan magazines, like *Silver Screen* and *Photoplay*. Even though I couldn't read English, I could get some sense of what the stories were about from the photos. I learned to recognize stars like Greta Garbo, Jean Arthur, Gary Cooper, Robert Taylor, Irene Dunne, Ginger Rogers, Fred Astaire, Jeanette MacDonald and Nelson Eddy and believed that the roles they played represented the way people really lived in America.

In this still relatively liberal period when Japan's free press had not yet been muzzled by the military, Japanese magazines like *Shin-seinen*, which means "The New Young Men," still featured photos of seminaked girls, love stories, and articles about American movies and movie stars and life in Europe and the United States. During the puritanical war years, old copies of such magazines were treasured by students and passed from hand to hand. With its samurai codes and glorification of suicidal death in combat, the military did its best to stamp out the influence of the West. But among young Japanese, fascination with the West—and with sex—never quite died.

Of all the American movies I saw in that era, perhaps none made as great an impression as the Deanna Durbin musical *One Hundred Men and a Girl*. It was the last American movie shown in Korea before the start of World War II and for me summed up all the romantic notions I had developed about life in America. Since it was years before I was able to see another American movie, its images lingered in my mind like a private movie of my own. Recently I found a videotape version of it and bored my family playing it over and over on our VCR. It brought back memories of my childhood in Korea and of the mythical America I inherited from my father and grandfather.

Though I shared in their dream of America, in my own childhood fantasy games I was still very Japanese. I often played the role of Futabayama, the sumo wrestler still considered to have been the greatest champion of all time. Poor Koji, four years younger and of course much smaller, was always the opponent Futabayama defeated. It takes a child's wild imagination to see me, age about ten, as a sumo wrestler. Even today, with a spare tire of my own, I weigh about 150 pounds.

Minolta entered my life at about this time through a Minoltaflex camera. I'd been using a toy camera known as a Togo, which was designed for children and named for Admiral Togo, a popular hero among young people because of his exploits in the 1904–05 war against Russia. I showed an interest in photography serious enough for one of my uncles, Seichi Kusumoto, who lived with us in Seoul, to teach me how to use his Minoltaflex, a twin-lens reflex camera based on the German Rolleiflex. I was soon taking snapshots whenever friends or relatives visited. People were always my favorite subject. When we went on class trips to scenic or historic sites, the pictures I took were dominated by my fellow students rather than monuments or scenery. Sadly, all the photos I took, and the camera itself, were lost in the aftermath of World War II.

From the Japanese point of view, that war began not on December 7, 1941, but in July 1937 when Japanese troops on maneuvers at Lukouch'iao, outside Peking, were fired on by Chinese troops. As a child, I could never understand how Japanese troops could have been on maneuvers in China. I later learned that other foreign powers, including the United States, Great Britain, France, and Germany, all had military units in China during this period, using the excuse of protecting their nationals who had economic interests there.

The incident at Lukouch'iao began the full-scale Sino-Japanese War. As the march of militarism became louder, war games played with toy guns around our fortress towers of gauze-wrapped tires took on a new intensity and meaning. Even the Korean game we played with spinning tops kept in motion as we whipped them with strings became a form of warfare as tops were set on collision courses. The victor was the top that kept spinning after the inevitable crash sent the other top to the ground. Sometimes both tops fell, but from all our history lessons we believed that Japan had never been defeated and would never fall.

While war clouds gathered across the rest of the world, this was a relatively prosperous and happy time for our family, isolated as we were in Korea. We bought a summer home outside Seoul for weekends. The house was near a bridge that spanned the Han River, which we knew by the Japanese name, Kanko. The gardens had their own small waterfall and Japanese pond. It was a big, sprawling structure with plenty of room for visiting relatives. Of course, my grandfather invited many friends. Often a geisha from the teahouse would come to help entertain our guests. The house itself resembled a traditional Japanese wood-frame teahouse with its sloping roof and long, rambling porch. One surviving though rather blurry photo shows a family group with geishas no doubt invited by my grandfather. I'm standing very stiffly in my militaristic school uniform. My grand-father, looking tipsy, holds my infant brother on his lap. From those old photos I can tell that my grandfather was still a handsome, vig-orous man, but at about this time he and my grandmother were preparing to retire to the family home in Tanabe.

In the splendid isolation of Seoul, with the assembly plant in full swing, our employees started calling my father "The Henry Ford of Korea." The name stuck, and my father was very proud of it, even through the war years, when we had to be quiet about it. When we left the country, as refugees after the war, our Korean friends revived the name in the presentation they made to my father at our farewell party.

I can remember the celebrations among the Japanese community in Seoul when Nanking fell in December 1937. There were parades with flags waving by day and lanterns flashing by night and shouts of "banzai"—"long life of ten thousand years." For us kids, it was all very exciting, and it was only many years later that I learned with shame of the atrocities committed by Japanese soldiers at Nanking.

In 1939 the government completely banned American automotive imports. My father had anticipated this move and had stocked enough spare parts to maintain a service operation and keep Korea's Fords running throughout the war. It was during one of the family's summer visits to Tanabe, also probably in 1939, that I had my first encounter with the realities of war. We had gone to spend some time at what is still a famous hot spring, Shirahama, outside Tanabe. The Japanese Red Cross had brought a group of twenty to thirty severely wounded soldiers from the war in China to recuperate at the spa. Many had lost limbs. Some still had open wounds and we could see blood that had soaked through their bandages. My father asked Koji and me to offer some money to buy *sake* for one group of soldiers. They were grateful and very moved. We expressed our sorrow, but the soldiers told us they were lucky. They had survived. They had been treated well. And they were home. Many of their comrades had not been so lucky.

I was still young, probably eleven or twelve, and still capable of being caught up in the romantic excitement, in the tales of heroism of a distant war. Until that time my idea of war had been colored by the glamorous legends of World War I aces like Captain Eddie Rick-enbacker and Baron von Richthofen and of Japan's Admiral Togo. Arms outstretched, I was a fighter plane, circling spare parts and stacks of tires in the body shop, machine guns chattering through my clenched teeth. Hands cupped to my eyes, I was Admiral Togo on the bridge of his battleship, the famous *Mikasa*. I didn't know that war could mean young men not much older than I with blood soaking through their bandages. But after that meeting, the war was never again quite so distant. I didn't suspect it at the time, but this was to be my last visit to Tanabe till after the war. Then we would be refugees, poor, hungry, but, like these soldiers, feeling lucky to be alive.

2

The War Years

Our middle school was as militaristic as the colonial government. I entered in April 1941, unaware, of course, how much my life and the world would change in that year. Elementary school had been difficult enough, but our Japanese middle school was the best and most demanding in Korea. My class at the Seoul Middle School had two hundred students, including a half-dozen exceptionally brilliant Koreans who spoke excellent Japanese. On our first day, the dean told us that we had all been the number one or number two student in our elementary schools. For six years I had been the number one or number two student. Now I was surrounded by students who were all used to being at the top of their class. I was thirteen and, though I didn't yet realize it, I would never again be a number one student.

Our school operated on the principles made famous by General Maresuke Nogi, a highly respected hero of the 1904–05 war with Russia. General Nogi had been a brave but not particularly brilliant commander. His two sons were killed in the war, and he himself lost more men under his command than did any other general. But he was the Emperor's favorite and revered for his strong samurai spirit.

After Japan's victory in the war, General Nogi was named dean of the Gakushuin School for members of the royal family. He was the author of books designed to mold the behavior of young Japanese in a spartan, samurai spirit. His own spirit dominated our school, and his ideas were severe. An army officer was assigned to each class. The time set aside for military training and work to help the war effort increased steadily. Even during the height of the war, when I was caught up in patriotic fervor and dreamed of being a fighter pilot, the severe militarism of our school, which was so much like a miniature reflection of our government, seemed misguided to me.

We always had to wash in cold water. The school gym was unheated, and we were not allowed to wear socks while training in *kendo*, a form of dueling with a broad sword. This was supposed to make us tough. Such ideas would have been bad enough in Tokyo, but in the much colder winters of Seoul they were a form of torture. I considered them unreasonable and, when winter came, took the dangerous step of saying so to our army officer. I was fortunate. My punishment was limited to standing at attention for three hours in the hallway.

Needless to say, there were no girls in our school. In fact, none of my formal education was in a co-ed setting. We had no foreign-language instruction in elementary school, but when I started middle school, I also started to study English. With my fascination for America, I was anxious to learn. But on Monday, December 8, 1941—according to Eastern Hemisphere calendars—I heard the incredible news while on my thirty-minute walk from home to school. People were running out of stores and homes with great excitement. Someone stopped me to ask if I had heard what had happened. I shook my head dumbly and was invited inside to hear the radio. Military music ended and the announcer came on to tell us: "Early this morning Japanese navy and army forces engaged in war with the United States and the British."

Many Japanese were stunned. Though we were aware of growing tensions with the United States, we had always been taught, and our military had always been trained, to prepare for war with our ancient enemy, Russia, and with its modern form of government, communism. Japan's alliance with Germany in 1936, which Italy joined the next year, was called by the Japanese the Anti-Comintern Pact, a reference to the Communist International formed by the Soviets in 1919. As schoolchildren we played a game with a glass-covered maze in which we tried to guide a tiny metal ball from one end to the other. The one section from which there was no escape without forfeiting the game was called the Comintern, clearly a place of evil.

Our German ally's nonaggression pact with the Soviet Union in 1939 clouded the issue. In April 1941 Japan signed a similar pact with the Soviets, only to be embarrassed two months later when Germany invaded Russia. My own view was further confused by the awe and fondness for the United States that had prevailed in my household.

I feared for my country. I was so filled with notions of the technological superiority of the United States—just consider our wonderful Fords—and with the greatness of America that I was sure Japan would be defeated. But the attitude in my home was ambivalent. A photo of Admiral Togo hung on our living room wall; a record of one of his speeches competed with Schubert for playing time on the phonograph; and our admiration for our German allies was strong.

Other ideas were hammered into my head in school and through government propaganda. After generations of being trained to hate the Russians, we now had other enemies, what our propaganda called the ABCD—America, Britain, China, and the Dutch. Their economic sanctions cut off our foreign trade and our source of oil. We had been trained to fight the Russians but we had been driven to fight the Americans with little preparation. We knew it would not be as easy to defeat the Americans as it had been to defeat the Russians when my grandfather was a soldier, but we had no choice. The longer we waited, the fewer oil reserves our military would have and the less chance we would have of victory. We had to strike quickly, and our first target had to be our most dangerous enemy, the United States. We were taught that we must fight the United States the way we would fight against a devil. It was amazing to see how some people who had thought the United States was so wonderful quickly did a 180-degree about-face. But even at the height of the war, despite the best efforts of our government, I doubt that many Japanese ever learned to hate Americans quite as much as we were supposed to.

Our teachers, aided by Japan's early victories, were persuasive. Their arguments centered on naval power, which really meant battleship power. How foolish we were. If our own stunning success at Pearl Harbor had proven anything, it was the supremacy of air power. Our fleet inflicted relatively little damage and was most effective as an escort for our attack planes. Characteristically, our planes con-

centrated on the American battleships, virtually wiping them out.
But they missed the aircraft carriers, which turned out to be the
most important weapons in the war of the Pacific.

Though Admiral Yamamoto believed in air power, other admirals
went on believing in the invincibility of Japan's great battleships.
Though a generation older, they had had the same education I was
receiving. We had all learned the wonderful stories about the battleship *Mikasa* in the one-sided victories over Russia early in the
century. On a visit to the port of Yokosuka, my father had shown
me the *Mikasa*, and it made a strong impression on my young mind.
Though Japan recognized the growing importance of air power, it
was Japanese battleships that appeared on postage stamps.

In school we were taught that Japan could never lose a war and
in fact in its twenty-six-hundred-year history had never lost a battle.
Even the heroic General Nogi had lost a battle or two to the Russians
but we were never taught about that. We were told that our two
super-battleships with their long-range "big guns" could defeat any
enemy. These were the sixty-eight-thousand-ton *Musashi* and the
Yamato with eighteen-inch guns, but during the war we were never
told their names or their size.

We were told, however, that the Americans had nothing like
them, that even though American technology could produce such
ships, they would be too big to get through the Panama Canal to
reach the Pacific. Hearing this, I was among the students who
cheered. We weren't reminded about what relatively small Japanese
attack planes had done to huge American battleships at Pearl Harbor.
Like Admiral Yamamoto, my father believed in the importance of
air power. As a patriotic Japanese, he supported the war, but as a
loyal Ford dealer, he was skeptical of Japan's ability to match American industrial might. Datsun/Nissan, then Japan's only automobile
manufacturer, had become a fairly serious competitor of our Ford
agency. My father looked down on Datsun, however, convinced that
Japan could never compete with American technology. Datsun produced a very small car with a low-horsepower engine. Ford, on the
other hand, could make engines strong enough to power cars as big
as the four-door Lincoln.

"Japan can't make big car engines like Ford does," my father
would say in the privacy of our home. "How can we make engines
big enough for airplanes that can fight the Americans?"

But by then I was a true, if confused, believer, seeing myself as a heroic fighter pilot in the victorious Japanese air force while still harboring the dream of one day taking over my father's Ford dealership, visiting Detroit, and returning with more examples of America's unbeatable technology.

Among the first signs we had that Japan and its allies might not be invincible came when the dean of our school called a meeting of all the students to announce that Admiral Yamamoto had been killed in action. He gave no details. Most of us wept. Admiral Yamamoto had been the war's greatest hero, built up by the media and our teachers during the war. Only after the war did we learn the full dimensions of that tragedy. By June 1942 American cryptographers had broken Japanese military codes, and had intercepted and defeated a Japanese fleet preparing to attack Midway Island to the northwest of Hawaii. The Americans knew Admiral Yamamoto's schedule on a flight from Saipan to New Guinea. Even at the risk of revealing that they might have the codes, the Americans decided to attack. Not only Admiral Yamamoto but all his top staff, the brains of the Japanese navy, were aboard the two Mitsubishi bombers that, along with the six Zero fighter escorts, were attacked by thirty-six P-38s. Both bombers were destroyed.

The other news that struck a fearful chord came from Russia early in 1943. We had been hearing of the great German successes in pushing the Soviet army back deep into Russia—to within artillery range of Moscow, Leningrad, and Stalingrad. But suddenly, Radio Tokyo was playing Beethoven's Fifth Symphony with its mournful, funereal tones. Then we were told Radio Berlin had announced that the German army at Stalingrad had been overrun. Another hero we had heard much of, Field Marshal Paulus, had been captured. To the Japanese, this was a matter of great shame. To be killed in action, as Admiral Yamamoto had been, was tragic, but it was also a point of honor. To be captured was a humiliation. The death of Admiral Yamamoto and the capture of Field Marshal Paulus made some of us wonder if the Axis powers were unconquerable, as we had been taught. None of us ever spoke of our doubts, and our outward lives went on as before.

Virtually all entertainment was banned. Groups of students, accompanied by a teacher, occasionally went to see a war movie. A boy seen walking with a girl could be punished by police or teachers. Any hint of romance was considered soft and unmanly. Popular music was banned and stiff, military marches echoed endlessly on the military-controlled radio. In February 1942 the government banned the teaching of English, not only to students but even to military intelligence officers. It was typical of the nationalistic fervor that gripped the country with a determination to stamp out corrupting foreign influences. It was also a very foolish move and completely the opposite of what the Americans were doing. The American military began intensive Japanese-language lessons for bright young enlisted men and officer candidates. This proved a great boon both during the latter stages of the war and during the years of the American military occupation of Japan. The Japanese approach, however, did indicate that the military had no serious hope of conquering and occupying the United States. Had that been part of the military's plan, they surely would have wanted to train a cadre of people who would have been able to speak the language.

I was a young adult in college before I really had an opportunity to study English. Japanese of my generation, no matter how long we may live in the United States, will never have the fluency in English of the postwar generation, who started younger and studied continuously.

Baseball was another victim of the war. The game had become popular in Japan during the period of rapid Westernization in the 1920s. College teams were more closely followed than the professional clubs of that era, and the rivalry between my father's school, Keio University, and Waseda was a match-up so popular that it provided the story line for a children's record that I played over and over again on the family Victrola. By the time I was growing up, baseball was also being played avidly among the Japanese in Korea, and I was familiar with the names of legendary American heroes like Lou Gehrig and Babe Ruth. But the military government banned baseball during the war because it was an American game. And so at the age of twelve I lost out on both English and baseball. And who knows? With my physique I might have made a good shortstop.

I try to blame my overly protective father for my lack of athletic skill. I try to blame World War II for my lack of ability in English. Perhaps, like the rest of us, I shouldn't blame anyone but me for my shortcomings. I would include in this lesson those who sometimes blame Franklin D. Roosevelt for Japan's involvement in World War II. To this day a few Japanese believe that our country was forced into World War II by the series of economic sanctions imposed by the United States at the urging of President Roosevelt. Scrap-iron and oil shipments to Japan had been limited in July 1940 in the wake of continuing Japanese aggression in China. When Japan seized southern Indochina in July 1941, the United States, Great Britain, and the Netherlands imposed a total oil embargo. Japan, then as now, had to import virtually all of its sources of energy and had to act quickly to ensure a steady source of oil. Otherwise, the country would have collapsed.

With hindsight, it does appear that the goal of Japan's wartime leaders was to carve out military and hence economic domination of what was termed the Greater East Asia Co-Prosperity Sphere. The immediate target was not the United States or even its territory of Hawaii, but Dutch Indonesia, a target that could not be conquered unless potential British and American resistance was first neutralized.

By mid-1941 political alliances and military conquests had moved Japan into the fires of war. America had not, after all, forced Japan to invade China or to move into Indochina. But by cutting off Japan's oil supplies, the United States may have motivated Japan's military to strike out in a new direction.

Postwar studies indicate that some leaders of the Japanese military believed the American will to fight would soon be sapped because the United States had become so weakened by pacifist and isolationist sentiments. They believed that even if America's technological strength and economic resources would make the United States difficult to defeat in battle, the political will was lacking for prolonged and severe warfare. America would negotiate a peace settlement, giving Japan effective control of East Asia. They were very wrong.

Not knowing America, not even willing to study its language or to try to understand its culture and history, the Japanese military had no hope of accurately predicting what America would do. Thirty years later there may have been limits to America's willingness to continue the war in Vietnam. In the 1940s, there were no limits to America's commitment and will to fight.

By May 1942 Japan had occupied or surrounded virtually all of the so-called Co-Prosperity Sphere, including Dutch Indonesia with its rich oil reserves. But then, with the June 1942 Battle of Midway and the death of Admiral Yamamoto, the Americans stopped Japan's advances, only six months after they had begun with an impressive string of victories. Three long, terrible years of suffering remained, however.

In many ways, we were much better off in Korea than our countrymen in Japan. The devastation of the war never reached Korea. With its strong agricultural base, food, though rationed, was much more plentiful than in Japan, even though great quantities of Korean produce were shipped to Japan. For relatively wealthy families like ours, the black market was also a reliable source of food, more so than its counterpart in Japan. This point was brought home to me when Tetsuo Matsukata, son of Duke Shokuma Matsukata, visited our family in Seoul. Duke Matsukata was a younger son of the famous and influential Masayoshi Matsukata, twice a prime minister and a brilliant samurai, farmer, financial minister, and political leader. (Many years later, Duke Matsukata's daughter, Haru, married Edwin O. Reischauer, who became the American ambassador to Japan.) Tetsuo Matsukata, a member of this wealthy and well-connected family, was impressed that my own much more modest family could afford white rice in Korea. Brown rice was the best that the Matsukata family could manage in wartime Japan.

More significantly, no one in our family went to war. My father was too old. I was too young—just barely. Our family home was in Tanabe, which had no industry or military installations. The city was never bombed.

As the operations of our Ford agency declined to service and repairs, my father launched another enterprise in 1943, an asbestos mining and processing operation. If we had continued in that business, today our family might be facing lawsuits for causing cancer.

More and more of our school hours were devoted to military training and silly work that was supposed to help the war effort. During my last two years in high school, we spent 80 percent of our time digging out the roots of pine trees that were pressed to extract resin that would be turned into grease for airplane engines. Lack of fuel was still Japan's major problem. Our country had gone to war because of oil. We had occupied Indonesia because of oil. But American submarines and airplanes were sinking our tankers anyway. And so now we were digging up pine roots because of oil. I asked one of our teachers how much our efforts helped. He said two days' work could help keep an airplane engine running for five minutes. We knew we were losing the war, but we went on digging up roots.

Another awkward effort to conserve fuel resources angered my father. Gasoline had become totally unavailable. As a result, the military government directed that motor vehicles be equipped with charcoal-burning fuel tanks that were attached to the back of the car. They looked like bulky, old-fashioned, kitchen stoves. Starting these charcoal burners was difficult and could be dangerous. They had to start "cooking" long before they generated enough gas to get the car moving. They were foul-smelling and gave off great clouds of thick, black smoke with explosions that sounded like gunfire.

"It's not a car anymore. It looks more like a cow," said my father, looking at his once handsome four-door Ford with its ugly new fuel tank.

The Ford sign on the front wall of our agency was another victim of the war. The military government made us take it down, but the imprint of the letters was still visible against the building. The government ordered us to repaint the building. My father said he would but never got around to doing it, which turned out to be a blessing when the first Americans arrived after the war.

In 1945, I was seventeen, old enough for the military draft. I still dreamed of being a fighter pilot, though Japan had few planes left and barely any fuel to fly them. But I also dreamed of succeeding my father, both in business and at Keio University. In my last year of high school, I applied both to Keio, in hopes that the war would end, and to the Army Air Force Officer Candidate School, in case the war continued and I was drafted into the military. I was accepted by both but notified the authorities that I would attend the Army Air Force School at the Tokorozawa Army Air Base. Given the atmosphere that prevailed in school and in the Japanese community in Seoul, I really had no other choice. But within myself, the choice was not so clear-cut. While the romantic in me said yes to the idea of going to war, the realist said no.

Had I entered the military then, I would have been trained not as a fighter pilot but as a kamikaze. And not even as a kamikaze pilot, for there was not enough fuel for planes. Small boats that were little more than a torpedo with a cockpit, a motor, and a rudder were being prepared for final suicidal assaults on an invading American fleet. Had the war lasted a few months longer, I might have died the proud death of a young kamikaze.

The kamikaze concept may sound irrational, but fuel was in such short supply that training for new pilots was limited. The Japanese

Zero fighter planes, with their thousand-horsepower engines, had been a match for the equally low-powered P-40 Flying Tigers and Grumman F4F Wildcats that were the American fighters when the war began. But it turned out that my father had been right about America's industrial capabilities. The next generation of American fighters, like the P-51 Mustang, the Grumman F6F Hellcat and the Corsair, soon took to the skies. Their two-thousand-horsepower engines, fueled by higher-octane fuels than Japan had, made them far superior to the Zeros still in the sky. Poorly trained Japanese pilots in inferior warplanes were on virtually suicidal missions every time they took off. In this context, the kamikaze program was a well-calculated alternative. Since death was nearly always inevitable anyway, the idea of turning the Zero into a guided bomb, targeted at vulnerable ships, had a certain terrible logic to it. The kamikaze pilots preferred to die this way rather than to be shot out of the sky on a mission that accomplished nothing. In my heart I know I would have accepted the fate of the kamikaze.

In April I was called up for military service. I went to Pusan to wait for the ship that would take me to Japan. I waited, but the ship never came. There were no communications from Japan, only rumors in Pusan that the ship had been sunk by an American submarine. For two weeks I waited, then I returned to Seoul. Further instructions never arrived.

Even from the heavily censored newspapers and military radio, we knew the war was going badly for Japan. In typical phrases we were told that heroic Japanese forces had "changed their route" or "moved in another direction" away from Guadalcanal, Saipan, Iwo Jima, Leyte, Manila, Okinawa. Nevertheless, we believed that the powerful Japanese fleet was being held back for a last-ditch defense of the home islands that would turn back the overextended Americans and change the course of the war. Of course, we didn't know that most of the fleet had already been sunk.

Then, on August 8 on Eastern calendars, radio news broadcasts told us of an air raid the previous day on Hiroshima. The broadcaster said only a few American planes had been involved but that a new type of bomb had done great damage. He gave few details, but we smelled something wrong. Usually, when we were told anything about American air raids on Japanese cities, it was that great numbers of American planes had attacked but, because of heroic Japanese defenders, little damage had been done and many American planes were shot down. Now we were being told the opposite. An American plane had dropped one bomb and great damage had been done.

A week later, it was announced that the Emperor was going to speak to the people on the radio. We were astounded. The Emperor had always been considered a god who stayed above the concerns of government and isolated from his people. Now, for the first time ever, an emperor of Japan was going to speak on the radio. Rumors swept Seoul about what he would say. Opinion was split. Many thought he would make an inspiring address to spur the war effort. Others thought he would announce that the war was over. My father invited many people to our house to listen to the Emperor's radio broadcast, even though we feared that if he announced Japan's surrender, it would mean a great loss of face, particularly in front of our Korean employees.

At noon the Emperor's thin, high-pitched voice came crackling over the radio. He spoke in the convoluted language of the court and at first it sounded as though he might be calling for new and extraordinary sacrifices to continue the war.

"To our good and loyal subjects," he began. "Pondering deeply the general trends of the world and the actual conditions in our empire today, We have decided to effect a settlement of the present situation by resorting to an extraordinary measure."

All this sounded as though it might be building up to a command to fight on no matter what the consequences. Then he said, "We have ordered the acceptance of the Joint Declaration of the powers." That mystified us for, of course, no one had any idea what this reference to the Potsdam declaration meant. But then the Emperor described the "new and most cruel bomb" the Allies had used.

"Should we continue to fight," he added, "it would not only result in an ultimate collapse and the obliteration of the Japanese nation, but also it would lead to the total extinction of human civilization." Then we knew it was over.

The war ended that day. The Emperor had told us we would be called on to "endure the unendurable and suffer the insufferable." He was right.

3

Home to Japan

The war came home to us only after the war was over. Korea had never been bombed. Food was plentiful. Our family was prosperous, and when the war ended we had the good fortune of being occupied by the American military. Our Japanese compatriots in the northern parts of Korea and in Manchuria were not so lucky. Those areas were taken over by the Russians.

Many Japanese refugees began to pour into Seoul from the north and with them stories of atrocities and rumors that the Russians were on their way to occupy all of Korea. Japan's nonaggression pact with the Soviet Union had remained in effect all through the war. At Yalta in February 1945 the Russians had agreed to enter the war against Japan. But they waited. On August 9, the day the second atomic bomb fell, this time on Nagasaki, with the war clearly over Russia broke its nonaggression treaty, declared war on Japan, and within five days occupied most of Manchuria and northern Korea. Japanese refugees told frightening stories about the Soviet soldiers, many of whom seemed to be criminal types forced into the military. It appeared that the Russians were determined to reoccupy all the territories they had lost to Japan since 1894. Unaware that the Rus-

24

sians and Americans had made an agreement at Yalta effectively dividing Korea at the 38th parallel, we expected these barbarian troops to sweep over us within a few days.

Young boys like myself, who had finished middle school and expected to be drafted, were in a kind of limbo, with nothing to do and no real idea of what was happening in the world around us. We used to meet and talk about what would happen to us—and to Japan. One evening we heard a rumor that Russian soldiers had parachuted into an area near Seoul. There were about six of us, all the same age and all from the same school, talking about what we should do. One boy, very much in favor of the militaristic approach that had been drummed into us at school, said that since we had already been called up for military service it was our duty to get weapons and go north to fight the Russians.

A dead silence fell on the group. In my heart I was thinking this was a crazy idea, but I was afraid to say anything out loud. To say no to such an idea would have been thought of as an expression of cowardice. Then one of my friends who was cleverer than the rest of us said it would be against the samurai spirit to go on fighting now that the war was over. He reminded us that it was the code of the samurai to fight bravely to the end but, if defeated, to give respect to the winner. He was very eloquent and mentioned the traditions that surround May 5, Boys Day, in Japan, when flags in the shape of a carp are flown all over the country. Though small, the carp is a very strong fish that will fight hard against the fisherman's hook. But once it's been pulled onto the boat, the carp stops jumping and accepts death quietly. The carp is said to have the spirit of the samurai, and this is the spirit that Japanese boys are taught to have. My friend said that since the Emperor had decided to surrender, it was the samurai's duty to obey.

We all agreed. My friend's eloquence may have saved our lives and certainly allowed us all to save face, including the boy who suggested we go off to fight the Russians. During the years of the occupation, there must have been many Japanese who consoled themselves with the thought that it was the samurai's duty to respect the victor. Such an attitude may help to explain why the years of the American occupation were so successful and so peaceful. But then it's also true that the American soldiers did not behave as the Soviets did.

Japanese shrines and schools in Seoul soon overflowed with pitiful refugees from the north. Our family took in three middle-aged men, one of whom had lost his wife in a way he would never discuss. From the stories of killing and rape that the refugees did tell, from the women who had shaved their heads and dressed in men's filthy clothes, from the injuries that hobbled many, from their hunger and total lack of possessions, we could sense the horror that appeared to be coming our way.

The men we took into our home had escaped with nothing but their lives. We did everything we could to make them comfortable. But they were frightened and bitter and communicated little about what they had suffered. Many had feared the Koreans would turn on them with long-repressed hostility. But the Japanese refugees encountered relatively few reprisals from the Koreans they had ruled for four decades.

Our own fear continued even when the first Americans arrived in early September. For years we had been taught that Americans were the great devil. We expected the worst. Then the GIs arrived in their jeeps with their open faces and their generosity, their Hershey chocolates and Wrigley chewing gum and Lucky Strike cigarettes. The Ford agency faced the road that led to the Japanese military police headquarters, which the Americans took over in a peaceful transition. One group of Americans, passing the agency, spotted the still visible imprint of the Ford sign on our building. They pulled up in their jeeps. My father with his excellent English greeted them warmly, and we soon had new and important friends, particularly the leader of that first group of Americans, Colonel Bennett. Our cold fears began to melt. These men weren't Soviet barbarians. They meant us no harm and turned out to be kind, outgoing, and curious about the strange people they were among.

My family entertained the GIs in our home often. These were the first Americans I can remember meeting, and I was fascinated. They were so big. I was shy among them but watched closely, impressed by my father's ability to talk with them and his instinctive understanding of our new friends. The Americans also were impressed with my father's English and his knowledge of the United States, particularly since he had never visited their country. My father had a good speaking voice and an excellent memory. Though Shakespeare was his favorite, my father loved to recite lengthy passages from English literature both high and low in style. The Americans felt they had found an unlikely home away from home.

Since his own days in the military, my grandfather had collected Japanese swords. Many were highly valuable and, after his return to Japan, we still had a few handsome swords in our home in Seoul. Only officers could carry such swords. My grandfather, assuming Koji and I would follow his path into the military, left the swords for us. Such swords were believed to embody the spirit of the samurai warrior and were carried with great honor by kamikaze pilots. Had I entered the military and been trained as a kamikaze, I might well have carried one of those swords—to my death.

To us the swords were a treasure, but to the American military they were potential weapons. The American Army of Occupation passed a regulation that Japanese could not keep any weapons, including ceremonial swords. My father made the best of the situation by presenting one of our swords to Colonel Bennett as a gift. The next day the colonel returned with some of his aides, asking if they could have the other swords. Colonel Bennett also asked my father for certificates, tracing the history of each sword and verifying that they had been given as personal gifts. My father's written English was even more fluent than his spoken English, and Colonel Bennett was very happy with the beautiful certificates he created.

Through these difficult times, the Korean employees at the Ford agency remained kind and sympathetic to our family. When we had all huddled around the radio, listening to the Emperor tell us that the war was over, we had all been very quiet. Our Korean friends had turned away, averting their eyes, and silently left. They had not wanted to see our family lose face. I saw no expressions of joy by Koreans over the fact that the foreigners who had occupied their country had been defeated. The Koreans had no more idea of what the end of the war would mean for them than we did. Many feared they might just be exchanging one foreign occupier for another, and from what they had heard about the Americans from Japanese wartime propaganda, they had every reason to fear the worst. Even in that period between the Japanese surrender and the arrival of the first Americans, there were no riots or looting. And when the Americans did arrive and we began to see newsreels of Japanese prisoners of war, long lines of uniformed men with no weapons and their heads bowed, I would try to hide my face when the movies were over and the lights came up. And still the Koreans showed no sense of gloating or hostility.

But one day a group of angry and potentially violent workers from my father's asbestos operation suddenly arrived at our home in Seoul. The asbestos operation was about 120 miles from our home, and we never had the close relationship with the workers there that we did with the employees at the Ford agency and assembly plant. In retrospect, it seems possible to me that they may have been forced laborers, for there were many such workers in mining operations, factories, and military construction. It wasn't unusual for the Japanese military to round up able-bodied Korean men for labor battalions. Many were sent to Japan, and others were forced to work in Korea.

In any event, they were angry and hostile, demanding severance pay and making violent threats. My father met them outside the agency. It was clearly a dangerous situation. I wanted to go to my father, but my mother wouldn't let me out the door. Instead she sent word to the American military, pleading for help. Colonel Bennett soon arrived with a group of American soldiers in their jeeps. They rescued my father and dispersed the asbestos workers. I was more impressed than ever by American power and by the apparent willingness of our "devil" enemies to be our friends and even our protectors.

Allied postwar policies, set at conferences in Cairo in November 1943 and at Potsdam in July 1945, called for the liberation of all territories occupied by Japan since 1894 and promised that Korea would become a free and independent nation. The Americans in the south and the Russians in the north set about repatriating all Japanese. We had no choice but to leave. Our last night in Korea was a sad but memorable evening. Our Ford employees gave a farewell dinner for us. What I remember best was the big cake and my father urging us to enjoy it. "I don't know when we may have our next cake," he told us, "because I hear there is no sugar in Japan."

My father had decided to turn over to the most loyal and efficient of our Korean employees, Junmo Inn and Hichisei Zen, what was left of the family auto and truck business. Mr. Inn evidently made the most of his opportunity, for he later became president of the Automotive Association of Korea.

We knew we could take virtually nothing with us, so we packed all our most valuable treasures, including the Minoltaflex camera I'd become so fond of and all the photos I had taken, into boxes that we stored in our home, which we also turned over to our Korean employees.

Though I have many sharp memories of my boyhood years, I have never returned to Korea. Koji made a visit in the early 1970s but could find virtually no trace of our past. The building that housed the Ford dealership and our childhood home had been destroyed by fire during the Korean War, when Seoul, spared in World War II, became a battleground. The building that had been our service department and the movie theater across the street had survived. With our home had gone all those family treasures we had packed away, including the photos I took that might unlock more boyhood memories. My only pictures of those days are those dating to my grandparents' era that they had brought back to Japan with them when they retired in 1937.

Japanese are not very good at being refugees. In our two-thousand-year history, we had had no experience at surrendering or losing a war. More experienced refugees would have traded their possessions for jewelry and diamonds that could have been easily hidden and carried to our new home. We were allowed to take only hand-held luggage and one thousand yen each, the equivalent then of an average man's salary for about five months. We carried virtually nothing with us but food and clothing, and that might have been another mistake because we were so visibly much better off than the other refugees. Our Korean employees drove our family and our three adopted refugees to the railroad station in an open truck. My father had tears in his eyes as he said to my mother, "Don't look back." The banner our employees had attached to the side of the truck read, with a sad irony, "Henry Ford Is Leaving Korea."

The train we rode from Seoul south to the port of Pusan was packed with refugees, nearly all from the north and in pitiful condition. We were conspicuous with our relatively good clothes and all our baggage. Most of our companions had nothing and soon began to stare at us with such cold eyes that I was frightened by the envy and tension around us. Nearly all, like my own family, had been relatively well off until the final days of the war when the Soviet soldiers fell upon them. We had more than enough food for ourselves but hardly enough for all those who had nothing.

When we arrived in Pusan, there was no boat waiting to take us to Japan. We learned that we might have to wait several days, and there were no accommodations for the refugees. Once again, my father's English and the kindness of the American soldiers saved us. My father was able to get help not only for our family, but for all the refugees. All were treated well because my father was able to talk to the Americans. Once again I saw how the power of language and an understanding of people can change a difficult situation into a favorable one. When the others saw my father's successful efforts to get food and shelter for all, their cold anger toward us vanished. We were accepted among them through the rest of our ordeal in getting back to Japan.

When the ship that would take us home finally arrived, we had another lesson in what it meant to be a defeated people. The *Kainei Maru* had been a coal carrier, hastily converted to carry refugees. The ship was as jammed as the train had been and even dirtier. Remnants of coal dust clung to it even though the GIs hosed it down from top to bottom before we boarded. It was a twelve-hour trip from Pusan to the southern Japanese port of Shimonoseki. We had tatami mats to sleep on and plenty of food. I even met two sisters about my own age who were from Kyushu Island. With no sisters of my own and no chance for contact with girls in school, it was one of my first opportunities ever to talk to young girls. There were no soldiers or police to challenge us for being together in defiance of the puritanical regulations of the war years.

As we sailed toward postwar Japan, I never looked back.

II

A HIGHER EDUCATION

1945–1954

4

The Lessons of War

Being hosed down with DDT can't be called a pleasant experience. But when the American GIs sprayed us for lice at the Japanese port of Shimonoseki, no one objected. We were like the carp, accepting our defeat; but we also recognized that the Americans were spraying us to protect Japan from any diseases we might be carrying. They sprayed our clothes and under our clothes with a nozzle and all our belongings, except our food.

We stayed overnight in Shimonoseki, sleeping in the station, cooking in a big field outside. We had the rice we had brought in rucksacks from Korea, and we could buy vegetables and firewood locally. Acrid smoke fires curled into the night air, and all across that empty field, families huddled around the cooking fires, like nomads, preparing meals as best they could. It was a strange way to return to Japan, especially for a family like mine who had lived so well in Korea. Some of the refugees my family had adopted back in Seoul were from Kyushu Island. They left us in Shimonoseki as did the young girls I had met on the boat. I was seventeen and of course had very romantic feelings about them, all mixed up with the confused

33

feelings I had about the war and about my family returning to Japan as refugees.

The next day, we traveled by train to Tanabe. The first leg of our twelve-hour trip, snaking up the coast from Shimonoseki to Osaka, now takes only three hours by modern trains. I had made that trip many times before the war on our summer vacations, and I knew the only scheduled stop was Hiroshima. I hoped we wouldn't stop there that day. People spoke of the stories they had heard of radiation sickness. This was in late September, about six weeks after the bomb had fallen, and we were afraid even to travel through the area. It was early evening, about six o'clock, and there was still plenty of light. Curiosity mixed with our fear. Though frightened, we wanted to see for ourselves. We didn't know much about radiation, but we believed the stories we had heard that no life, not even grass, could return to the area for twenty years or more. Many agreed that with this kind of weapon there would be no more war. They thought this weapon was so powerful it would be beyond the control of humans.

This was my first visit to Japan since 1939, when we had encountered the wounded soldiers recuperating at the hot spring at Shirahama. Now I was about to see not just one group of severely wounded soldiers but an entire city destroyed by a single bomb. The train was very crowded. A haunting quiet crept through the cars of that packed, noisy train as we approached Hiroshima. We could catch only shadowy glimpses of buildings that had survived the blast, hollowed out like skeletons. In the hush that enveloped us, we became strangely aware of the creaking, rhythmic, clacking sounds of the wheels as we rolled through the outskirts of what had been a busy city. The train slowed. We stopped.

We were at a place where the railroad station once must have been. We saw people walking around, and someone shouted, "Look, there are people out there."

That made me less afraid. I had no way of knowing if they were survivors of the blast or rescue workers who had arrived later. They wore no protective clothing against the dangers of radiation. There was a makeshift tower, and our steam engine took on water. I could see no coal chute, but I assume that somehow the train's fuel supply must also have been replenished.

No one left the train, and no one boarded. We had again fallen silent. No one in my family spoke. We avoided each other's eyes as we stared out on the grim wasteland that stretched before us. We could see only a few gutted buildings. Layers of ash seemed to cover the barren earth but, perhaps fortunately, there were no apparent breezes to stir it up. From my earlier trips through Hiroshima I was used to seeing crowded streets and a busy station. It was strange that day to see so few people at the station and none beyond it. None of the people moving by the train looked up at us. No one aboard tried to wave to those outside. Though I had no camera, I am still haunted by the ghostly, skeletal images of the surviving buildings rising up over long, flat stretches where nothing stood.

Years later, Hiroshima took on a special importance in my life, but then its impact was one that I shared with all the victims of war who rode that train. We were Japanese. We had been defeated by an awesome power that we could only begin to understand. The illusions of the war years—dreams of empire, legends of invincibility—all had vanished, as utterly as Hiroshima, in a mushroom cloud. The train moved on toward Osaka. The desolate images lingered.

It must have been well after midnight when we arrived at Osaka, the major city nearest our home in Tanabe. Before the war, I had been used to seeing Osaka at night as a brightly lit city. But as our train pulled in I saw only a few flickering lights that might have been cooking fires. The station in Osaka had not been bombed, and we stayed there overnight. We were able to buy fish and firewood but no vegetables from vendors in a big open square outside the station. I drew water from a nozzle on a wall of the station, and my mother cooked what was left of the rice we had brought from Korea to eat with our fish. It was strange, but in that respect the refugees were better off than those who lived in Osaka who had no rice.

In the morning we could see that few people lived in Osaka anymore. Almost nothing remained of Japan's greatest industrial city. Prewar Osaka was much more modern than Hiroshima, where nearly all the buildings were made of wood. The only buildings we could see still standing in Osaka were concrete-and-steel skeletons gutted by fire. For Koji and me, the nights sleeping at the stations in Shimonoseki and Osaka had been an adventure. With the comfort of our tatami mats and cooking fires, it had been like an overnight outing, a school camping trip. Our parents kept telling us that once we got to Tanabe everything would be all right. But I think they must have been trying to reassure themselves, rather than us, for Koji and I were having fun.

Dawn brought a very different perspective. There were no shops but many street vendors with black-market goods piled on rickety tables. Many of the people looked as hollowed out by hunger and despair as the buildings had been by saturation firebombing. We saw many gray-faced men, who must have been veterans, still wearing tattered uniforms. Except for those of an occasional vendor trying hard to make a sale, I never saw anyone's eyes. People shuffled by with bowed heads.

We changed trains in Osaka, again hugging the coast but now heading south toward Tanabe, and, for the first time, we began to see parts of Japan that had been spared. Wakayama, the capital of Wakayama prefecture, had been bombed, but most of the region had not been touched. Basically, it is a poor area with no industries but great beauty. Pine-forested hills rise sharply just beyond the narrow, coastal flatlands. Though the mountains limit the amount of arable farmland, the economy is based on agriculture—plums and oranges—and fishing. At Tanabe, we found a haven from the ravages of war.

Tanabe was exactly as I had remembered it from the years before the war when we visited every summer. Lumber yards and the fishing boats harbored in the gracefully curving bay provided the basis for an economy that had supported a population of about thirty-five thousand before the military draft took its toll. Because it was poor, Tanabe was better off than most parts of Japan after the war. There had been nothing there worth bombing.

We arrived in late afternoon and were immediately reminded that there had been a war. There were no taxis. But we were all good walkers and set out on foot toward my grandparents' house, which was between the station and the sea, a walk of about twenty-five minutes. I could smell the clean salt air and filled my lungs deeply for the first time since I had realized our train was drawing close to Hiroshima. Though it was our first visit in six years, we encountered some familiar faces, obviously surprised to see members of the prosperous Kusumoto family burdened with rucksacks and looking tired and grimy. I didn't mind. Just being in this beautiful, familiar little city had lifted my spirits.

Tanabe is the kind of city where people don't bother locking their doors. When we got to my grandparents' sprawling, nineteenth-century house, my mother led us up the steps, opened the door, and walked in. My grandparents had no idea we were coming—in fact, no idea whether we were dead or alive. My mother burst into tears when she saw her parents. They were overjoyed to see us, and that evening a grand family reunion marked the beginning of a new era.

Luck or foresight had again been with my grandfather, for right around the beginning of the war he had bought a fishing boat. By the end of the war boats were scarce, and many fishermen wanted to rent my grandfather's boat. Since currency had little value, he rented the boat in return for fish. Almost every day we had plenty of fresh fish. City people used to come to the provinces to exchange clothes for fish and other food. And in Tanabe my grandfather could also exchange some of the fish for rice, fruit, vegetables, and *sake*. He still liked his *sake*, and his closest friend in town, S. Tamaki, owned the brewery that turned scarce rice into scarcer *sake*.

My grandparents' house had been built long before by American missionaries. It was typically Japanese in style but oddly situated on a quarter-acre plot. Japanese usually build their houses on the northern corner of their land with the biggest part of the house open and facing south to receive as much sun as possible. This house had been built squarely in the center of the plot. There were orange trees and phoenix trees around it and a pond stocked with carp. My grandparents and one servant had been living alone in the house, which was easily big enough to take in the four Kusumoto refugees from Korea. We settled in and I set about rediscovering Tanabe.

The three-story city hall, which my grandfather had built on his return from Korea, was then the tallest building in town. The narrow, twisting streets dated from the era of the feudal daimyo who wanted them that way for strategic purposes, to confuse and slow the advance of any potential enemies. I sought out the city hall and the Shinto shrine to which my grandfather, though not a religious man, had donated two huge rock lanterns, which stood like a symbolic gateway before the shrine. Tanabe is far enough to the south to enjoy a warm, almost tropical climate: the air is soft, and the sea breezes are fresh. I knew the ravages of war were not far away, but it was wonderful to be in a city at peace.

The Japanese death toll during the war has been estimated at two million, one-third of them civilians. Forty percent of the area of the cities had been destroyed, and urban population had dropped by over 50 percent. There was virtually no coal or oil and industry was at a standstill. Farmers were short of equipment and fertilizer, and food was hard to find, particularly in the major cities. Rice was scarce, and there were many other shortages, including a shortage of electric power. For periods each night sections of the city would be blacked out, but we always knew the schedule in advance and could arrange our evening around the dark. Life was easy in Tanabe.

At that time, there were no American soldiers in the area. But about six months later, in the spring of 1946, Tanabe became a repatriation point for soldiers taken prisoner overseas. By then, the fears that most Japanese had of raping, pillaging American barbarians had become less intense. Victors and vanquished, though still wary of each other, were learning to get along. A small group of Americans was stationed in Tanabe to supervise the quiet return of soldiers who had marched off to war with bands playing and flags flying and pretty girls cheering. Most major Japanese ports, like Kobe and Yokohama, had been completely destroyed. Before they were rebuilt, small ports like Tanabe handled most shipping. American Liberty ships, chartered by the Japanese government, were used to bring our soldiers home.

The tiny harbor could handle only one of the rather small Liberty ships at a time. For a few months we used to see about three ships a week. There were no more parades, no more flags waving, no more bands blaring, and the girls were more interested in the big, conquering Americans with their friendly smiles, Hershey bars, and nylon stockings than in the sad, shamed, defeated Japanese. There was never any mention in the newspaper or over the air about these arrivals, and returning soldiers had virtually no contact with the people of Tanabe. I was one of the few who watched—from a distance. Our soldiers, still in their tattered uniforms, returned with bowed heads, without fanfare. They were very quiet, respecting the victor in the true samurai spirit. They usually stayed in Tanabe overnight, camping on the docks, never coming downtown, and left by train in the morning. My heart went out to them, and I knew that, but for the grace of a few years, I might have been among them, unless I had met my fate as a kamikaze.

The GIs did come into town and, as the feudal warlords of old had planned, often got lost in the maze of narrow, winding streets. I'd picked up some English by this point and sometimes served as a guide for the bewildered Americans. My father, despite his pride in his excellent English, stayed away. I think that for a while, like the carp hooked by a fisherman, my father had given up the struggle.

My grandfather was so happy that we were all back together that he never mentioned what we had lost. In our household, and in Japan itself, defeat in the war and the loss of Korea were taboo subjects. This was very typical. We never said Japan "lost" the war. Instead, we spoke of "the end" of the war.

My father did very little in those days. Our family owned timberland on a hillside near Tanabe. My father supported our family by selling timber, contracting out to others the whole job from cutting to distribution to replanting. My grandfather had been impressed with all that my father had accomplished in Korea, but now, except for selling off timber, my father had no regular job. The loss of our fortune and status in Korea may have dampened his initiative and made him cautious about starting up again. My grandfather was not pleased with his adopted son. And he was not alone.

Many people asked my father to use the family savings to start a factory to make soap from fish oil. Tanabe had plenty of fish, and soap was another of those products that Japan was virtually without. But my father was a conservative man, not given to hasty investments. In this case, his conservatism turned out to be wise. Other local investors did start a soap factory in Tanabe, and for a while, despite the fact that it was not a very good soap, the product sold. But soon the major soap company went back into business in a big way, making soap from animal fat and investing far more heavily in advertising than the local companies could. In a few years all those small local factories shut down. Had my father invested, our family would have been among those wiped out.

I had been in Tanabe for only a few weeks when I made my first unsuccessful effort to begin my university career. Though I had been accepted at Keio while we were still in Korea, with the chaotic communications of that immediate postwar period the only way for me to check on my status was to go to the university. Just to get a train ticket required a forty-eight-hour wait on line. Koji and I took turns holding a place and each of my parents took an occasional shift till finally we had a ticket. I took a rucksack of food and set out. The train was packed when it arrived at the station. The only way to get in and out was through the windows. Even on trains that had bathrooms, there was no way to get to them. Travel was very difficult for women and, under those conditions, it was virtually forbidden for young girls to travel at all. It took five tough hours to get from Tanabe to Osaka, where I changed to an even more crowded train for the twelve-hour ordeal to Tokyo.

The firebombings had left the capital with virtually no available housing, so it had been arranged for me to stay with the Mizuta family, friends of my father's, who had a villa in Atami, a spa about two hours from Tokyo—another of those havens that had never been bombed. I got off the train at Atami and spent the night there. I left early the next morning for Tokyo, climbing through the window to get onto another packed train. Though horribly crowded, the trains were already working well and running on time, one of the first signs of postwar recovery. But the downtown railroad station was gone, replaced by a jerry-built covered platform. And between the station and Keio University's downtown campus, which was a brisk walk of about fifteen minutes, I did not see a single building left standing. It was like walking numbly through a desert; I stared straight ahead, trying not to see what wasn't there. The destruction of Tokyo, accomplished over a period of time primarily by firebombing, was even more devastating than that of Hiroshima and Nagasaki. The dramatic impact of those two atomic bombs overshadowed the horrible loss of life in the firebombings of Dresden in Germany and Tokyo and Osaka in Japan. Conventional warfare, as we now call it, in contrast to atomic warfare, should be gruesome enough to convince mankind never again to repeat the madness of a world war.

The Keio campus itself also had been badly damaged. Virtually every building had been destroyed except the library, which now doubled as the administration building. I found that the records of my application and my acceptance for admission were in order, and I was given a certificate as a student. I tried to catch the last half of that school year, commuting from Atami. But this meant getting on line every morning at four to wait for a train ticket. One of the Mizuta family's servants did this for me one day, but I felt so sorry about that that I decided I had better give up and wait for the next school year to begin in April 1946. After only three days of school, I headed back to Tanabe.

By then I had no food left and felt ashamed to ask the Mizutas, for I knew how scarce food was in the region around Tokyo. I made the long train trip with a growling stomach. The only people on board who seemed to have food were Koreans and Chinese. They had probably been among the many Asians from occupied territories who were brought to Japan as forced laborers during the war. They had been liberated by the American GIs and given special privileges. I watched as one family opened a box of food that included a fine white rice that we call silver rice. It was rare at that time. To the hungry Japanese like myself on the train, it was clear that the Koreans and Chinese were on the side of the winners, the tall, generous Americans who were helping us all but who were especially helpful to those non-Japanese who had been trapped in Japan during the war.

That winter there were great fears of starvation. Newspapers predicted that ten million people would die of hunger. But in a famous cable General Douglas MacArthur, Supreme Commander of the Allied Powers (SCAP), demanded that Washington send 3.5 million tons of food immediately or send bullets and guns to put down the hunger riots that would otherwise be inevitable. When the response was slow, MacArthur cabled again: "Give me bread or give me bullets." The food came quickly. No one starved. By the next year, agriculture had begun to recover, helped in part by the land reform imposed by MacArthur's general headquarters. Few Americans realize the extent to which MacArthur is a hero in my country or the degree of absolute power he held in Japan during the postwar years. Without his leadership, Japan might never have recovered from the devastation of the war.

I still remember my feelings during that long and depressing train ride back from Tokyo. I realized that because of the war my college education would be delayed by at least a year and suffered hunger pangs while Koreans and Chinese around me enjoyed silver rice. I knew for sure we had lost the war and that we had a long road back to recovery.

When I returned to Tanabe, I came down with a severe, inexplicable fever. The doctors called in to treat me could never explain its cause, but years later my mother told me the doctors advised my father and her to accept the probability of my death. The only treatment they could recommend was to apply ice to my head to try to cool down the fever. My father sat by my bedside twenty-four hours a day for more than two weeks, holding a plastic bag of ice to my head, which rested on a pillow filled with ice water. I experienced a recurring dream of my body floating downward through heavy air but always being saved by someone who caught hold of my head and pulled me up. In moments of consciousness I was aware of my father but then would float back again into the deep.

Slowly, the fever began to ebb. The doctors could no more explain my recovery than they could account for the illness. My father told me that he believed the difficulties of our trip from Korea, followed so soon by my trek to Tokyo, had worn me out and weakened my resistance. He was my only real doctor through that period and may well have saved my life.

As I recovered, I had little to do except renew my close ties with my grandparents and to get to know our other relatives and our new home city. That period blurs in my mind, but I do remember taking several excursions across the bay from Tanabe to Shirahama, the spa where we had encountered the wounded veterans of the China campaign. Small boats made the twenty-minute trip every hour. Though it was a pleasant outing, I was haunted by my memories of those young men and drawn to the scene as I continued to struggle with the ambivalent feelings of fascination and fear about the appeal of war to the adventurous spirit and the horror of war to the rational mind. That struggle still burns like a fever within me to this day. It may explain how my dread of Japan's military government can co-exist with my respect for the American military man who ruled Japan from 1945 to 1951.

5

MacArthur's Japan

In the occupation period after World War II, Japanese used to joke about what we called the American 3-S Policy: sports, sex, and screen. It was considered a modern variation on the Roman empire's idea of giving the people circuses to distract them from the fact that they couldn't afford bread. Though sports didn't much appeal to me, in those days I saw as many American movies as possible. And I will never forget my first exposure to the second s.

During the war years, we not only had no American movies and no baseball, but Japanese women also became nearly invisible. Just as I was reaching my teens and becoming interested in girls, the *mompe*, a particularly ugly but practical form of kimono, became the universal uniform for women. It covered the entire body and was cut like a loose and unlovely sack. You couldn't even guess, much less see, what a woman in a *mompe* looked like. Makeup was not available and, supposedly to conserve electric energy, the permanent wave was banned. In short, feminine charm was outlawed.

After the war, for the first time in history, Japanese theaters began to have what were called nude shows. Not striptease, because the nudes couldn't move. I was in college, about nineteen or twenty years old, when I managed to see my first nude show. It was at the Teito Theater in the Shinjuku district of Tokyo. The show was supposed to be a drama set in Roman times and the girl, nude from the waist up, was supposed to be a statue that was part of the set. The other performers acted out the story. The theater was so quiet you could hear a pin drop, but no one was paying any attention to the story.

I had never before seen the bare breasts of a young girl. What can I say? The experience haunts me still.

Critics of the 3-S Policy claimed that Douglas MacArthur was trying to spoil the Japanese people. For others, like me, the 3-S Policy brought us what we considered the first fruits of democracy. If we were being spoiled, I had no objection. Quite apart from the 3-S Policy, my own life and my own way of thinking have been enormously affected by MacArthur's contributions to Japan.

Few Americans are aware of MacArthur's role as what might be described as a benevolent, left-wing emperor of Japan. Though MacArthur himself was politically conservative, he turned what had been a feudal society into a liberal democracy. There is considerable irony, of course, in the fact that it took a dictator to give Japan a truly democratic form of government.

I believe no ruler has ever exercised so much one-man authority over the Japanese people. From the end of the war in 1945 until his departure on April 16, 1951, MacArthur had extensive control over eighty million Japanese. Japanese emperors have always had to contend with rival power structures that could temper their authority. Though MacArthur had comparable problems with political figures and the press back in the United States, his authority within Japan was virtually unchallenged. In addition, MacArthur had the resources of the world's most powerful nation at his disposal. Direct United States aid to Japan was only one-third that given to West Germany, which had only one-fifth as many people as Japan. Nevertheless, MacArthur was in a position to do more for the people of Japan than any previous ruler. And he did do more.

The form of government established by the constitution drafted by MacArthur's staff at GHQ took more from the British system than the American. MacArthur insisted that the new constitution retain the Imperial system as a symbol of tradition and unity but shorn of its trappings of divinity and militarism. The Diet became a popularly elected parliament with full legislative powers. The relatively brief period of the Taisho democracy in the 1920s had far less impact than the democratic reforms launched by what Japanese call the MacArthur Constitution, reforms which have taken a firm hold over a period of more than forty years.

The land reform put through under MacArthur was far more sweeping and effective in its results than that achieved in China under Mao Tse-tung. He also abolished the feudal aristocracy and broke up the giant "money clique" monopolies known as *zaibatsu*. The constitution imposed by MacArthur gave Japanese women for the first time in history the right to vote and to run for elective office.

In recent years, political figures and other public opinion leaders in the United States and Western Europe have frequently complained that Japan does not bear a fair share of the military defense burden. They tend to forget that Japan's limited home-defense forces result from American policy decisions imposed on the country in the aftermath of World War II. General MacArthur, though he himself was a war hero, wrote in his memoirs, "For years I have believed that war should be abolished as an outmoded means of resolving disputes . . . and my abhorrence reached its height with the perfection of the atom bomb." Like many Japanese, I agree with him.

MacArthur, in those postwar days, acted more like a traditional Japanese emperor than Emperor Hirohito did. For the first time in history, a Japanese emperor began to appear frequently in public, no longer hidden behind the "Bamboo Screen" of the Imperial Palace. MacArthur, by contrast, rarely ventured beyond the Dai Ichi Insurance Company building across from the Imperial Palace, where he made his headquarters, and the American embassy, where he lived. Hundreds of Japanese gathered each day, hoping to catch a glimpse of him as his Packard limousine went from the embassy to his headquarters. But few ever saw him.

Emperor Hirohito renounced his divinity and began appearing at baseball games, flower shows, and trade fairs, like an American politician—up to a point. There was no backslapping, handshaking, or baby-kissing. One incident illustrates the limits.

The Emperor was scheduled to visit a steel mill organized by a Communist trade union. The trade unionists earnestly debated whether they should express their equality with the once divine Emperor by shaking hands. They agreed that the leader of the union should insist on shaking hands. When the Emperor was introduced, the union leader extended his hand. The Emperor held back and said softly, "I would prefer that we greet each other in the Japanese way." The two men bowed to each other.

But the Emperor was far less aloof than MacArthur; whose head-quarters became known as "Dai Ichi," which might be translated as "The Great Number One," and, needless to say, his license plate was also 1. He was not only the most powerful man in Japan but also the most popular and was soon revered by many as our surrogate emperor.

At first, however, my own perspective was influenced less by what I read than by a photograph that shocked the entire nation. It showed Emperor Hirohito, formally attired in morning coat, dwarfed by a towering, tieless MacArthur. When I saw that photograph, I realized that spiritually, as well as physically, Japan had been defeated and, like many Japanese, I felt anger at the lack of respect shown by MacArthur.

But MacArthur believed it was important for the people of Japan to have a closer relationship with their emperor to give them a sense of continuity and stability during the occupation. His understanding of this aspect of the Japanese character greatly helped the peaceful relations that prevailed throughout the occupation. During seven years of occupation, no U.S. soldier was intentionally killed in Japan.

Perhaps never before in history have wartime adversaries, conqueror and conquered, become so close. But it was MacArthur's great sense never to act like a conqueror, but like a leader. Far from humiliating the Emperor, as that photo made me think he had done, MacArthur saved his life, by resisting pressures from within Japan and in the United States to try him as a war criminal, and became his friend. It was, in human terms, an emblem of what America did for Japan.

MacArthur, meanwhile, played emperor for us in the traditional manner. Though there were strong moves by conservative Republicans to nominate MacArthur for president in the United States, he probably would have made a poor presidential candidate. But his imperial style was perfect for Japan. As former ambassador Edwin O. Reischauer has written, "MacArthur turned out to be the most radical, one might even say socialistic, leader the United States ever produced. But of course revolutionary change is easier to effect through arbitrary military power in someone else's country than through democratic means at home."

During an era when left-wing opinions were under harsh attack on many fronts in the United States, MacArthur made it possible for Socialists and Communists to exercise unprecedented political freedom and influence in Japan. The Communist party newspaper, *Akahata,* flourished under the MacArthur Constitution, which guaranteed freedom of the press. Though Communist influence is greatly diminished in today's prosperous Japan, these traditions continue. Japanese voters can listen to—or ignore—a greater variety of significant political voices than can voters in America, where only two not very different political parties have any real influence. I must admit that in Japan, though voters can listen to many voices, the majority invariably votes for the somewhat misnamed and rather conservative Liberal party. But it does seem to me that Japan grants a wider degree of freedom to a broader range of political opinion than is the practice in the United States.

This may be fairly typical. What Japanese learn from America, and we have learned much, we tend to adapt and often improve on. But there's no doubt that we learned true democracy from America. The word did not even exist in our language. As adapted into Japanese, the word sounds like "demo-krassie," which is how it usually comes out when I try to say it in English. But even if most Japanese can't pronounce it correctly, even after forty years of practicing it, we are indebted to the Americans who gave our feudal society the great gift of democracy.

In October 1945, MacArthur told the new prime minister, seventy-three-year-old Baron Kijuro Shidehara, that he wanted constitutional changes to allow for a series of reforms that included the unionization of labor and educational reforms to achieve "a system under which government becomes the servant rather than the master of the people." According to MacArthur's biographer William Manchester, MacArthur personally drafted the new education bill.

All Japanese have many reasons to be grateful to the rule of "The American Caesar," General Douglas MacArthur, during the postwar years. My family—and Minolta, the company I soon went to work for—have special things to be grateful for, including my father's career as an elected official. Partly as a result of MacArthur's educational reforms, my father, "The Henry Ford of Korea," found his way out of his personal postwar slump through politics. In an effort to counter the impact of militarism on national educational policy, MacArthur introduced an important decentralization of the educational bureaucracy. The system no longer exists, but for several years local school boards were elected on the basis of prefecture— almost a form of states' rights, American-style, applied to education in Japan.

My father decided to run in the first such election, which was held in 1948. The Kusumoto name was well known and respected in Wakayama prefecture, largely because of my grandfather's generosity in building the new city hall in Tanabe. My father was one of the few university graduates in the area at that time, and he had the reputation of being a staunch conservative and a good family man who neither drank nor smoked. He was a very successful candidate. Elected to two successive terms, he became an active member of the school board. He also became known as an effective opponent of Communist party influence in the teachers' union—which at the time was a major issue in Japan. He developed close ties with the governor and other top government officials of the ruling Liberal party. Later on these contacts helped him when he again became active in the auto business.

Though my father was among the many Japanese who admired MacArthur, I suspect that at one time he might have thought the general was a bit soft on the Communists. Perhaps he was. A pun on the general's name in Japanese, *Macassur*, identified him in those days as a "left red."

After the war, the teachers' union was a prime target of the Communists. They were aware of the extent to which the military had used the schools to control the minds of the young, and saw the school system as a key to control of the future. In the early days of the occupation, MacArthur's GHQ had released all political prisoners. The Americans identified as allies all opponents of the military regime. Many Communists were among those released, and they soon took advantage not only of the political amnesty but also of the reforms MacArthur sought, particularly in politics, education, and the liberalization of the press. The Communist party did gain control of the teachers' union and continued to dominate the union until recent years.

My father enjoyed his career as an elected official in the education system, but he was less happy about the role of the Communists in the teachers' union. The current American concept of the Japanese employee as an uncomplaining partner in a cooperative labor-management system geared to efficiency and productivity ignores the turbulent period of postwar strikes, protests, and factory take-overs by angry workers. Like their American counterparts in the same period, Japanese workers in the postwar years were militant in their demands.

In Japan, under MacArthur, Communists were allowed to operate politically with far greater freedom than they could in the United States. For a time, they were the dominant force in the labor movement. But MacArthur was shrewd in his handling of the Communists. He let them defeat themselves. The Communist party made a big mistake by demanding that Emperor Hirohito be tried and hung as a war criminal. Though the MacArthur Constitution and Hirohito himself had demystified the Emperor, he was still held in great esteem by the vast majority of our people. The Communist party's adherence to Moscow also undermined them when the Russians' postwar policies proved so hostile to Japan.

MacArthur's own socialistic reforms, his expansion of the voting franchise to include women and younger people, and the protection provided by the constitution to a wide range of civil liberties also undercut the appeal of the Communist party. So did MacArthur's effort to aid Japanese industry, which gradually began providing more secure and better-paying jobs. Joseph M. Dodge, a former president of the American Banking Association, became a consultant to MacArthur and developed comprehensive plans to stabilize industry and control government budgets.

Shortages of everything from food to factories had fueled a runaway inflation. Dodge advocated strict control over government budgets as one means of controlling inflation. An even tougher measure, made possible only by MacArthur's absolute power, was a freeze on all money in banks. On February 11, 1946, the government issued a new, devalued currency and declared all old currency worthless. My family, good savers like most Japanese, was hit hard by the devaluation, but there was no way to escape the freeze. Within a few years, measures like these brought inflation under control.

MacArthur also severely restricted visas to Japan for American businessmen. He wanted to protect Japanese firms by not allowing American companies to come in and take control. He believed that the prosperity of Japan was important for world peace and predicted that in the future the Pacific would be far more important to American trade than the Atlantic. This was an amazing position in the late 1940s, but time has proved him right. MacArthur's policies eventually enabled Japan to achieve what our country had miserably failed to achieve through war—the creation of an East Asian Co-Prosperity Sphere in which Japan is the dominant economic power.

MacArthur's apparently left-wing policies were strongly influenced by a GHQ staff that included many ardent liberals who had developed their ideals as young bureaucrats during Franklin Roosevelt's "New Deal" administration. They were bright and hardworking and had the experience MacArthur needed in setting up a civilian administration. Though their political philosophy differed sharply from MacArthur's, he let them put their ideas into play as an effective way of undercutting the appeal of Japan's homegrown Communists and their Soviet models. With hindsight, it is possible to see the consistency in MacArthur's political philosophy.

Few younger Japanese realize how much we owe to MacArthur and American generosity during the occupation. The truth about the occupation is neglected in our schools, where many teachers accept the left-wing view that the occupation was an example of American imperialism. In fact, MacArthur was determined that Japan would not be taken over by American economic interests and made sure that it didn't happen. If more people in Japan realized the role America played in helping us to rebuild our industries, our current disputes over trade, defense, and other issues could be worked out in a less hostile atmosphere. Even in the 1960s, when American industries were pressing for protection against imports, presidents Kennedy and Johnson resisted and kept America's markets open, giving Japan a chance to expand its export economy.

Despite his *"Macassur"* reputation in postwar Japan, the general was always staunchly anti-Communist. He parted company with the "armchair general" variety of American conservatives only as a tactician and field commander. In postwar Japan, he was in the front lines of a struggle against conditions that were ripe for the development of communism. After centuries of exploitation by big landowners, tenant farmers were open to appeals for revolution. Land reform, breaking up the big holdings and giving individual farmers a stake in ownership, undercut the appeal of collectivization. Individual political freedom for all, including Socialists and Communists, gave even the left-wingers a stake in the democratic process, undercutting the appeal of centralized political control, which the Communists advocated. MacArthur apparently sensed that in the particular circumstances prevailing in postwar Japan, liberal reforms were a more effective buffer against communism than a more traditionally conservative approach. Therefore, the general gave his idealistic staff members free rein—up to a point.

MacArthur's policies toward unions changed abruptly on the eve of a planned national strike. Teachers and other public employees—in power plants, utilities, and the railroads—were to be in the vanguard of 250,000 strikers, and another 1.5 million workers were to stage sympathy strikes. On January 31, 1947, MacArthur issued a strongly worded order banning the strike, which was to have begun at dawn. The president of the labor federation, bowing to MacArthur's absolute power, made an emotional radio broadcast, calling off the strike. MacArthur immediately urged the government to pass a bill banning strikes by public employees, including teachers. Needless to say, my father was pleased.

From that point on, MacArthur's rule took on a more obviously conservative tone. But by then land reform and the new constitution were firmly in place. For Japan, there has been no turning back from the course of liberal democracy charted for our country by Douglas MacArthur.

6

How to Succeed at College Without Really Studying

My higher education began in April 1946 under difficult circumstances at Keio University in downtown Tokyo. Keio, the oldest private university in Japan, is thought of as a rich man's college. It is very expensive, but in those days it hardly seemed fancy. The only buildings on campus that survived the war were the library and one small building known as the "Free Speech Auditorium." Traditionally, it has been Japan's nearest equivalent of London's Hyde Park as a place where people can speak freely on any subject, no matter how controversial.

For the first two years our classes were held in a surviving high school building with bombed-out windows. Fortunately, it was spring and not nearly as cold as it had been in our school in Korea. When winter came, however, we wore coats and gloves, which made note-taking difficult. So many people had been killed, and so many families had fled Tokyo when the massive bombings began in late 1944, that there were relatively few younger students left in the city. Since food and housing were more available in the countryside, the migration of families back to the city was slow in getting under way. With its urban, industrial base wiped out, Japan had again become an agricultural country. The availability of our windowless high school was a sad reminder of the devastation that had rained down on the cities.

No dormitories had survived the war, and I was lucky to be taken in by the Hashimoto family, who lived in Shibuya, a nice district but about an hour's train ride from campus. Jusaburo Hashimoto was also a Keio graduate. He did not know my father directly but through a common friend agreed to take me in. It turned out that the main reason for his generosity was to give him a chance to recruit me for Keio's rugby team, which he sponsored. Rugby is not exactly the national pastime in Japan, and I'm not exactly a natural athlete. But I didn't want to offend my benefactor. Reluctantly, I went to my first practice with members of the senior class. They told me with great enthusiasm what a wonderful but rugged game rugby was. They assured me with gaping smiles that I would lose teeth, that my nose would be bent out of shape but could be fixed with a steel stick inserted in what was left of the bone. I shivered. That was the end of my very brief rugby career.

I was grateful that Mr. Hashimoto didn't throw me out of his house, but I was about to engage on a daily basis in a sport nearly as rough as rugby—commuting to school on the packed playing fields of the National Railroad and its feeder lines. My normal route involved taking one train from a station near the Hashimotos' home, then changing at the main Shibuya station for the National Railroad. At each platform, professional "pushers" shoved us into already jammed cars. Often, I would have to wait while three or four trains went through before I could get myself wedged into one of the cars.

I tried taking a train in the opposite direction, hoping I could board at a station farther up the line where the train might be less crowded. But I got caught. I tried to argue my way out of paying the extra fare but I lost. I wound up just as packed in as usual and a bit poorer.

My next tactic worked better. I started walking to the main station. Like all students during the war years, I had been trained as a "walking soldier" and was used to hiking great distances. Though I rarely walk anywhere today, in those days, like most of my generation, I was great at brisk, long walks. That early training may explain why so many Japanese men in my age bracket tend to live long lives and are very healthy.

Food was an even bigger problem than transportation. Two

daughters in the Hashimoto family used to travel to the countryside every Sunday to buy potatoes and other vegetables that might be available on the black market. Rice was strictly controlled and much more difficult to get. For those who could afford it, Korean and Chinese restaurants were the best places to get rice and noodles since the Koreans and Chinese were generally allowed to ignore Japanese rationing laws. One of the tragic stories of the time was of a judge who had starved to death because his honor made it impossible for him to deal on the black market. No one could survive in those days without the black market, which was another of the factors that contributed to runaway inflation until MacArthur's drastic measures stopped it.

I must confess that for me college life was neither very pleasant nor very productive, at least not in academic terms. For one thing, we were poorly prepared for college. I had decided on a business career, hoping to follow in the footsteps of my grandfather and father. I majored in economics, which meant having to read texts in English by men like John Maynard Keynes. Of course, my study of English had been a casualty of the war. As a result, I limped through my college career, handicapped by an intellectual war wound. There was one economics teacher I paid attention to, though not when he was lecturing in academic terms.

Professor Kinbara had been a young scholar in Germany after World War I. Japan had taken a very sensible approach to that conflict. It sided with the Allied powers but stayed away from most of the shooting. Saipan and the South Pacific islands around it were a German colony at that time, and Japan contributed to the Allied war effort by seizing them. Japan also dispatched a few warships to the Mediterranean, but its most important role was as a supplier of arms and equipment to the other Allied powers, expanding its economic empire but avoiding the negative costs of heavy involvement in armed conflict. Basically, in 1914, Japan decided to make money, not war, an approach that would have served it well two decades later when the clouds of World War II began to gather.

Japan was relatively prosperous when young Kinbara set off for Germany after World War I. The Japanese yen was strong and the German mark had been weakened by inflation. As a result, Kinbara, rather than living like the usual impoverished scholar, lived like a king. At Keio, he loved to tell stories about his many German girlfriends.

His well-taught lessons on the economics of romance were reinforced by field trips I made on my own in Tokyo, where American
GIs, as young as our professor had been after World War I, also
lived like kings. It wasn't unusual to see fuzzy-cheeked American
soldiers walking through Tokyo with a lovely Japanese girl on each
arm. Most Japanese were shabbily dressed, but not the girls strolling
with their American boyfriends. They wore Western-style clothes in
bright colors and high-heeled shoes instead of sandals—and, of
course, nylon stockings.

One of the most fascinating sights you could see was the daily
spectacle at the intersection of Owari-cho and Ginza streets in downtown Tokyo. Before the war, when I visited Tokyo on summer vacations from Korea, this corner was the center of Tokyo's most
elegant shopping district, the equivalent of New York's Fifth Avenue
and Fifty-seventh Street. Today, that elegant corner is again dominated by the circular tower of the Sanai women's wear shop and the
world's greatest concentration of neon signs. But in 1946 the only
shops were the tables that street vendors used to display their meager, black-market goods. Shells of bombed and fire-charred buildings
dotted the mostly flattened landscape. The traffic lights had also been
blown away, but the American military had built a makeshift kiosk
with an open platform in the middle of the intersection. One at a
time, tall, invariably handsome and incredibly healthy-looking military policemen, in neatly pressed olive uniforms and dazzling white
helmets, white gloves, white belts, and white holsters for their .45-
caliber automatics, took turns on the platform directing traffic with
a style and flair that a ballet dancer might envy. And they performed
before an audience of dazzled young Japanese girls. The young women
would watch the American on the platform, then turn to glance at
the hungry-looking, poorly dressed Japanese men waiting to cross
the street with bowed heads and hunched shoulders. Young girls
would come to that corner with no other purpose than to watch the
powerful choreography that controlled traffic with such authority.
Apart from the pedestrians, virtually all of the traffic was made up
of American military jeeps, trucks, and command cars.

For me, the show wasn't just the whistle-blowing, arm-waving
dancer on the platform but also the girls who watched in fascination
and the sad, defeated Japanese men they glanced at with a barely
noticeable shake of the head. Burned-out men shuffled past burned-
out buildings, averting their eyes, jealous of the power of the Amer-

ican GIs to attract the young girls but knowing they could not compete and that there was nothing they could say. The seeds of Japan's postwar recovery may have been sown on that corner of the Ginza in 1946.

During my college years, most Japanese were still at a loss, not knowing what to do to escape from the daily struggle just to earn enough to buy food for survival at black-market prices. Though we were jealous of the GIs, the generosity they showed to their Japanese girlfriends was also at work on a more profound level. The economic help and political liberalization America provided under General MacArthur's direction enabled Japan to begin to rebuild both the economy and the confidence that had been shattered by war.

While I did not learn a lot from my classes at college, I did learn a lot watching that daily spectacle on the Ginza. When we finally graduated from Keio, the dean in his commencement address bluntly told us we were the worst class in the history of the university. He said that in normal times most of us would not even have been eligible for graduation. Our poor preparation was not the only reason that college contributed little to my education. Americans have some strong misconceptions about the superiority of Japanese education. Elementary and secondary school education is rigorous by American standards, but it depends too strongly on rote memorization. Even at the graduate level, originality and creativity are not encouraged. To me it isn't surprising that the only Japanese to make major contributions to science and mathematics have done so while working at American universities.

In Japan college is considered a time for relaxation rather than grinding study. Getting into college is the tough part. But students, after knocking themselves out to qualify for college, are traditionally entitled to four years of socializing, making contacts and generally enjoying themselves before settling into the adult grind of long hours and hard work. In these terms, my career at Keio was a great success. I made contacts and friendships that have meant very much to me. But most of my learning was accomplished by copying from my friends' notebooks. Fortunately, my real education was going on elsewhere.

During college vacation in the summer of 1949, my military career finally began at the site of the Tokorazawa Army Air Base, which I'd been heading for when the war ended back in August 1945. Only I wasn't joining the Japanese military. I was going to work as a houseboy for Captain Michael Bolint of the U.S. Number Five Fighter Wing at what was then called Johnson Air Force Base. A friend of mine from Tanabe had a part-time job at the base and told me of its advantages. "You get to eat good American food, and the family I work for even takes me to the movies." The chance to see all those good American movies meant even more to me than the chance to eat. I was happy to be hired for what was supposed to be just a summer job.

When the Korean War began on June 25, 1950, I was still working for the Bolints. Though he never spoke of it, I had to assume that Captain Bolint's many missions took him over my old homeland. The Bolints were wonderful people, and their six-year-old daughter, Teddie, became one of my most important teachers. After all, she had been studying English all her life, and I learned a lot from her. She was a cute little girl with blond hair and I enjoyed taking photos of her. At the time I had a Minolta 35-mm focal-plane camera. I had chosen a Minolta because of my fondness for the Minoltaflex I had used as a child in Korea. Perhaps it was just coincidence, but I sometimes wonder if, with those Minolta cameras, fate was already moving me toward the career I would ultimately follow.

Captain Bolint was able to buy Ansco/Kodak film at the PX, so I had plenty of opportunities to practice my photography. There was a period when I thought this might become my career. Theo, Teddie's mother, used to compliment me on my pictures. I might have become a good photojournalist, though I lacked the creative instincts of an art photographer.

My job left me plenty of spare time for taking Teddie around the base, practicing my English and my photography, and learning more about America and Americans. Though I loved my job, I was afraid to tell my parents that I was working as a houseboy. It wasn't what they had in mind when they sent their son off to an expensive university. I was proud of the photographs I had of myself in my houseboy's white uniform, but I never sent any to my parents. Instead, I told them I was working at the university library, which sounded properly intellectual. Later, when I had graduated and was no longer working as a houseboy, I told them the truth and showed them my houseboy photos.

There were many advantages to working for the American military, not just for me, but also for the Hashimoto family, whom I had been living with. While I stuffed myself on American food, they were able to use my ration coupons to supplement the family's food allowance. Since I was living in newly built dormitories for workers, the Hashimotos also had a bit more room in their house.

The job wasn't difficult. The Bolints also had a Japanese maid who took care of most of the housework. My main responsibility was taking care of Captain Bolint's car, a green Nash that I washed every other day. The Japanese houseboys were very competitive about the cars they looked after, each boasting that his employer had the best car.

Since I knew more about cars than the others did, I sounded more convincing than most in my pride about my boss's car. Working on that car brought back to me again that American smell I had known in our Ford body shop in Korea. It was also in the Bolint household that I saw my first washing machine and vacuum cleaner, products that no Japanese at the time, no matter how wealthy, had the privilege of owning. But most impressive of all, the Bolints also introduced me to one of the great wonders of the world: the Sears Roebuck catalog. I was astounded at this encyclopedia of riches and amazed that ordinary Americans could own such things. With the Bolints' help, I ordered myself a light gray, almost white, double-breasted gabardine suit and a fancy pair of shoes to go with it. A pair of shoes in those days cost the average Japanese a month's salary, but I was able to order very inexpensively what I was sure were the best shoes in the world. In my new outfit, I looked like a California nisei.

This became my real school, preparing me for America, where my business career would develop. It turned out that the Bolints weren't movie fans, so I didn't get to see all those movies that had been my main reason for taking the job. But I had no regrets. In fact, I enjoyed what I was doing so much that I stretched that summer job into nearly two full years. I arranged with the Bolints to have three days off a week to attend classes. It wasn't unusual for students not to attend all their classes. Primarily because of the shortage of food and housing, some students might be away from the university for weeks at a time.

I managed to see more than my share of movies, many of them American, at regular Japanese theaters and also took advantage of the university's movie club. Though we did get invited to previews at special discounts, my real interest in the club was less in seeing movies than in getting to meet the stars of the movie industry. At the time, along with thinking about becoming a photographer, I had a dream of being a movie director. One day the club arranged a student visit to the studio of Akira Kurosawa, who is best known in America for films like *Rashomon*, *The Seven Samurai*, and *Ran*, his version of Shakespeare's *King Lear*. Kurosawa was not yet famous but greatly admired by students of film. We spent a wonderful half-day at his studio. To me it was all glamorous and inspiring, but I knew there was maybe one chance in ten thousand of my ever becoming a great film director.

I became very close to the Bolint family and will never forget April 15, 1950, my twenty-second birthday. I felt like part of the family as the Bolints gave me a party, complete with a big cake and everyone singing "Happy Birthday." I was close to tears and very happy. Later, when I was in America, I learned that Captain Bolint, by then promoted to major, was stationed in Düsseldorf, Germany. But I was never able to get in touch with him. Perhaps he, or Teddie, may one day read this book and find me.

Near the end of my senior year, I borrowed the notebooks of my friends and began studying extra hours. I managed to graduate as an average student in the worst class in the university's history. Despite my own shortcomings as a student, I will always be grateful to Keio for the traditions it bred in me and, quite frankly, for the contacts it afforded me. I was soon to meet the most important of those contacts, the alumnus Kazuo Tashima, the founder of Minolta, who became both a second father and a business mentor to me.

7

Growing Up with Minolta

Since I had not been a very good student, there was little chance of my joining one of the major trading companies to fulfill my dream of going to the United States. They were among the few Japanese firms that had offices in America. I had gone to the school placement office to try to arrange an appointment with the Mitsui shipping company. But I was told that Mitsui would only consider the top twenty students. I was a long way from the top twenty. After that, my father and Mr. Hashimoto took over.

Jusaboro Hashimoto and my father had agreed that my interest in photography might lead to something. Mr. Hashimoto knew Kazuo Tashima, founder of the Osaka-based company that produced the Minolta line of cameras. Housing by that time was somewhat easier to come by in Osaka than in Tokyo and Mr. Tashima's firm, which was then known as Chiyoda Kogaku Seiko, was the only camera company in the Osaka area. And so Mr. Hashimoto arranged an interview for me with his friend and fellow Keio alumnus. I hoped it would turn out better than Mr. Hashimoto's efforts to recruit me for his rugby team. But my first impression of the firm that had created my Minolta 35-mm camera wasn't promising.

Minolta, like Keio University, was headquartered in a high school, one that had survived the massive March 14, 1945, firebombing of central Osaka. Three of Minolta's main plants in the Osaka area had been destroyed in air raids, and, at my interview, Mr. Tashima told me he had decided the safest place to relocate would be in downtown Osaka, where there was nothing left worth bombing. I can still see the charred insides of the burned-out Kyuhoji National School building. Mr. Tashima, a solid, conservatively dressed man in his mid-fifties, sensed my disappointment.

"Our headquarters may be shabby-looking," he said, "but we are concentrating on building new factories. Someday we may have better-looking offices, but for the time being we are more interested in our manufacturing plants." Mr. Tashima had a way of sitting sometimes with his fists clenched on the desk before him. It gave him a very severe appearance.

I was nervous at that first meeting. I had never before been in the presence of the president of an important company. Mr. Tashima was a stocky man, not much taller than I, but I felt small in his presence that day. His Western-style suit looked as though it had been cut from fine British textiles. Even when sitting behind his desk in that unimpressive office in a fire-charred building, he was an imposing figure. From the first, however, his words were warm and friendly. I felt that he was studying me closely, even as he tried to put me at ease.

He asked about my command of English. My nervousness increased. I smiled and mumbled a few words, something like, "Oh, yes. I study English very nicely."

"That's very excellent," said Mr. Tashima, very formally.

Luckily for me, though he understood English fairly well, Mr. Tashima was never really comfortable with the language. He wasn't able to spot my shortcomings as the conversation quickly reverted to Japanese.

We discovered we had much in common. We were both graduates of Keio and both our families were originally from Wakayama prefecture. My father, just about the same age as Mr. Tashima, was also a Keio graduate. Mr. Tashima was impressed by the fact that I had been using Minolta cameras since I was a child and, to my surprise, by the fact that I had worked with the American military, even if only as a domestic servant.

"Getting along with the American soldiers is very important," he said. "They are our most important customers." He let that topic drop and it was several months before I understood the importance of what he had said.

We talked for at least half an hour. He told me a bit about the history of his company and how it had grown through military contracts during the war when employment increased from one thousand to four thousand. But the postwar recovery had been slow in taking hold. He said his company had an excess of employees. The labor unrest prevalent throughout the country had also created problems; a strike in 1950 had contributed to the severe financial difficulties his company faced.

"We aren't hiring at all," he said.

My heart sank. My hopes had been building even though I realized our interview was not at all part of the usual process for hiring new graduates. In a company the size of Mr. Tashima's, hiring normally would have been handled by a personnel administrator. There would have been tests to take and academic records to consider. Mr. Tashima and I just talked. I began to wonder if our meeting was merely a courtesy interview granted out of friendship for Mr. Hashimoto.

"Mr. Hashimoto has told me some interesting things about you," Mr. Tashima said. "Perhaps we can arrange something."

He was silent for a moment, then he began telling me about his family's firm, an import-export company known as Tashima Shoten. Based in the port city of Kobe, the firm had an Osaka branch with offices in the same building as Mr. Tashima's camera company.

"Until we can open up something here, perhaps we can arrange something for you at Tashima Shoten." He smiled and added, "I used to work there myself. It isn't a bad place to start."

I left his office that day not quite knowing what to expect. Chiyoda Kogaku Seiko and its Minolta cameras were very well known. No matter what the job or the salary, the prestige of working for the company that made Minolta cameras would be very high. I didn't know what to expect of Tashima Shoten. But jobs were scarce and I was grateful when, three months after my graduation, Mr. Tashima introduced me to his uncle, Katsumi Tashima, who ran Tashima Shoten, and I was given a job.

I started in June 1951. It turned out to be great for me, working for an import-export firm and getting an apprenticeship in international trade that I could not have obtained at the time from Minolta, which had no real export business. My job at Tashima Shoten provided experience in the details of foreign trade that would be so helpful to me later at Minolta. I handled correspondence and cables from foreign buyers, licenses, foreign-currency exchange, and all the details involved in building international trade. French may be the language of international diplomacy, but English is the language of international trade, and my new job gave me plenty of opportunity to practice my second language.

For the eighteen months that I worked with Tashima Shoten I saw a great deal of Mr. Tashima, who was also known as KT. Tashima Shoten was located on the fourth floor of the building and the camera and optics firm occupied the first three. I met with Mr. Tashima almost every day and occasionally spent time with him in the evening. My relationship with him slowly changed, and, through our many long conversations, KT became almost a father to me, teaching me, counseling me, helping me to understand the business world, and giving me a chance to get to know him. Though I have met many important people in my life, no one has impressed me more than KT.

Knowing a bit about KT's life is essential to understanding my own story, for he has had enormous impact on virtually everything that has happened to me since the first day I met him. He was born on November 20, 1899, in Hikata-machi, which is now known as the city of Kainan, about twenty miles north of my grandparents' home in Tanabe. He graduated from Keio in March 1923 and worked briefly for the Dentsu News Agency as a bookkeeper in its advertising division in Tokyo. This was the forerunner of today's Dentsu, the world's largest advertising agency. The great earthquake of September 1, 1923, destroyed much of Tokyo, including the Dentsu offices. KT's family, frightened by the earthquake, brought their son back to Kobe to join Tashima Shoten, the import-export firm his father had founded there in 1920.

In 1927, at the age of twenty-eight, KT made his first trip abroad, traveling to the Middle East and Europe for Tashima Shoten, as part of a trade mission organized by the city of Kobe to promote the export of Japanese silk, cotton, knit goods, cheap toys, handmade novelties, and other products. While in Paris, he toured an optics plant and was fascinated by the technology. KT saw binoculars and range finders being made for the Japanese army and was ashamed that there was nothing like this being done in Japan. He began to dream of producing high-grade optical products, including cameras. At the time the Japanese market was dominated by the Leica and other German products. When his father opposed the idea of such a venture under the auspices of Tashima Shoten, young KT set off on his own. As the oldest son, KT would have become president of his father's trading company. But he had a vision of a Japan capable of producing manufactured products it could be proud of, like the industrial countries of Europe that he had visited. He also believed that Japan desperately needed products that it could export. As industrialization increased in Japan during the 1920s, the country's dependence on imported oil also increased. The only way to get the foreign exchange needed to pay for fuel imports was to increase exports. KT was convinced that quality cameras could become one of those exports.

Back in Japan KT met two Germans, both named Wilhelm but known, respectively, as Willy and Billy. Willy Heilemann imported German products into Japan through the port of Kobe. His friend, Billy Neumann, was an engineer experienced in optics. Together, KT and his German friends formed Nichi-Doku Shashinki Shoten, the Japanese-German Camera Company. It was officially established November 11, 1928, with about thirty employees. Relying heavily on imported German optical technology, they turned out their first products, a bellows camera called the Nifcalette, in March 1929. Within three months, they had increased production from one camera a day to one hundred. But their timing could not have been worse. The October 1929 stock market crash in the United States, followed by the drying up of international credit and a wave of protectionist legislation, initiated by the United States with the Smoot-Hawley Tariff Act of 1930, crippled international trade. The Great Depression of the 1930s, affecting virtually every country in the world, was under way.

As KT would recall, "Our Japanese-German Camera Company was a small boat which set sail right into a storm." But somehow the small boat survived. In July 1931, KT restructured the privately held firm as a joint venture under the name Molta Goshi Kaisha. Later that year, however, Heilemann and Neumann left the company to set up their own firm, manufacturing camera parts. KT reorganized his company, relying on the skill of young Japanese technicians.

From the first, KT was export-minded even though the company did not become seriously involved in exports until after the war. But KT's experience with his father's trading company convinced him that whether it was silk or manufactured products, Japan's domestic markets were not strong enough to support an expanding economy. Densely populated, mountainous and rocky, with little land fit for farming and hardly any oil or iron ore, Japan, much like the British Isles, had to develop an export economy to pay for the imports it needed just to survive. Problems with imports have often been the mother of invention in Japan. The first major success of KT's company is a good example of this. By 1933 it had become impossible to import the sheepskin needed to make the bellows for those early cameras. No substitutes had the necessary flexibility and strength. At KT's urging, the skeptical company engineers, using synthetic resins to produce a form of Bakelite, set about developing the world's first rigid-material bellows. Their attempt worked.

The Minolta Vest, introduced in January 1934, was a big hit in Japan. The name "Minolta" had first been used for a new camera model the year before. KT coined the term from a combination of Japanese and foreign sounds. The Minolta factory outside Osaka was then surrounded by rice fields. The Japanese expression for ripening fields of rice (*minoru-ta*) comes close to the sound of Minol-ta. (Keep in mind the *l* sound that Westerners hear when Japanese attempt to say foreign words with the letter *r*.)

The phrase in Japanese conjures up a lovely image of waving, windswept fields of green rice shoots. KT used to say that he was inspired in part by a Japanese saying often cited by his mother. "The ripest ears of rice bow their heads lowest," meaning that the wisest and most successful people are the most humble. There is some vanity in such humility, of course, but then we all have a bit of ego in us. There is also an English-language acronym in the name Minolta, coming from the key initial letters in "(M)achinery and (IN)struments (O)ptica(L) by (TA)shima."

The Minolta Vest popularized the name Minolta within Japan, and Minolta cameras soon began showing up in other parts of the world, though the company was still a long way from having a serious export arm. By 1937, the company was able to expand and diversify. Reorganized that year as Chiyoda Kogaku Seiko, K.K. (Chiyoda Optics and Fine Engineering, Ltd.), the firm built a lens factory at Sakai and introduced the first Japanese-made twin-lens camera, the Minoltaflex, the camera I used as a child in Korea.

By 1938 Germany had occupied Czechoslovakia and Austria and Japanese troops had plunged into China. The flow of imports was slowing, which forced Japan—and Minolta—to become more self-reliant. KT was soon producing binoculars for naval officers and military range finders, replacing those French products he had seen being manufactured for the Japanese military years before. In 1942 Minolta opened its optical glass factory at Itami. The government banned the manufacture of commercial cameras, and the industry became totally devoted to the war effort.

During the war years, Minolta and its main rival, Nippon Kogaku, the makers of Nikon, were adopted by rival branches of the armed forces. Minolta worked primarily for the army and air force; Nippon Kogaku worked mostly for the navy. Minolta agreed to develop an aerial camera for the air force. Nippon Kogaku went to work on a range finder for the *Yamato*-class battleships with their famous eighteen-inch guns. By that time the Japanese camera companies were making excellent lenses, some better than what the Germans were producing. The navy was confident that no other country could produce the long-distance range finders being used on the *Yamato*. This may have been true, but what the Japanese military didn't realize was that the British and the Americans were developing radar, an electronic tracking device that made range finders obsolete. Given Japan's dominance in electronics today, it is ironic that during the war industry concentrated perhaps too much on optics and not nearly enough on electronics.

Military spending during the war years greatly improved the technological capabilities of Japan's camera companies. But there was a devastating trade-off. The saturation bombing of the Osaka industrial area in the spring of 1945 wiped out Minolta's industrial capacity. Digging through the rubble of bombed-out factories to salvage fire-blackened components, KT began the slow process of rebuilding. He soon received a helping hand from an unexpected source—General Douglas MacArthur.

During the occupation, General MacArthur was troubled by the fact that American servicemen spent most of their free time—and money—drinking and chasing girls. This meant good business for Japanese bar girls, but General MacArthur had other ideas. He concluded that part of the problem was that in war-torn Japan with its shattered economy there was little else for American servicemen to spend their money on. This was somewhat less of a problem in Europe, where the economy had been less devastated and the benefits of the Marshall Plan were already taking effect. Leica cameras and

Swiss watches were particularly popular items at American military-post exchanges in Europe. MacArthur reasoned that every camera or watch bought by a serviceman at a military PX would mean that much less money he could spend drinking and chasing girls.

Neutral Switzerland had been spared by the war and its precision machine tool industry was an important factor in the quick recovery of the European economy. Part of MacArthur's dream for Japan was that it would become the Switzerland of Asia, politically neutral, peaceful, prosperous, and democratic. He was well aware that Japan was poor in raw materials and even poorer in sources of energy. Since the country was also densely populated and, after the war, unemployment was high, MacArthur reasoned that labor-intensive industries would be ideal to get the economy back on its feet. Coupled with his desire to give servicemen something to spend their money on, this convinced him to develop Japan's camera and watch industries.

General MacArthur obtained loans from the U.S. government and issued special import licenses so that Japanese firms could import precision tools from Switzerland. The Japanese manufacturers that benefited most from this generous American policy were the makers of Minolta, Nikon, and Canon cameras and Seiko watches. The Japanese companies had to agree that 80 percent of their production would go to the American military PXs for sale to servicemen. Only the remaining 20 percent could be sold on the domestic market. In effect, this meant that 80 percent of production was earmarked for export.

The Minolta 35-mm I started using while working for Captain Bolint was the first Japanese camera to be modeled after the German Leica. One drawback of the Leica was the inconvenience of loading film from the bottom. Minolta solved this problem with a back cover that opened out.

Another inconvenience of the Leica was that its film frames were double the size of motion-picture frames, with long horizontals. When enlarged, both sides had to be cut in the printing process. The Minolta used a more natural film format that provided forty exposures rather than the Leica's thirty-six. A few months later, Nikon came out with a camera following the Minolta format. Though Nikon had previously made a wide range of precision optical instruments, including camera lenses for other manufacturers, it did not market its first commercial camera, known as the Nikon I, until 1948. Only about 750 of these cameras were produced. The Nikon I has become a rare collector's item and sells for over $3,000.

GIs in Japan began buying these Nikon and Minolta cameras, which became known as Japanese format cameras, and some made their way back to America. Color was becoming popular but prints were so expensive that most people took slides. But Kodak did not adopt its film to accommodate the Japanese format. In many respects these "Japanese format" cameras were a good idea but they weren't right for the American market. MacArthur's GHQ intervened and ordered Nikon and Minolta to change the format for their sales to PX outlets.

Though Japanese optics had improved greatly during the war, our postwar cameras were not so good mechanically. Shutters and film winders did not function very well, and electronically we were far behind the Americans. But by the time I graduated from college and was ready to start my career, three factors already mentioned had laid the groundwork for Japan's later emergence as the world's finest producer of cameras: the importing of European lenses, technology, and engineers to get the industry off the ground—the first important step, taken by KT himself; wartime spending by the Japanese military, which had helped the industry expand; and, most recently, MacArthur's intervention in obtaining precision Swiss machine tools and opening an "export" market with the military post exchanges, which brought in badly needed foreign currency.

Even while I was working with Tashima Shoten, my work began to involve Minolta cameras. Cameras were still in short supply in Japan during those years. Knowing of the family connection, customers of Tashima Shoten often asked if we could help them get a Minolta camera, which sold at a premium on the domestic market. It became part of my job to keep our customers happy by getting them expensive cameras from KT. So in a very small way my career in the camera industry began with domestic sales for Minolta.

By the end of 1952 KT was ready to move me into Minolta. My job was in the "export department," which really meant selling to the PXs. Miura Trading Company, Minolta's domestically based trading company, would bring American "buyers" to Minolta to discuss camera and equipment sales. These buyers were, of course, military men dealing for the PXs. Much of my job was order-filling paperwork, and I spent about a third of my time making tin-lined wooden crates for shipping cameras. I became expert at handling a hammer and nails. But, since I spoke English and knew a bit about the American military from my job with the Bolint family, KT assigned me the task of entertaining our GI buyers at Osaka nightclubs. It was good training for my later work with American camera dealers.

My initial reaction to KT's unimpressive offices changed completely as I learned to understand his priorities in rebuilding the company. The new lens-polishing plant at Sakai, where the original plant had been destroyed during the war, was very modern with air-conditioning and humidity control, not for comfort but for improved manufacturing processes. I am still struck by the extent to which conditions in Japanese manufacturing facilities are much more modern and efficient than what I have seen in American factories. Japan's industrial base had been totally destroyed during the war. America's had not been touched. After the war, America went on using plant facilities that were already showing their age. Japan, of necessity, started fresh with up-to-date technology and modern, highly productive industrial plants.

With KT as my tutor I began an intense apprenticeship in the camera industry. He instilled in me his belief in the importance of exports and taught me more and more about the operations of his firm. Recovery from the war had been slow, but in 1947 the firm became the first Japanese camera company to turn out a postwar camera, the Semi III, an update of its prewar Auto-Semi, a folding camera designed for the 6-by-4.5-cm format using 120 film. Perhaps more important than the camera itself was a modest export order for 170 cameras for a distributor in South Africa—Japan's first postwar camera exports.

KT also taught me the importance of market share and smooth labor-management relations as he struggled to resolve another strike in 1952. Wages, traditionally low in Japan, still had not caught up with the effects of the severe postwar inflation. The workers' demands were understandable, but strikes were a luxury that a country as poor as Japan and a struggling company like Minolta could not afford. KT saw the strike as a threat to Minolta's market share more than as a threat to its profitability. To KT increased market share wasn't a goal in itself but a means of achieving lower unit production costs. As production volume increases in an efficient factory, unit costs go down, giving a manufacturer greater opportunity to compete on prices. Which in turn creates opportunities for further increases in market share. Eventually, this does get translated into greater profits.

KT was determined to reach a compromise with Minolta's employees in order to avoid a long strike. He knew that in the highly competitive Japanese camera industry other companies would soon begin to move in on Minolta's hard-won share of what was then a limited domestic market. He also knew it was often harder to regain lost market share than to win it in the first place. KT reached a reasonable settlement with his workers and got back to the business of building Minolta's market share.

In my conversations with KT, I realized that he had a vision of America that paralleled some of my own dreams. We were surrounded by evidence of America's destructive power at war, but we also saw America's willingness and ability to rebuild what it had destroyed. The American military played as dominant a role in Japan's recovery as it had in the outcome of the war.

In April 1951, two months before I began work with Tashima Shoten, General MacArthur had been ordered home after his conflict with President Truman over the conduct of the Korean War. The Japanese press, though no longer censored, had not reported on the growing differences between President Truman and MacArthur. So the firing itself came as a shock to us. The second big surprise was that a civilian could fire a military leader of MacArthur's stature. It was another lesson for us in what democracy means and greatly increased our respect for the American system, even though we sympathized with MacArthur.

In September, at an international conference in San Francisco, the United States and Japan formally agreed to a peace treaty that paved the way for the end of the occupation. As it happened, however, as a result of the Korean War there were more GIs than ever in Japan, a fact that had a profound effect on the economy of Japan and the fortunes of Minolta. During the first year of the Korean War, the American military bought nearly $800 million in various supplies from Japanese firms. By the end of 1954, nearly $3 billion in U.S. military purchases had bolstered the Japanese economy with what amounted to "exports" that brought in foreign exchange even though the sales were made within Japan. From 1945 to 1955 American military expenditures in Japan more than doubled the amount of U.S. economic aid.

During the next decade, American military expenditures in

Japan increased by another $3.2 billion. During the Vietnam War, they increased by still another $3 billion. By today's standards those amounts may seem small, but they made a huge difference to the struggling Japanese economy. Though virtually every segment of the economy benefited, many of these expenditures went for sophisticated military equipment and helped Japan to build a high-tech industrial capacity with peacetime applications in such important industries as steel, shipbuilding, electronics, and autos.

My father was among those who benefited from the resurgence of the auto industry. There were few men with any experience in motor vehicle dealerships in Japan at that time. My father's reputation as a successful auto industry entrepreneur had come to the attention of officials at the Prince auto company, which was owned by Japan's Bridgestone tire firm.

My father became the Prince dealer for Wakayama prefecture. He was so successful in Wakayama that he later moved to Osaka and took over the dealership there. He then became head of Prince operations based in Kyoto. After those many years when my grandfather thought his adopted son and son-in-law was doing nothing in Tanabe, my father was once again a highly active and successful businessman. Prince later merged with Nissan, and my father moved into the Nissan corporate structure.

Many new car companies blossomed during the 1950s. The supposedly all-wise and all-powerful Ministry of Trade and Industry (MITI) decided there was too much competition. Most of the industry simply ignored MITI's efforts to arrange a series of mergers to create just two competing firms. Americans who accept the myth of "Japan, Inc." attribute enormous power to MITI, but its real importance is as a source of suggestions and coordination, rather than as an all-powerful economic czar. Japan hasn't known a czar since MacArthur left.

Meanwhile, I kept dreaming of America, knowing that KT was looking for someone to establish Minolta in the United States. Finally, in January 1954, KT told me he had made his choice.

"I've decided you would be the best candidate for us to export to America," he said.

I must admit it was the most exciting day of my life, though KT's decision did cause me some problems within Minolta. The man who was then manager of our export department was jealous of me. From the first KT had treated me almost like a son rather than merely an employee. Then, at a young age and with little experience, I was given this choice assignment. The export manager, who was my immediate boss both in Japan and during my first assignment to America, continued to be a problem for me for many years.

I could sense trouble coming, but KT believed that younger men were best suited for the rigors of overseas travel. There were people within Minolta who considered my American pilgrimage to be KT's folly, a costly adventure with little hope of return undertaken at the expense of the growing domestic market. Some ill will continues even to this day, and I must admit there is some truth to the view that Minolta might have done more to build up its domestic market in the 1950s.

But back in 1954 I wasn't thinking much about Minolta's domestic sales. All I knew was that the son of "The Henry Ford of Korea" was on his way to the United States, a family dream of success come true.

III

A PIONEER
IN AMERICA

1954–1958

8

The Land of Opportunity

I caught my first real sense of America the day I boarded the SS *President Wilson* in Yokohama harbor in February 1954. The whole family had come to see me off. There must have been a hundred relatives and friends, for in those days it was the dream of every Japanese to see America, the land of opportunity. At an official exchange rate of 360 to the dollar, the yen was weak, and Japan, still recovering from the war, was very poor. Only high government officials, the heads of major corporations, movie stars, and a handful of students, most of them Fulbright scholars, ever made the trip. I had no such claim to privilege.

There was a special status involved in sailing aboard the SS *President Wilson*. It was the pride of the United States President Line, and not long before Crown Prince Akihito had been a passenger. The photograph of him boarding the ship had become famous, and naturally my relatives and friends took many photos of me that day. I had been told that in the United States all the businessmen wore hats. So I went out shopping for an American-style hat and found a big, expensive Stetson fedora. The hat looked nearly as big as I did.

KT was there to see me off, along with some of the members of the board of directors. I had also received many cables and letters, congratulating me on my assignment and wishing me good luck. I felt like a real celebrity, though I was really just a traveling salesman.

The scene was especially festive because one of my fellow passengers, an elderly, tiny Japanese lady, was the founder of a popular sect known as the Dancing Religion. In the confusion of the postwar era, new religions had sprung up in Japan. Many famous people became adherents of this group, including my boyhood hero, the grand champion sumo wrestler Futabayama. Sect members danced themselves into trancelike states said to put them at one with the Infinite Being, to relieve tensions and even to cure headaches. Followers of the Dancing Religion carried on with the frenzy of disco dancers. There were at least a thousand on the dock that day, dancing madly, seeing their leader off. She had been invited to Hawaii, our first stop, by a group of her nisei adherents. I soon learned that, like me, she was traveling third class.

I was twenty-six, a real greenhorn, who spoke English haltingly, a merchant with a figurative pack on his back heading off to the United States. My luggage included two blue aluminum suitcases loaded with four dozen Minolta cameras, plus flash attachments and extra lenses, that I hoped to sell in America. All were excellent: the Minolta 35, a focal-plane camera with interchangeable lenses that was similar to the Leica; the Semi-Minolta, which used 120 film; the Konan 16, a subminiature "spy camera"; and the Minoltaflex, the camera I had used myself as a young boy in Korea. Good cameras all, but none, I would discover later, really suitable for the American market.

I was the first member of my family ever to go to the United States, but we had been moving in that direction since my grandfather's time. We followed a strange route: from Japan to Korea and back, then on to America over three generations. My father and mother were among the crowd that saw me off as I struggled up the gangplank with my luggage. From the deck, I waved a final goodbye, feeling no sadness at leaving but only excitement over sailing to the promised land of America and enjoying my last glance at the wild gyrations of the Dancing Religion's adherents. It was only later, when my father told me that my mother had been crying as I climbed the gangplank, that I felt guilty about my feelings that day. Even as I made my awkward passage down steep, narrow steps to my third-class cabin in the bowels of the ship, I was thrilled.

Minolta had spent the extra money for me to travel "special third class" so that I had a semiprivate room. The tiny room had bunk beds, and I was content with my cramped lower berth. I had wanted to sail on an American ship, even third class, to begin to get the feeling of America as soon as possible. To me, that cabin aboard the big, 17,500-ton *President Wilson* seemed luxurious, and I felt I was already in the United States. Of course, all the Americans on board were in first class. Most of my fellow passengers in third class were Chinese. My cabin mate was a nisei from Canada, and the pursers, waiters, and other staff were all Oriental.

I tried to go up to the first-class deck, but the signs told me it was strictly "off limits." It was possible to climb to the top deck, but there, on those first days out with rough seas and biting February winds, I was alone with the ship's smoking funnels. By the second and third days out, many passengers were seasick. Luckily, I never was.

When we sailed into tropical weather, three days out of Yokohama, I had some company on the sunny "boat" deck, including some first-class passengers. But I realized it was still an impossible distance from third class to first. Hawaii was nearly twenty-five hundred nautical miles away and San Francisco nearly twice that distance. I might have thought I was already in America, but in reality I still had a long way to go.

So did Japan, I reflected. With considerable help from the United States, Japan had become for the first time in its history a democratic, egalitarian society, fired by the ideals of industrial enterprise and slowly moving on the path of economic recovery. But we were still considered a source of junk products and cheap toys.

My assignment was to establish Minolta in the United States, starting with a trade show in Chicago that March sponsored by the Master Photo Dealers and Finishers Association (MPDFA). My resources included forty-eight cameras, with lenses and accessories, plus $1,000 in precious American currency given to me by KT. KT thought that the $1,000 would cover my start-up expenses and then I would earn my own way by selling Minolta cameras. It wouldn't work out quite that way, but I did have an additional, secret resource. Unknown to Minolta, or the authorities, my father had given me five hundred American dollars, which he must have obtained illegally on the black market at the going exchange rate of 420 yen to the dollar, considerably above the official rate of 360, which prevailed with little change till the 1970s. I appreciated my father's sacrifice. Since all bank accounts were still frozen to control inflation, my family had little disposable income.

With my fifteen hundred American dollars, however, I felt very rich indeed. Soon after we set sail, I started spending them, modestly. All the bowing and smiling, all those good-byes had left me thirsty. I bought my first American beer. During the war, Japan had only one beer, Dai Nippon, a very good beer as a matter of fact. The name means "Great Japan," which is typical of the militaristic way of naming things during that period. Later the company split at the insistence of the American military when it broke up the old Japanese monopolies. But to the Japanese there was still only one beer. We never thought to ask for a brand name, so I went to the third-class bar and asked for a beer. The bartender said, "What kind?" I had no idea what he meant. So I repeated my order. "Beer, please."

"I heard you. What kind of beer do you want?"

"Yes, beer, please."

The bartender shrugged, pulled an icy bottle from the well under the counter, and poured me my first American beer. A Rheingold. I liked it. Light and dry, it was ice-cold and excellent for my thirst. As I remember, it cost about twenty cents, tax free. After that, when I wanted a beer I always asked for Rheingold, still not realizing that America could have more than one beer. I had a similar experience when we finally docked in Hawaii a week later.

Hawaii's Waikiki Beach was a famous, romantic destination for wealthy Japanese, particularly honeymooners. The Royal Hawaiian Hotel, known to Japanese as "The White Hotel," though it is actually closer to pink, is mentioned in the Japanese song "The Romantic Route to Hawaii." I wanted to see it. Waikiki is quite a distance from the Aloha Tower, where the ship docked. It was a clear, sunny day and after the cold, gray weather I had left in Japan, Hawaii seemed very pleasant. I decided to walk to save taxi fare, though many other passengers did take cabs to Waikiki. It turned out to be a two-hour trek and quite warm. Seeing the congestion of Waikiki today, it is hard to realize that only thirty years ago there was nothing much there.

But I kept walking, impressed by the bright colors, the greens and blues and reds of the flowers and the brilliant white and soft pastels of the buildings. Japan, in the early 1950s, was drab, gray, and dull. By contrast, Hawaii was a visual paradise. Of course, I was taking photographs as I went. All in color. Never before had I taken so many pictures in color. Film in Japan was expensive then, especially color. But on the *President Wilson* I had bought several rolls of Kodak color for slides, a film I still use today.

As I walked, I saw my first example of American automation, a cement truck groaning down the road, its huge revolving cylinder mixing cement as it went. I was so impressed that I wrote to my parents, telling them about this cement factory on wheels that could transport its product at the same time it was manufacturing it. I had never seen anything like it.

Before I was halfway to my destination, I began to feel the heat of that tropical sun. This time my taste was for ice cream. I went into a drugstore and asked, as I would at home, for a dish of ice cream. The man behind the counter said, "What flavor?" I hadn't learned anything from my experience on the *President Wilson*. Japanese consumers today are fussy about their preferences in liquors, beer, and ice cream, and the varieties are endless. But during the war, in ice cream as in beer, we had only one choice. Ice cream meant vanilla. The man in the drugstore repeated his question, "What flavor?"

I thought he must have meant, "How much?" So I said, "One dollar." In those days a serving of ice cream cost maybe fifteen or twenty cents. So I wound up with a huge dish. I don't remember the flavor, but I'm sure it wasn't vanilla. The color and the taste were much richer. It had the smell of America.

And San Francisco turned out to be the real thing. I fell in love with the city even though I was there for only a few hours. As we sailed into the harbor, the sight of the Golden Gate Bridge brought the first- and third-class passengers together in great numbers on the top deck. I have since heard many stories of European immigrants being thrilled by their first sight of the Statue of Liberty as they sailed into New York harbor. For me, arriving from the East, the Golden Gate Bridge produced that same shiver of recognition. This was America. Some passengers cheered; many wept—including me, as I tried to concentrate on taking my photographs.

Not long after, for the first time, after many dreams, my feet were on the solid earth of the continental United States. At the time, of course, I had no idea how important America would be in my life. I had time that day only for first impressions.

I had some spare time and managed to see a bit of San Francisco before I took a bus to the airport. Naturally, the beauty of the city impressed me, but I was struck even more by something that I did not see. If Japan had been victorious in World War II, downtown Tokyo and every other major city today would be crowded with giant statues of General Tojo and Admiral Yamamoto and other military leaders of that era. I expected to see many such monuments in San Francisco, but I saw none. The impression I got that day, which has been pretty well confirmed since, was that the United States did not turn its modern military heroes into great symbols of the nation. In the years since, I have seen very few World War II monuments. One exception is the sculpture in Washington, D.C., of the raising of the American flag at Iwo Jima. And the figures in that monument are ordinary fighting men, not great generals or admirals.

Perhaps it is something in America's democratic traditions that makes the United States hesitate to elevate its recent military heroes to the status of national idols. In the twentieth century only one American general, Dwight D. Eisenhower, has been elected president. The United States has never allowed the military to rule the way Japan did in the years leading to World War II.

Along with war monuments, as a Japanese arriving here so soon after that horrible war, I had expected to encounter some degree of hostility. I encountered none. In fact, I was struck most of all by how friendly and helpful people were. I had no idea of how anything in America really worked. On top of that, my English was very limited and my accent almost impossible to understand.

I had to catch a plane to New York, where I would be met by a representative of Kanematsu, a trading company that Minolta had been in touch with. And I had to find a way to safely ship my valuable cameras, for taking them on the plane as excess baggage would have been far too expensive. People went out of their way, first to understand me, then to help me, taking me to a shipping company right there on the dock where I was able to make the necessary arrangements.

Maybe I've led a charmed life in America. I've heard many stories of foreigners with limited English being cheated by taxi drivers, being robbed of their luggage, or at least being snubbed, ignored, or subjected to verbal abuse and ethnic slurs. None of that has ever happened to me. Even in the New York City area, where I have lived for most of my adult life, I rarely see the abrasive hostility that city is so famous for. Once, when I was first living in New York, I was stopped on the street by a woman who thought I was Chinese. She began yelling at me and for a moment I was quite frightened. She had lost a grandson in the Korean War and blamed the Chinese for his death. I explained to her that I was Japanese, and she left me alone. Certainly I was a wide-eyed pilgrim, a pioneer like my grandfather in Korea, making my way through this country with awe and wonder when I first arrived. I am less naïve now, but I may still be something of a pilgrim, still fascinated by this country and its people. Maybe that's why I've been so lucky in my encounters, at least so far.

Certainly I was very naïve that first day when I arrived in San Francisco. In fact, I was about to make another silly mistake. At the airport, I boarded a plane for the first time in my life. I was young, shy, stiff and trying very hard to be proper. When the time came to serve the meal, the stewardess asked me, in what I now recognize as a typical American way, "Are you hungry?" To me, that seemed like a very personal question. But more important, I was afraid she thought I was some poor, starving Japanese who needed a free meal. So I said, very stiffly, "No."

"Then you don't want anything?"

"No."

I can see myself. Back straight as a ramrod. Fists clenched, pressed against my knees. Staring straight ahead. And my stomach rumbling.

The first leg of our flight on a DC-6B propeller-driven plane was six hours, San Francisco to Chicago. When I saw that everyone else was eating, my hunger only got worse. I knew I had made a stupid mistake, but I was too embarrassed to admit it and ask for something to eat. Fortunately, they fed us again between Chicago and New York. This time, I graciously accepted.

We landed at what was then called Idlewild airport, today's JFK. Idlewild was then a barren, windswept terminal with only two gates, more like a bus stop than an international airport. I was met by a young Japanese representative of Kanematsu & Company. Later I met William J. Daly, the American Kanematsu employee I would work most closely with. Bill Daly turned out to be a young man only a few years older than I but every bit as stiff and formal, which I hadn't expected in an American. He became my ears and my voice in America, but I used to have to joke with him a lot to get him to relax. That must have made me a bit more relaxed, too. I nicknamed him "Rock," because it was almost impossible to get him to change his mind about anything. As he tried to educate me to American ways, we would sometimes argue. But I could never get him to change his views. He was a wonderful guide, very honest and a very good friend. He stayed with Kanematsu for twenty-five years and later became active in public education in Fort Lee, New Jersey, where we both now live.

Minolta's relationship with Kanematsu was typical of the way a Japanese company got started in the export business. Minolta and Kanematsu had the same bank back in Japan. It was the Kobe Bank that encouraged Minolta to work with Kanematsu. We call this the convoy system, or *keiretsu* in Japanese: a manufacturer, a bank, and a trading company setting sail together to begin an export venture. Virtually every Japanese company now operating in America went through a similar process. Banks play a much more important role in venture financing in Japan than they do in the United States. In fact, only recently have American banks begun to make an extensive effort to encourage export development through consulting services and financing. But in the early 1950s, even though KT was international in his thinking and dreamed of Minolta becoming a major exporter, it was our bank that made it possible for the company to enter the global market.

The bank's assistance included providing the precious foreign currency, the thousand dollars I carried with me for Minolta's low-budget invasion of the American market. Minolta, then unknown in the United States, could not arrange a foreign-currency credit line. But the Kobe Bank, operating through American banks, could provide foreign currency in our behalf. Through such arrangements, a Japanese manufacturer does not have to struggle alone to establish itself in a new country.

Bill Daly had found a room for me in what was then a very good residential hotel, the Park Crescent on Broadway in the West Eighties. My rent was $100 a month. I opened my suitcase and set out to sell Minolta to America.

9

Beating a Path

The Kanematsu trading company had its office down in the financial district, at 150 Broadway. Bill Daly made a desk available for me there. Our first priority was to plan our trip to Chicago to introduce Minolta at the Master Photo Dealers and Finishers Association trade show at the Conrad Hilton Hotel. Lugging my two big suitcases packed with cameras and accessories, we took the train to Chicago. Bill had arranged for a small display space in the ballroom where the show took place.

The MPDFA show in 1954 was every bit as big as the shows of its successor organization, the Photo Marketing Association (PMA), are today. I thought it would provide a wonderful opportunity for me to meet many of the top people in the photo industry. There were important people at the show, but, as it turned out, I did not get to meet many of them. We had an area nine feet square that I can't refer to as a booth because we had hardly anything more than a table and a couple of chairs. Not even a sign to say who we were. In fact, the people in the booths around us were annoyed because our stall looked so shabby. Bill Daly went out to find a decorator who cut a Minolta sign out of cardboard, and I rented two glass showcases from

MPDFA. So there we were: two people, one sign, two showcases with four excellent Minolta cameras. Nobody paid any attention to us at all.

I was about to learn an important lesson. I had come to America believing in the old saying that if you build a better mousetrap, the world will beat a path to your door. I discovered that even with a first-class mousetrap, you still have to beat a path to your customer's door. I had all these wonderful cameras, and I certainly knew something about photography. But I knew nothing about the American market, about American consumers or American distributors. My primary mission at the MPDFA show was to find an American distributor for Minolta. None showed up. None beat a path to our booth.

So instead I sent Bill Daly around to the other booths to see if he could kidnap one. No luck. Eventually Bill did manage to get Max Zell and his boss, Abe Feigerson, of Anglo Photo in Canada, to take a look at our cameras. At the time, Anglo Photo distributed only a German camera, the Iloca, which no longer exists. Max Zell did show some interest in my Minoltas. Later that year I visited him in Montreal and he became Minolta's first foreign distributor. But only for Canada. Abe and Max later added Nikon and Yashica to their line and became very successful.

There were other important people at the show but I was able to do little more than introduce myself to most of them, including Norman Lipton, then head of the German Camera Industry Association. Noboru Hamashima of Nippon Kogaku, makers of the Nikon camera, had a small booth with his American distributor, Joseph Ehrenreich, who later played a big role in my life. Hamashima had arrived in the United States a few months before I did, the first Japanese camera representative to set up shop here permanently. Ehrenreich, a major distributor based in New York City, had agreed to handle the Nikon, which was an important first step for the Japanese camera industry. His marketing expertise was another big factor in establishing Nikon in the vast American market.

Nikon, like Minolta, owes much of its worldwide success to America. David Duncan and Carl Mydans, famous photographers for *Life*, which was the world's largest-selling magazine, gave Nikon a big boost during the Korean War. Passing through Japan, they picked up Nikkor lenses designed for the German Leica. The fact that *Life* photographers were using lenses made by Nippon Kogaku helped

Nikon establish its reputation, particularly among professional news photographers, in the United States. To the best of my knowledge, Al Levin was the first American to sell a serious line of Japanese cameras in the United States. For several years, starting in 1948, he was Nikon's one-man sales force, until he recommended Nikon to Joseph Ehrenreich. After Ehrenreich became Nikon's distributor in 1950, Levin joined him as a salesman.

Though Nikon was there at the 1954 camera show, overall the Japanese presence wasn't significant. There was nothing as insignificant at the show, however, as Minolta's presence. When I left Chicago to return to New York, I still had forty-eight unsold cameras, no American distributor, and a dwindling supply of dollars.

Back in New York, I began making the rounds of the many big independent camera distributors then headquartered in the city. One after the other, they refused to meet me. Finally, I managed to see some of the people at one of the important distributors, Intercontinental. At the time, Intercontinental handled a fully automatic German camera called Robot. They asked me if Minolta had anything similar. I told them no and that was the end of that.

There were times when I was so discouraged by our lack of sales that I was ready to send a report to Japan recommending that we abandon this idea of exporting to America. Through a third source, I had heard reports that back at Minolta in Japan there was criticism of KT for getting the company involved in the United States. It was said that the effort to break into the American market had become KT's "expensive hobby." I felt sad for KT and responsible for the criticism since I was his man in America.

I tried everything I could think of, reaching out beyond the established camera distributors to such long-shot possibilities as the Bulova Watch Company and even Columbia Records. Because of Bulova's reputation for high-quality, precision instruments, I thought it might recognize a kindred spirit in Minolta. Back home Minolta had been involved in joint efforts with the Japanese watch company, Citizen, and, in the United States, Bulova had an excellent distribution system in jewelry, drug, and department stores, as well as in specialized watch shops. Bulova never quite saw it my way, however. I did come a bit closer with Columbia Records. Columbia also had a good distribution system through department and sporting goods stores like Davega, a popular chain that has since disappeared from

the scene. I did my best to sell the idea that stores carrying records
might also be interested in cameras. The Columbia marketing people
showed definite interest, but nothing ever came of it.

Though Japanese are famous for their patience and long-term
planning and investment strategies, I was an inexperienced young
man in his twenties and my own patience and resolve had been beaten
down by frustration. I worked hard during the day, but in the evening
I headed for Times Square to escape in fantasy in its glittering old
movie palaces.

New York was an enchanted city for me. For years on the wall
of my home in Japan I had a detailed map of Manhattan. I studied
that map like a general planning a battle and, without ever having
been there, I could tell you exactly how to get from Rockefeller
Center to the old Paramount Theater or from Penn Station to the
Waldorf-Astoria. By then I had seen hundreds of American movies,
particularly during my years as a not very energetic college student.
Japanese theaters often had double and even triple features, and I
once figured out that I saw an average of over three hundred films
a year, most of them American. Many of my favorites were set in
New York: *The Naked City*, *A Tree Grows in Brooklyn*, *Miracle on
34th Street*, and great old musicals like *42nd Street* and *Broadway
Melody*. Naturally, having seen such realistic Hollywood portraits of
New York many times, I felt I knew the city well. When I first
arrived in New York, I felt as if I had come home, for this had been
my dream for many years. I've since discovered that in this respect
I'm like many Americans who come to New York from the hinterlands
to seek their fortune when they are young and are almost as naïve
about the real city as I was.

Since a ride cost only fifteen cents, I would take the subway to
Times Square. People make a joke about the way I still pronounce
it. To American ears it sounds as if I'm saying "Times Scare." People
say my pronunciation is appropriate because many find that part of
New York a bit scary. But to me in 1954, it was wonderful. All the
bright lights, and particularly the giant Camel sign with the man
blowing smoke out over Broadway, cast a spell over me that has
lasted to this day. In those days especially, New York was the shining
center of the world. The 1950s have been called the American Decade,
a period when the United States accounted for 45 percent of the
world's gross national product. Broadway was still very much the

Great White Way and at night I walked along it in absolute amaze-
ment.

Though the subway was cheap, most evenings I walked from my
hotel down Broadway to midtown and Times Square. For me, it was
a great thrill to walk past the wonderful old theaters and through
the lobbies of hotels like the Waldorf-Astoria, which I knew about
from the big-band broadcasts from its Starlight Roof, and the old
Pennsylvania Hotel on Seventh Avenue across from Penn Station.
From my maps I not only knew where the Pennsylvania was, but
from the old Glenn Miller record I even knew the phone number—
PEnnsylvania 6–5000. The hotel, now called the Penta, still has the
same phone number in a digitized version. Tommy Dorsey was playing there when I first visited the famous hotel, but I couldn't afford
to hear him or to go to the Waldorf's Starlight Roof or, when I went
to Chicago, to the Empire Room at the Palmer House, but I could
walk through the lobbies, hearing the music in my head. Many Japanese are big-band fans as a result of the wonderful Armed Forces
Broadcasting radio programs we used to hear as young men during
the years of the American occupation. For years during the war we
had heard nothing but military marches and heavy militaristic themes
on Japanese radio. We were amazed that the American military didn't
do the same thing but instead gave us all this wonderful, upbeat
swing. To this day in the New York area many Japanese of my
generation keep their radios tuned to stations like WNEW and
WPAT, where we are most likely to hear music from the big-band
era.

One song in particular, Artie Shaw's recording of Cole Porter's
"Begin the Beguine," became a symbol for the Japanese of their
country's new beginning in the postwar era. Books have been written
about it in Japan, including at least one that takes its title from the
song, but few Americans are aware of the impact that American
idealism, American democracy, and American culture have had on
Japan.

I began to fear that perhaps America was just a fantasy, both for
me and for KT. I might well have written a fatal report recommending
that we give up on our American dream but for the encouragement
I received during an otherwise frustrating call on a New York photo
dealer. The late Joseph Ehrenreich was the owner of the 32nd Street

Penn Camera Store, then a major American dealership. As I mentioned, we had met at his Nikon booth at the MPDFA show in Chicago. He had pioneered as the first American distributor of a serious Japanese camera. He is one of the few foreigners to have been awarded the Japanese medal known as the Third Order of the Sacred Treasure Emperor's Medal. With good cause, he has been called "The Father of the Japanese Camera Industry in America." Personally, I consider him my "American-Jewish godfather." I called on him several times in New York, though I never sold him any cameras. On one of those visits I told him how discouraged I was and said I had been thinking that maybe I should give up and go back to Japan.

"Don't give up," he said to me. I've never forgotten his words. "This is a big country. Give it a chance. Stay at least one more year."

It was good advice but by no means the last good deed that Mr. Ehrenreich would do for me. I would, thanks in large part to him, eventually stay in America long enough to discover just how big a country it really is, not just in size, but in heart and generosity. Meanwhile, I did the best I could to learn as much as possible about the American camera market. I talked to dealers, to customers, and, perhaps most helpfully of all, to journalists on the major trade publications. I had little else to do, so I wrote detailed reports on everything I learned, including Intercontinental's question about Minolta's ability to provide an automatic camera. As it turned out, partly because of that report, Minolta Japan soon did produce its first automatic camera.

The distribution list on those early reports is as interesting as their contents. Addressed to Steve Tashima, KT's brother, who was then our director of sales, they also went to managers in production, sales, finance, administration, purchasing, accounting, product research, consumer research, and to our factory manager. These reports included such vital matters as a request for more camera boxes to replace some that "did not look new" and might make dealers suspect that the cameras in them weren't new either. Much of the material in those reports was equally trivial, but KT attached such importance to the American market that he wanted all departments informed and involved.

In one of my reports I proposed the idea of developing a special exposure meter for our subminiature cameras. These were the Minolta 16 series of so-called spy cameras, 16-mm cameras that were popular but probably not up to the standards of James Bond. Our engineers replied that an exposure meter does not help a great deal with subminiatures. I argued back that this was not a technical matter but a "question of marketing." I never did win that fight. In retrospect, I think the engineers were right.

My big success with the spy cameras came in early 1958 when we persuaded Sears Roebuck to drop the German-made Minox subminiature from its popular mail-order catalog in favor of the Minolta 16. This was our first success with a major American retailer and, with Sears's vast marketing reach behind it, the little spy camera sold very well. Just being in the Sears catalog was an excellent form of advertising for us, getting the Minolta name before more consumers than any advertising we could have afforded on our own at the time. And beating out a German-made camera helped our reputation in the industry.

In retrospect, some of my early reports seem very amusing. I remember one in which I discussed the steam that rises from manhole covers on the streets of Manhattan. I described this in great detail to show how wasteful Americans were. I thought the steam was rising because someone down under the street was carelessly running hot water all the time. It was years later before I found out that the steam we see at street level is generated by all the gas and electric power lines underground. This excess energy, rather than being wasted, is channeled to provide what in New York is known as "city steam heat" to commercial buildings.

But at least some of my reports were a bit more on target. Burt Keppler, himself the son of a famous photographer, was then a journalist with *Modern Photography*. In 1987 he would startle the industry by switching to its archrival, *Popular Photography*. At the time he was highly critical of Minolta. He said the cameras were too heavy and were equipped only for use with a flashbulb rather than with the electronic flash then coming into vogue. I hadn't even known the electronic flash existed until I came to the United States. With a flashbulb, the shutter must be timed to wait three milliseconds, the time it takes for the bulb to go off, before opening. With the electronic flash, light and exposure must be instantaneous.

In my report to Japan, I said Minolta cameras, designed only for the flashbulb, must be changed if we were to have any success in the American market. Though I didn't realize it at the time, almost everything I suggested in my reports was taken very seriously. I had the full support of KT, and it was this spirit that eventually put

Minolta so far ahead in the export business, turning KT's "expensive hobby" into the pillar of our company.

Minolta surprised me. Within ten months, in time for the MPDFA show at Atlantic City in March 1955, our engineers developed a handmade model of the Minolta Autocord, the first twin-lens reflex camera specifically designed for the American market, with one of the first X-sync shutters for use with the electronic flash. The Japanese firm that later became world-famous for its Citizen watches helped Minolta develop the X-sync shutter. Since the shutter had no application in Japan, where the electronic flash was not yet widely available, it was developed solely for the American market.

Our engineers also set about developing the Minolta A, a 35-mm camera. Also specially designed for export to America, it was light in weight, with automatic features like those in the Autocord· that advanced the film and cocked the shutter in one motion. Yes, we had some excellent Japanese mousetraps when I first came to America with those two suitcases. But we had to adapt our product line to the American market before we could start beating a path to our customer's door.

Not knowing what impact I was having back in Japan, I went on knocking on doors, writing my reports, borrowing more dollars when necessary from Kanematsu, and, in the evenings, going to the movies. After six months of not making any headway, I realized that a young man like myself, working alone, was not enough. I asked KT to come over to help me out. He agreed and in September 1954 made his first trip to the United States. He must have floated another foreign-exchange credit from the Kobe Bank, because he flew over first class and I certainly hadn't earned any dollars for him.

With the founder of this little-known but clearly first-class camera manufacturer coming to the United States, the trade press saw the makings of a good story. It was relatively easy to arrange interviews for KT, and one important publication, *Photo Dealer*, even threw a party for him. Stories about Minolta began to appear in *Photo Dealer*, *Popular Photography*, *Modern Photography*, *Photo Trade News*, *U.S. Camera*, and other publications. This was my first lesson in the importance of public relations, a discipline little used or understood in Japan even today.

With KT on the scene in New York, for the first time the big guys were beginning to pay some attention to Minolta. At the reception given by *Photo Dealer*, KT and I met Larry Fink, president of FR Corporation, a manufacturer of photochemicals for the amateur darkroom enthusiast. Gus Wolfman of *Photo Dealer* made the introduction. FR had just started its own distribution network and wanted an additional line. It was about to go into electronic flash attachments, and KT had informed me that, based on my reports, Minolta would soon have a camera to accommodate the electronic flash. Larry expressed an interest in Minolta and by the end of that year we had signed a contract. At the next MPDFA show at Atlantic City, we officially introduced Minolta to the American market, distributed by FR Corporation.

Originally, Larry Fink wanted to sell our cameras under his firm's name. KT and I absolutely refused. But, given the reputation that Japanese cameras had in the United States at the time, we knew Larry had a point. Without an American name behind the camera, we could get no trust from the American consumer. KT and I decided on a compromise. We kept the Minolta name, but in tags on the camera and in our advertising we specified a twin warranty, backed by both Minolta and its American distributor, FR Corporation. We had made a beginning.

By then Larry Fink had given me my Americanized first name, creating a pattern that has since become a Minolta tradition. "Sadahei Kusumoto" is a bit difficult for Americans to pronounce. Even worse, from my point of view, is the American tendency to shorten long names. Often, my last name would be reduced to Kusu, which isn't bad since that's the name of a tree common in Japan. But Americans often misspell and mispronounce my name as Kusomoto. And in Japanese *kuso* means "shit"; *moto* means "fundamental." My full family name, Kusumoto, can be rendered as "Roots of the Tree." But mispronounced as Kusomoto, it means "Fundamental Shit." Larry took my first initial and came up with the simplest American name he could think of. He said Sam would be particularly appropriate because most of the major camera distributors and local dealers in America happen to be Jewish. Occasionally, I still get letters addressed to Samuel Kusomoto, however.

We weren't as lonely at the MPDFA show in Atlantic City as we had been the previous year in Chicago. We were drawing plenty of interest, but we still weren't signing up dealers or selling cameras. The dozen Minolta Autocords and twelve Minolta A cameras I had with me were handmade pilot production models. They got such a workout as I demonstrated them that they were constantly breaking down.

Paul R. Perlowin, national sales manager for FR Corporation, had recruited a sales force of about twenty, all with good backgrounds in the photo industry. They were impressed with our cameras. The Minolta A, designed to sell for fifty dollars, was a range-finder 35-mm with a lens so excellent that our salesmen compared it with the famous German-made lens, the Tessar. But the mechanics of the handmade models were not quite up to the day-long demonstrations of a camera show. I spent every night in my Atlantic City hotel room repairing cameras for the next day's show. Fortunately, I had been well trained. Before I left Japan, KT had ordered Minolta's chief of engineering to teach me everything he could about camera technology and repair. I visited our chief engineer's home every night after regular working hours. By the time I left for the United States, I was capable of earning my living as a camera repairman. As it turned out, that's just about what happened.

When we started to advertise in cooperation with FR Corporation in March 1955, we still weren't able to sell to camera stores. But I was swamped by requests for repair service from the thousands of American servicemen who had bought Minolta cameras at PXs in Korea and Japan. In effect, these cameras were Minolta's first exports. The servicemen rotated tours of duty fairly rapidly and many took dozens of cameras and watches home with them. Since none of these Japanese companies, except Nikon, had a representative in the United States, there was no way for the cameras to be repaired. At least until I got here.

Until my repair business began to grow, I had almost no income in America. Fixing cameras was much simpler in those days. Virtually all the Japanese cameras on the market were mechanical rather than electronic. My tool kit consisted of one screwdriver. I had nothing to measure shutter speed, not even for the new X-sync shutter. So of necessity I became expert at clicking, listening, and guessing. I must have gotten pretty good at it because I was soon repairing other manufacturers' cameras as well.

My other main source of income came from the limited number of cameras that the Japanese government allowed to be sent without excise tax to the United States as samples. These cameras I sold at cost to friends, including the doorman at my hotel. Even with this income, I still had to borrow money from Kanematsu to keep going.

The climate in the United States tends to be much drier than in Japan. This caused the glues used on our cameras to dry out, creating distortions in the range-finder image on our new automatic cameras. Every camera had to be adjusted. Minolta couldn't afford to send over a service repairman; but with my booming repair business I needed help and did have some cash to hire someone—at least someone inexpensive. The Japanese community in New York was small, numbering not many more than two hundred, mostly students and a few businessmen and government representatives. I went up to Columbia University looking for a Japanese student who needed a part-time job and discovered Ken Fukae, a student at the Graduate School of Journalism. He was bright, eager, hungry and knew absolutely nothing about cameras. I offered him a terrible salary that he accepted immediately, asking when he could go to work. I knew I had made the right choice. He proved to be technically gifted and hardworking, just what I needed. Ken, a year older than I, had actually been taken into the military near the end of the war and trained to be a kamikaze. But, like me, he had been lucky. The war ended before he had a chance to meet a hero's death. Ken went on to become a vice-president of Minolta Corporation in the United States, specializing in technical innovations in business equipment, a field we were not even thinking about when Ken first joined Minolta in 1955. He now has his own successful business equipment importing and distribution firm, Kentech, based near Minolta headquarters in New Jersey.

Later that year, as business began to pick up a bit, Minolta sent over a service repair technician who became known as "Beefsteak" Nishida. Despite that manly sounding nickname, he was even slighter in build than I. Beefsteak spoke not one word of English when he arrived, nor did he ever learn. But as long as we avoided seafood restaurants he could eat. He liked beef and, fortunately, the Japanese word for "beefsteak" is *beefsteak*.

Not long after his arrival, I went through a very sad experience with Beefsteak. I received a cable from our home office telling me that his father had died. I had to break the news to him, which was bad enough. But I also knew there was no way that Minolta could afford to send him home for the funeral. In Japanese tradition, it is a matter of great shame for a son not to attend his father's funeral. This was particularly true in Beefsteak's case. As the eldest son, he was expected to be on hand to take care of all the funeral arrangements. Beefsteak did not say anything when I told him of his father's death. But he looked into my eyes. I knew the question he was asking with that pleading look. I had to shake my head—no. Neither of us spoke, but we both understood. Today, if one of our Japanese employees in America hears that a close relative back home has taken ill or died, Minolta without question pays for his trip home, and if the employee is married, we pick up the bill for the entire family to return to Japan. But in 1955, we couldn't afford to send Beefsteak home. I tried to console him, telling him that I was sure his mother was proud that of all the Minolta technicians in Japan, he was the one chosen to be sent to America, the most important assignment he could be given. Beefsteak nodded, but I realized that my words could only be of cold comfort. That night I took him to dinner, but he barely touched his steak.

Slowly, business improved, and Katsusaburo "Ken" Nakamura arrived as my assistant. He was just a year younger than I, and we became close friends and colleagues, young bachelors on the loose in New York, too poor to get into much trouble but enjoying ourselves anyway. In 1959, a year after I returned to Japan, Minolta Corporation was formed as the American branch of our parent company, with Ken as its first president. He is now back in Japan and is a director of the company. It was Ken who discovered Akio Miyabayashi, a student at New York University. We hired him as a part-time driver. Yes, by then we actually had some deliveries to make. He is typical of the bright young people Minolta hired and developed. He is now my counterpart in Europe, heading Minolta's operations there. In the late 1950s New York nurtured the incredibly youthful nucleus of what would become Minolta's extensive foreign operations. Minolta's experience is just one example of America's role as a training ground for leaders of Japanese industry. We learned about exporting from America. Meanwhile, America forgot.

10

Early American Mentors

During my early years in the United States, Jesse Wilkes was one of the Americans who did the most to help me learn how to sell Japanese cameras to Americans. With his partner, Lou Shappe, Jesse ran an agency that specialized in the photo industry. Shappe-Wilkes was the perfect agency for us at the time: specialized to the extent that it knew the American photo market inside out; big enough to have national reach, yet small enough to give its clients personal attention. Jesse, along with Bill Daly, was my guiding light in American-style marketing and merchandising. I had had some experience in selling before I came to America. But I still had to learn that there was a difference between selling and marketing.

Somehow I had gotten the idea that a good salesman is one who can sell the buyer more than he needs. I soon learned that in our business, at least, that's not so. Selling your dealer more than he needs will backfire. The dealer stuck with more inventory than he can handle will soon be disgruntled and will start discounting heavily in an unprofitable effort to move the merchandise you have overloaded him with. I had come to America thinking I was supposed to be just a salesman. But Americans were teaching me that my real function would be marketing, helping my customers—dealers and distributors—sell through to their customers.

Jesse Wilkes took the same ethical approach when it came to selling advertising to me. He realized that our limited advertising budget came as direct investment from Japan. Unlike the typical Madison Avenue agency, he never pushed for big advertising budgets, though it would have been easy to mislead anyone as naïve as I was then. He knew that our modest sales and limited number of retail outlets did not justify heavy advertising. Despite the meager income he received from us, Jesse was generous in the help and advice he gave us.

Co-op advertising, direct mail, point-of-purchase displays, contests, premiums, sales and service training, incentives for dealer personnel, and many of the other basic techniques of merchandising and marketing were relatively new to Japanese novices like me. A mystique has grown up about the secrets of Japanese manufacturing and managerial success. In truth, we have no secrets. But what we have learned about marketing from Americans has been even more important to Japan's success as an exporter than what we have learned about manufacturing.

For example, it was Paul Perlowin of FR Corporation who not only recruited and trained the sales force for Minolta cameras but also gave me some important advice about pricing for the American market. Minolta had planned to sell its Autocord for $100 in the United States and the Minolta A for $50. Wrong, said Paul Perlowin. The Autocord should be priced at $99.50 and the Minolta A at $49.95. I argued, thinking that was deceptive, making the camera look less expensive than it really was. But Paul insisted that American consumers were used to such pricing. He was right, of course, and that's what we did.

In the fall of 1956, Paul Perlowin and I looked at a map of the United States and in our minds drew a circle around it running from New York up to Boston, west to Chicago and San Francisco, then down through Los Angeles, San Diego, Houston, Miami and back to New York. We set out by plane to conquer America.

Flying was still a great adventure in the propeller-driven planes of the 1950s. On most airlines there was only one class of service, and it was excellent. When your reservations were made, you would get a call a day in advance to confirm them. If you were going to be on a dinner flight, you would be asked how you wanted your steak done or if you had any special food orders. Flights were longer, of course, and stewardesses had time to serve passengers more graciously than is common on some of today's crowded, hurried flights. Paul and I visited camera dealers in each of the cities where we stopped. Minolta's growing reputation opened many doors for us, a sharp change from two years before when hardly anyone knew what Minolta was. During that trip, which took three weeks, I saw not only how vast but also how beautiful America is. By the time we completed our swing, I thought we had done a pretty good job of introducing America and Minolta to each other. Camera stores around the country were featuring our $49.95 Minolta A and our $99.50 Autocord.

Our ads stressed the "fully automatic" system that advanced the film and cocked the shutter in one motion. Our American marketing experts taught us how important such phrases had become to American consumers in the early 1950s, when the automatic shift had become a big selling feature of the automobile industry.

Our only direct competition in selling quality cameras in the United States in the late 1950s came from the German firms. I remember how impressed I was when I met Jack Callahan, the United States sales manager for Franke & Heidecke, makers of Rolleiflex cameras. The firm was so successful he had his own private plane, which was quite unusual in those days. I hoped one day Minolta might do half as well as Rolleiflex, Leica, and the other German cameras, which then included Zeiss-Ikon, Exacta, Minox, Voigtlander, and Iloca. Today, only Leica offers any serious competition, but in those days the Germans were very strong, perhaps too strong.

Our journalist friends on the trade publications were helpful in getting us to understand the American market and the technological expectations of the serious American camera buyer. They used to tell us that the Germans didn't want to listen to advice. The Germans thought they knew everything, but the Japanese were more open— "with big ears and big eyes." Burt Keppler, then at *Modern Photography*, was highly respected at Minolta in Japan and we listened carefully to his advice on product development. Somewhat later, Norman Goldberg and Michel Frank of *Popular Photography* were also influential guides. All three became well known by reputation to Minolta's engineering department in Japan. In conversation, one of our engineers might say, "If we do it this way, I'm sure Norm and

Bert will like it." Our willingness to listen to our American friends helped us greatly.

American camera companies were not quite so friendly, though for the most part Minolta's quality 35-mm cameras were not in direct competition. The major American cameras—Kodak, Ansco, Cardon, Argus, Bolsey, Graflex, Mercury, and Universal—were relatively simple "boxes" for the mass market. Nevertheless, Argus and other firms lobbied strongly against imports.

Washington in those days was trying to help Japan, which then had a big trade deficit with the United States and needed to export to pay its debts. Today, that situation is reversed. The Japanese must remember the help given to us by America when we needed it most, even at times when it hurt some U.S. companies. People tend to forget what doesn't please them. Since I was there from the beginning, I remember everything, including American generosity when we had big deficits and had to borrow heavily from the United States.

In an annual postwar ritual, the Japanese prime minister would be photographed, waving and smiling from the deck of the Pan Am StratoCruiser, taking off again for Washington to ask for another loan. It was a big day for Japan in 1963. Prime Minister Hayato Ikeda arrived as usual in Washington but, for the first time, said that on this trip he wasn't begging for another loan, because the Japanese economy was at last self-sustaining. He thanked President Kennedy for all the help America had given. It was a moment that no Japanese should ever forget or ignore.

I must confess to having a fair number of obsessions. One of them is talking about the important role America has played in the postwar accomplishments of Japanese industry and the overall recovery of Japan from the wartime devastation we brought on ourselves with the invasion of China and the bombing of Pearl Harbor. I write newspaper articles about it, I talk to journalists about it, and I make speeches about it. This is one of the obsessions that fuels my motivational engines.

In the 1950s Washington didn't give in to pressure from American manufacturers to restrict Japanese camera imports. The principles of free trade prevailed and the world economy benefited. The economies of both the United States and Japan enjoyed a period of unprecedented growth.

*   *   *

I fulfilled a lifelong dream when in the spring of 1955 I bought my first American car, a brand-new Pontiac Star Chief. The sticker price was $4,000, but the dealer offered a low down payment and twenty-four months to pay, though I didn't keep the car that long. I traded it in for a swept-wing DeSoto and later switched to a Chrysler. If Detroit had known about me, I might have ranked as its favorite Japanese. I bought three different American cars during those first four years that I lived in the United States. Despite my heritage as the son and grandson of Ford dealers, I have never owned a Ford, a fact that angered my father. I guess the design of other cars just appealed to me more, especially that swept-wing DeSoto. It cost me as much to park my new car at a garage near Kanematsu's office in Manhattan as I had been paying for my hotel room.

The car was a necessity as well as a luxury. Many of the camera industry's distributors were on Long Island, and the only practical way to get to them was by car. But I must admit that having the car made me something of a celebrity. In New York's small Japanese community, we all knew each other and very few, particularly among the younger men, had a car. It soon became one of my responsibilities to pick up some of the Japanese arriving at Idlewild airport, everyone from students to movie stars. I know I was criticized by some for driving a big car at such a young age, but I had fun and met many important people.

One of them was the late Kiyoshi Ichimura, president of Riken Kogaku. He taught me something about myself when he came to New York soon after I bought my first car. At that time, Ricoh cameras were the company's only product, but Ichimura always had his eyes open for new ideas. I was asked to show him around New York, which I gladly did. As we drove through the streets of the city, he asked me what the most interesting difference was that I had noticed between New York and cities like Tokyo and Osaka. I headed for Fifth Avenue.

In Japan in those days, ladies' underwear was always hidden from public view. Even when housewives hung out the wash to dry, there were no "unmentionables" on the line. I showed Ichimura some of the shop windows along Fifth Avenue with attractive mannequins in lacy underclothes. Later I showed him some of the underwear ads in the the Sunday *New York Times*, ads that seemed to me as sexy as anything in *Playboy*.

I told him ladies' underwear was apparently much more in demand in New York than cameras. Camera stores were usually tucked away on side streets and were not a very prominent part of the New York scene. Ichimura said little but listened closely. Not long after, I discovered that Ichimura had something I lacked—the entrepreneurial spirit. Soon after his return to Japan, while continuing as president of Riken Kogaku, Ichimura established the first Sanai store, specializing in lingerie and featuring mannequins as sexy as any on Fifth Avenue. Sanai soon became Japan's first full-line ladies' wear store, and its towering, round building is the most famous in the elegant Ginza shopping district, where I had once watched American GIs directing traffic when the only "shops" in that bombed-out area were the tables of street vendors. Whenever I see that thriving store today, I think of the role I had in creating it. If I had been as enterprising as Ichimura, I might have taken that good idea myself and become rich on it. Today Sanai is a chain with branches all over the country.

Ichimura later created the Sanai Oil Company, which had the contract to provide all the fuel used at Haneda airport, Tokyo's main air terminal before Narita was built. Meanwhile, Ricoh, not doing too well with cameras, branched out into business equipment and became a highly regarded copier manufacturer.

In 1955 Minolta's progress in the United States got another boost, this time from a man whose impact on the Japanese camera industry has been enormous. Kinji Moriyama was the youngest member of the Diet, the Japanese parliament. He came to photography as a gifted enthusiast, but it was to become much more than a hobby. The camera industry was looking for a politician who would support its interests. As a new parliamentarian, the young Representative Moriyama had plenty of energy and enthusiasm but not much political power. His own interest in photography had inspired him to establish contacts with many manufacturers, distributors, and dealers in Japan. He realized that Japan needed to develop export industries to survive, and, like KT, he was convinced that the photo industry had the potential for exports. He persuaded many key people that helping the Japanese camera industry would help the Japanese nation.

Without Moriyama's accomplishments, my own work in New York would have gone on being frustrating. I often had the sense that I was beating my head against a stone wall built by years of American consumer experience with shoddy Japanese cameras. Moriyama's story became an important part of my story when his efforts began to change that perception. In 1954, he was instrumental in creating the Japan Camera Inspection Institute, sponsored by the industry to promote the development of higher-quality photographic products and to stop the export of what we considered to be toys as real cameras. Enabling legislation gave the institute the power to inspect all cameras slated for export. An export license was denied to all toy cameras. Moriyama was the founder and first chairman of the institute.

When Kinji Moriyama came to New York in 1955 with his wife, Mayumi, who is now equally famous in Japan, I met them at the airport and arranged his first meeting with the press. His purpose was to establish the Japan Camera Information and Service Center in New York City. Originally, the government put up 70 percent of the center's financing; the rest came from the photo industry, which later assumed all the costs. The center started operations in September 1955 at the Fifth Avenue offices of another example of a joint government/industry venture, the Japan External Trade Organization (JETRO). The center's official opening was in February 1956.

Until the center was established, I had felt very much alone in New York. From my point of view, the German cameras dominated the market so thoroughly that I thought Minolta and the other Japanese manufacturers had little chance of success. When Kinji Moriyama and his staff arrived, I had new friends from home whom I could depend on to bolster my spirits. The center also meant there would be another place, besides my desk at Kanematsu, where Japanese cameras could be taken for repair. The center gave Americans somewhere to go for service and information or to register complaints about Japanese photo equipment. This helped to build public confidence in Japanese cameras.

The staff that the Moriyamas brought to New York to help establish the center was impressive. It included young men sent by four major manufacturers: Minolta for technical services, Nikon for administration, Olympus for accounting and financial operations, and Konica for advertising. The Nikon representative, Takateru Koakimoto, and the Olympus representative, Toshiro Shimoyama, later became presidents of their companies. In fact, three men who became president of Nikon served their apprenticeship in the export business in America. In addition to Koakimoto, Noboru Hamashima, Nikon's first representative in the United States, whom I met when I arrived for the MPDFA Camera Show, and Shigetada Fukuoka, who worked for four years as an assistant to my mentor, Joseph Ehrenreich, also later became presidents of Nikon.

Joseph Ehrenreich sold his 32nd Street Penn Camera Store and established Ehrenreich Photo Industry, distributing both Nikon cameras and Fuji film. Some years later, after Ehrenreich's death, the firm employed a young assistant sent by Fuji named Minoru Ohnishi. Ohnishi later became president of Fuji. These leaders of companies that later became major exporters all served an apprenticeship in the United States, a career path later followed by several other Japanese who were their companies' first representatives in America. For the Japanese, America has become our training ground as well as our most important foreign market.

Another member of the original staff that the Moriyamas established at the center was a young secretary named Mariko. She later became the wife of Minolta's Ken Nakamura. And a young man who was Ken's assistant in New York for three years, Henry Tashima, replaced his father, KT, as president of Minolta in 1982. Henry has joined an elite circle of Japanese business leaders who spent several years in the United States, learning all they could about the world's most productive economy and biggest market. By contrast, I know of no American company headed by a man who spent his apprentice years in Japan. The camera industry wasn't the only one in those days to send to America bright young men with leadership potential, but it perhaps went further than any other industry in recognizing the importance of American methods and America's markets.

At his first meeting with the press in New York, Representative Moriyama took a fountain pen from his suit-coat pocket. "This is a Parker pen," he said. "Made in the USA. And my suit is made from British textiles. Both are excellent products. But please, when it comes to cameras, use Japanese." The reporters' laughter signaled the beginning of the Moriyamas' excellent relations with the press in the United States. I became close to the Moriyamas over the years and admired them greatly.

Representative Moriyama's political prestige grew steadily. He has twice been a cabinet member as minister of transportation and minister of science and technology. He was the first Japanese named Man of the Year by the Photo Manufacturers and Distributors Association in the United States and also the first to be elected to the Hall of Fame of the MPDFA. In 1987, he received the First Order of the Rising Sun Medal, the highest honor the Japanese government can bestow, which was to have been presented to him by the Emperor at the Royal Palace. A few days before he was scheduled to receive the medal, however, Representative Moriyama died of a sudden heart attack while playing golf. I was among the honorary pallbearers at his funeral in Tokyo. Prime Minister Yasuhiro Nakasone presided over the services.

Shortly after his death, he was succeeded as president of the Japan Camera Inspection Institute by his wife, who has been a member of the upper house of parliament since 1980, one of the first women elected to the Diet. Mrs. Moriyama began her career as a government official and was director general of the Women's Bureau of the Ministry of Labor. A graduate of Tokyo University, she speaks excellent English and was often her husband's interpreter.

Kinji Moriyama recognized the importance of American mentors in establishing the Japanese camera industry in the United States. He arranged for the award of an emperor's medal to the late Joseph Ehrenreich and also established the Frontier Club, which continues to meet every year in Tokyo. Members include Japanese who came to America to help establish the photo industry and a few Americans who helped in the early days, such as Henry A. Froelich of Philadelphia, who became America's first Konica distributor in 1952.

The Moriyamas lived in New York for about six months after they first arrived. They not only established the Japan Camera Information and Service Center but also arranged for the first Japan Camera Show. It was held in December 1955 in the office space the center then shared with JETRO. As more and more Japanese camera companies set up full-scale operations in the United States, the role of the center diminished. Its continuing responsibility has been to promote the development of the Japanese camera industry in the United States, and it is today the main sponsor of the annual Japan Camera Show in New York.

I took advantage of the improved public perception of Japanese cameras by working harder than ever at signing up new distributors. By March 31, 1956, the end of our 1955 fiscal year, Minolta had won a 40 percent share of the Japanese camera market in the United States. That sounds impressive. But it was a small market, and Nikon and Minolta had just about all of it. Minolta's net sales to distributors were only $720,000 that year—not much but a big improvement over the previous year, when we had virtually no sales.

Later that year, Minolta became the first Japanese company to advertise in both *Life* and *Playboy* magazines. In the case of *Playboy*, which had only begun publication in 1953, I must admit it was a personal choice. I enjoyed the magazine, and many camera buyers evidently agree with me. Through the years our *Playboy* ads have been very successful. *Life* was another story. In addition to having the world's largest circulation, it was widely respected for the quality of its photojournalism. Our ads no longer involved FR Corporation but were done by Jesse Wilkes. Now, rather than the "Double Guarantee" of FR and Minolta, our cameras carried the tag "As advertised in *Life*."

My "American-Jewish godfather," Joseph Ehrenreich, had been closely watching these developments. The positive publicity received by Japan in general and Minolta in particular accelerated the acceptance of Japanese cameras in the United States by at least two or three years.

Mr. Ehrenreich, who had encouraged me not to give up, soon gave me very good reason to be glad I had taken his advice. He introduced me to the proprietors of the Peerless camera store. Early in 1957 Peerless started handling Minolta. In a full-page *New York Times* advertisement, Peerless testified that Minolta cameras were as good as German cameras. Our resulting sales were much better than I could have expected.

Peerless was an industry leader, with the highest volume of camera sales in America. Many dealers previously reluctant to handle Japanese products followed Peerless's lead. But increasing competition soon proved to be the price of success.

Canon had opened a five-man office on Fifth Avenue late in 1955, trying to sell directly to retail outlets. The time wasn't ripe for direct distribution, however. Canon gave up the effort and signed up with Bell & Howell as its distributor. In 1957, Yashica introduced a twin reflex camera at a suggested retail price of $75, or $24.50 less than Paul Perlowin's pricing for the Minolta Autocord. Minolta and Nikon were no longer competing just against each other and the German and American manufacturers. Now we had serious competition from other Japanese firms. Ricoh, Konica, Pentax, Aires, Petri, Miranda, Mamiya, and Olympus were soon in the game. Minolta quickly lost its 40 percent share of the Japanese camera market in the United States.

KT began to visit the United States more frequently. On one of those visits, in May 1957, *The New York Times* ran a story about us, quoting me in the headline:

KUSUMOTO WROTE HOME
THAT CAMERA HAD
NO SEX APPEAL

The story, written by Bill Freeman, who covered marketing for the *Times*, described Jesse Wilkes's role in introducing us to trade editors during KT's first visit in September 1954 and brought the Minolta story up to date. A lot of our early history was packed into that story, including the role of the FR Corporation, Kanematsu, and Ken Nakamura. The headline referred to the complaints I had heard from American dealers about those first cameras I brought with me when I arrived from Japan.

Zensei Ushiyama, the president of Yashica, arrived in New York in the spring of 1956. He took a suite at the Waldorf-Astoria, an unusual move at the time. In 1954 I had pounded the pavement and knocked on a hundred doors to try to get American camera distributors to see me. Now Ushiyama sent out announcements inviting American camera distributors to come and see him at the Waldorf. And they came. Soon, three of the biggest—Raygram, Hornstein, and Intercontinental—signed up as Yashica distributors. Yashica became an instant success and a major competitor. Not only Ushiyama, but also his interpreter, Harry Gocho, became well known in the photo industry both in New York and back home in Japan.

In 1956, as Minolta continued to prosper, I moved out of my hotel and rented a room with a German-American family in Forest Hills. For my new home, I bought my first television set, an American-made, black-and-white RCA. I convinced myself that watching television helped me improve my English. Perhaps it did, but the most important thing I learned from the comedy shows I watched was that any mention of Japanese products brought an immediate laugh. We may have thought we were making progress in the camera industry, but to the American mass audience our reputation for shoddy goods was still a joke.

Though Minolta's market share slipped with increased Japanese competition, we were now dealing with a much bigger market for

Japanese cameras. Minolta sales shot up. And so did our spirits. Ken Nakamura and I freely roamed Manhattan, young men heady with the sweet smell of success, that distinctly American aroma. Minolta was still a small presence in this great country, and we were still poor. But we could sense the possibilities.

By that time Dick Ohtomo, who had also attended Keio University, was in New York representing Canon. Dick is a handsome man, an excellent singer, and a highly successful business executive. He has since worked for several different companies, which is unusual in Japan, and he has also been married to two of Japan's most beautiful women. His first wife had been Miss Tokyo. That marriage ended in divorce, I believe around the time that Dick met Mari Yoshimura, who became his second wife. Mari is a famous movie star and television personality in Japan. Though we worked for rival camera companies during those early days in New York, we became close friends. Dick later returned to Japan as an advertising man for Canon in the domestic market and played a key role in establishing Canon as a leading company. He left Canon to go to work for Pfizer as advertising manager for its Coty line of cosmetics in Japan and later held the same position for Coca-Cola. Dick came full circle back to the camera industry as president of the Japanese operations of Polaroid. Since his 1985 retirement from Polaroid, he has been a consultant to an American law firm and to Dartmouth College in Japan. The International College of Japan, seeking Americans to teach business courses to its English-speaking Japanese students, established a sister-school relationship with Dartmouth, and Dick now works with the Dartmouth extension office in Japan. My alma mater, Keio University, has similar relationships with two of America's best schools of business, Harvard and Stanford. Japan continues its passionate pursuit of learning how to succeed in business by trying American methods.

With the possible exception of Dick, the most successful of all the young Japanese who worked in New York in those days was probably Ike Hattori. Ike worked for Sekonic, which exported meters, and he had a desk next to mine at Kanematsu. He had more flexibility in his expenses than most of the other Japanese and usually managed to have a good time. The famous Takarazuka Theater group came to New York while on a world tour. This all-girl musical group based outside Osaka is considered an elite organization. The girls generally come from very good families and must be extremely talented to qualify. The troupe was featured in the American film *Sayonara* in which Marlon Brando fell in love with one of the Takarazuka stars. There were practically no Japanese women in New York in those days, and my young friends were all very excited. But no one got so excited as Ike. He fell in love with one of the singers.

Ike was always spontaneous and warmhearted. He had difficulty saying no and was so often late for appointments that we used to speak of "Hattori time" as meaning an indefinite "sometime" in the vague future. This was also a play on the family name of the owners of the firm that makes Seiko watches, which also happens to be Hattori. I wasn't too surprised by Ike's absence from his desk at Kanematsu shortly after the Takarazuka group left town. But I was surprised when he called me from Mexico City, where the troupe had its next stop. Ike had pursued his singer there. He returned to New York after a few days but kept up his pursuit by long-distance. He eventually married the girl, after his return to Japan.

Ike quit Sekonic and formed his own firm, importing American and European electronic products into Japan. In recent years trade in electronic products has flowed mostly the other way, but Ike had a good idea at the right time. He also had the entrepreneurial spirit. He put his idea to work and became wealthy. His firm, Electori, has been so successful that Ike drives both a Porsche and a Mercedes-Benz, which are far more expensive in Japan than they are in the United States.

After the struggles of my first two years in New York, I had begun to have a wonderful time with a small group of young Japanese friends whose difficulties, successes, and ambitions were similar to my own. Jesse Wilkes used to call us the samurai, young strangers in an alien land that had recently been our enemy in a devastating war. We all had problems with language and finances but, even though many of us worked for rival firms, we all had a great deal of loyalty to each other. We worked hard for our companies, but also for our industry and our country.

One of our favorite hangouts was a Greenwich Village restaurant called Kokoro tow Kokoro, which means "Heart to Heart." There was an American lady, whose name I can't recall, who sang popular songs in rather good Japanese, though she had never been to Japan. She was then in her fifties but she often had an admiring circle of young Japanese bachelors gathered around her piano, singing along with her. We all agreed that she was entitled to visit Japan and, among ourselves, regretted that we could not raise the money to send her. When I was back in New York in the early 1970s, more than a decade later, the restaurant and its American singer were still there. By that time many of the Japanese I knew were well enough off so that we could afford to pay for a trip to Japan for her. We made the offer, but she smiled and shook her head. "Why didn't you ask me ten years ago?" she said. "I'm too old for that kind of trip now." The restaurant is long gone, and so is the singer, who never saw the country she sang about so well.

One recurring reverie from my early years in America is inspired most often by a very un-Japanese sensation, the scent of perfume. For whatever reason, despite our thriving fashion and makeup industries, perfume still has not become popular among Japanese women. But I often remember one Sunday date I had with a girl named Irene when the Easter Parade was still fashionable on New York's Fifth Avenue. Irene worked in the office of my mentor, Jesse Wilkes. We both dressed up for the occasion. I had bought Irene an orchid, but what struck me most as we walked up the avenue, even more than the grand display of the latest fashions, was the intoxicating blend of perfumes worn by the women. We strolled past Saint Patrick's Cathedral, past the fashionable stores that line the avenue, and my head swam in this ocean of beautiful impressions. For a not very religious man, it was a very religious experience. With a lovely girl on my arm, I thought I was in heaven.

My co-worker, Ken Nakamura, and I had both grown up during the war years and entered middle school at about the time the Japanese military government prohibited the teaching of English. Though we have both lived many years in America, neither Ken nor I will ever speak English as well as younger-generation Japanese who learned the language fairly well as children before living abroad. Back in 1957, our English was even worse, but at Minolta in Japan, they thought I was improving rapidly. The copies they saw of my English-language correspondence seemed excellent. What they didn't know was that a young secretary at Kanematsu had also become the Minolta secretary. Her name was Augusta. We called her "Augie." She always corrected my English and did such a good job that she almost got me in trouble.

My bosses back at Minolta decided my English had become so good that I should start writing the instruction manuals for our cameras sold in America. This was totally beyond my ability, but I couldn't lose face by admitting it. Augie came to my rescue. We would gather instruction books for similar cameras put out by our competitors, cut and paste, and change them slightly. With Augie's help, the transitions and the parts I had to write myself were smoothed over. Nobody ever noticed that I was lifting from the competition.

Augie and I became very fond of each other. She lived in the Flatbush section of Brooklyn, and her parents, whom she visited often, lived way up in the Bronx. I was glad I had a car. We saw each other almost every night. In those days there were many drive-in movies in the New York area. Since I'm such a movie fan, the drive-ins were a favorite date spot. There was one near the Whitestone Bridge in the Bronx that we went to often, but I must admit that at a drive-in with Augie I seldom paid much attention to the movies.

Her family was warm and accepted me easily, though it was rare in the 1950s for an American girl to date an Oriental man. Augie was of Italian descent and a wonderful cook. She often cooked at my apartment, and I soon became addicted to one of her specialties, linguine and clam sauce. When I go to an Italian restaurant with people who know me, someone is likely to say, "I know what Sam's going to have. Linguine and clam sauce." They are usually right, but they don't know why.

Cute was a favorite word used to describe an attractive girl in the fifties, and Augie certainly fit the description. Whenever I used that word to describe her, she would say, "Of course. I take cute pills." She was very pretty, taller than I, and had a wonderful figure. I loved to photograph her, and the only indication I've ever seen of any artistic ability on my part was some of the lovely portraits I shot of her. But I suspect that the artistic value of those portraits had more to do with the model than with the photographer.

I also liked to sing Japanese love songs to Augie, though I'm not a very good singer. I would translate the songs for her and she began to recognize certain words. Nearly all Japanese love songs are sad and certain romantic words and images—moon, rain, mist, night or evening, gentle breezes, autumn, and a sailor sailing off into the fog or the setting sun—show up again and again in most of them.

Augie would often ask me to sing something for her, particularly when we were driving somewhere. Then I would translate the song and she would say, "There you go again with the moon and the mist and the rain." Driving with Augie in the rain, softly singing a Japanese love song, is one of my fondest memories. One of those songs that she asked to hear often went something like this:

> *I'm wearing a nice blue suit*
> *and going to town with my girl,*
> *having a drink of tea*
> *and seeing the newest movie.*
> *Everywhere we go, my sweet, pure girl*
> *looks like a lovely French doll.*
> *I cannot decide if I should confess*
> *how much I love her*
> *or if I should propose marriage.*
> *Maybe I should not.*
> *The wind of the night has a sweet smell.*
> *The moon in the sky looks like she enjoys*
> *her young life as much as we do.*

The title of the song was "Blue Suit." Augie and I took several trips together, including a visit to Montreal, where I introduced her to Max Zell and Abe Feigerson of Anglo Photo. From there, with me singing love songs, we drove on to Toronto and Niagara Falls.

> *I cannot decide if I should confess*
> *how much I love her*
> *or if I should propose marriage.*

Our trip to Niagara Falls wasn't quite a honeymoon, as it is for many young couples, but "Blue Suit" was an appropriate song.

There was a finished basement in the house I lived in in Forest Hills. I often hosted bachelor parties for the young Japanese community. We would round up as many as we could of the very few Japanese girls then in New York. Augie would often be the only American there, and she became well known in that tight little circle. The news of our relationship soon got back to Minolta headquarters in Osaka.

Much as I had come to love America, I knew I would soon have to return to Japan. KT wanted me to put what I was learning in the United States to use in our export department, helping Minolta to expand its operations in other parts of Asia and in Europe, as well as in North America. And my family had begun to remind me that I was thirty and still unmarried. They wanted to find a wife for me and see me settle down with a family. Minolta had the same concern, though for a somewhat different reason. KT was afraid I was about to take an American wife. In the atmosphere of the time, that might have been the end of my career, and, as I tried to think about it from the point of view of an American woman, I realized how unfair it would be for Augie to have to adapt to the low living standards and the lowly status of women that existed in Japan. Despite my dreams, I knew that life in Japan, with its cramped living quarters and the many restrictions our society places on women, would be difficult for Augie to endure. We would talk about it and then she would ask me to sing what had become her favorite song, "Blue Suit." I didn't have to translate it for her anymore. She understood that my time in America and our time together were coming to an end. We cried together often during those evenings.

Even as I began making preparations to leave for Japan in October 1958, I knew that one day I would return to America. But I had no idea when or under what circumstances. And I knew it would be terribly unfair to ask Augie to wait for me.

I'm not a conscientious letter writer, but Augie's mother and I did stay in touch after I returned to Japan. I never heard from Augie, but less than a year after I left, her mother wrote and told me that Augie had married someone else. I read that letter with a sad sense of relief. Feelings of guilt and loss still trouble me when I think of Augie. Knowing that our love was impossible, I felt happy that Augie had found someone else. But in 1967 her mother wrote to me again. She told me Augie had died of cancer. I was alone in the office working late one evening when I read the letter. It threw me into total shock. The letter fell from my hand. I had had no idea that Augie had been ill. And now she was gone.

I wanted to reach out to her. Absurdly, our song, "Blue Suit," started running through my mind. I tried to sing it, staring out a window at the misty lights of Osaka. The words choked in my throat. I reached down for the letter, crumpled it in my hand, and cried. I think about Augie often but, even today, I rarely talk about her. I can't, without feeling my throat tighten up and my eyes blinking back tears.

IV

THE GOLDEN YEARS

1958–1969

11

Our Man from America

When KT brought me back to Osaka in 1958, I discovered that my tour of duty in America would be both an asset and a source of problems. America had spoiled me in many ways. Everything from the richness and abundance of the food to the full-figured sexiness of the women reflected a nation of limitless size, success, and opportunities. I had indeed been seduced by America, and I suspect that to many Japanese I must have seemed like a born-in-America nisei. I must have also seemed like a pain in the neck, particularly to some of my senior colleagues at Minolta.

KT had wanted to bring me home both to put my American experience to work in helping Minolta expand its exports and to keep me from becoming so Americanized that my career with Minolta might be ruined. Though some instinct told me I would return to America one day, I was ready for the challenge of being back in Japan to help Minolta grow.

When I returned to Japan, I thought the obvious spot for me would be in the export department but involved with the American market rather than hammering nails and making crates as I had been doing a few years before. But KT was sensitive to the fact that

115

someone else, far senior to me, headed the department. Shigeo Sandow, the man who had been my boss before I went to America, had been jealous of my assignment. Though I had nominally reported to Mr. Sandow and to Minolta's director of sales, Shozo Tashima, I also had a direct pipeline to KT during my years in the United States. That had also been a source of resentment.

KT may have wanted me in exports, but he had other factors to consider, including the respect given to seniority in Japan. Moving me into exports, where I might be perceived as a challenge to Mr. Sandow, could have had a negative effect on the morale of other senior managers. Now that I'm in my sixties, I can see the advantages of the seniority system. It creates a sense of security that allows top managers to give younger workers credit for creative new ideas and hard work without feeling threatened by talented and ambitious juniors. On the other hand, it can make junior employees feel stifled because of the limited chances for advancement. For many years after World War II, this was a relatively minor problem in Japan. The war had killed off tens of thousands of men who had been managers and potential managers. And, during the occupation, General MacArthur had purged major Japanese industries of many senior managers who had been identified with the *zaibatsu*, the monopolies that had worked closely with the military to further Japanese imperialism. It was as though someone had cut loose with a double-barreled shotgun, thinning out the ranks of Japanese management and leaving a relatively open field for younger people to advance.

Today, I must admit, that is no longer the case. Young people have a slower and tougher road to advancement. I suspect that many do feel frustrated. That's how I felt three decades ago when my own career path seemed to be stalled.

Japan's devastating defeat in World War II turned many once warlike Japanese into pacifists. We want to avoid conflict, particularly within the corporation. So I went to KT with what I thought was an excellent idea. I asked KT to put me in charge of Minolta's advertising. He looked at me with a puzzled expression on his face.

"Why would you want to do that?" he asked.

I told him how excited I had been about what I had learned about advertising in America. With mentors like Jesse Wilkes, I had seen what effective marketing communications could do. And I believed I could help Minolta by putting those lessons to work in other markets.

"But that was America," said KT. "This is Japan. You know what the advertising industry is like here. There is so much corruption, kickbacks, bribery, so much temptation, I would hate to see you get involved. It could ruin your reputation—and your career."

With a moment's reflection, I did know what KT meant. In those days the advertising industry had an unwholesome reputation in Japan. Advertisers typically did their own creative work internally and used outside agencies mainly as space brokers. And the space brokers competed primarily on the basis of their kickbacks to corporate advertising managers.

KT might have thought I had been away from Japan too long to remember that fact, and the concerned expression on his face told me that in his fatherly way he wanted to protect my reputation. He described advertising as a "dirty business" and wondered again why I wanted to get into it. I must say that the advertising industry in Japan has changed greatly since then, mostly because of one agency—Dentsu.

In 1955, Hideo Yoshida, then president of Dentsu, sent two young men to New York to work as trainees at the American ad agency Young and Rubicam. Dentsu at that time was a small agency with a production and sales staff that worked with all clients. The salesmen at a Japanese agency often competed against each other as well as against other agencies in going after new business. "Gifts" often played a decisive role in determining who won the business. Young and Rubicam, like most American agencies, assigned an account executive to work with just one client or, at most, a small group of clients. The trainees sent to Y&R liked what they saw at the American agency and recommended to Yoshida that Dentsu adopt the American system. He followed their advice.

Dentsu reorganized its entire operation and began to compete for business, not on the basis of kickbacks but on the quality of its creative product. Top corporate officials soon recognized the value of Dentsu's capabilities—and honesty. Dentsu began to get more and more business. The results were typical of the way in which Japanese management profited from lessons learned from Americans. Dentsu has since become the world's biggest ad agency, retaining its close ties with Y&R in the process. The rest of the Japanese advertising industry had to follow Dentsu's lead, but that reformation was far from complete back in 1959. I quickly backed away from my request to handle Minolta's advertising.

I was beginning to feel that my wonderful times in America might turn out to be a liability. Minolta's export operations had changed greatly since I'd left in 1954. Though the U.S. military post exchange was still important, the United States itself was now Minolta's biggest export customer. Exports to Europe were just beginning through an office we had set up in Hamburg, Germany, again with the help of the trading company Kanematsu.

KT wasn't about to put me in the export department—or in advertising. But he did come up with a job for me. He put me in charge of a newly created sales planning department with a staff drawn from several areas of the company, including personnel, sales, and finance. KT wanted to coordinate sales plans with key departments from research and development through production, distribution, and advertising for both domestic and export markets. Today, Minolta in Japan has sales planning departments for each of its four product divisions—photo, copiers, office systems, and meters and measuring devices. But in 1958 it was a new concept for us, and at first I wasn't quite sure what to make of my new assignment.

I wondered if KT was just creating a job to keep me from feeling too frustrated about not being placed in charge of exports. But sales planning turned out to be a wonderful opportunity for me. For one thing, I was still involved with exports and at least marginally with advertising. And my new job gave me a greater opportunity than I'd had before to work with the people from R&D and the factory.

This was in the era when cameras were still relatively simple. To understand camera technology today you have to be an expert in computer engineering. But then I could still understand and even repair all our cameras. Minolta had become the first Japanese camera company to manufacture every part of its cameras, including the optical glass. We had also introduced the first Japanese-made planetarium in 1957 and in 1958 the SR-1, the first Minolta single-lens reflex camera with the bayonet lens mount system.

Minolta had begun to find its niche as the camera of choice for the serious amateur. Nikon developed an early lock on the professional market. Canon products ranged from inexpensive to top of the line, and the scores of other Japanese camera companies then in business scrambled to find a place for themselves.

This was a period of considerable innovation in the Japanese camera industry and Minolta was very much in the forefront. We introduced the revolutionary Minolta Auto Wide in 1958. It was a

One-year-old Sam Kusumoto in 1929 with a Boys Day display of samurai dolls and artifacts depicting phases in Japanese history.

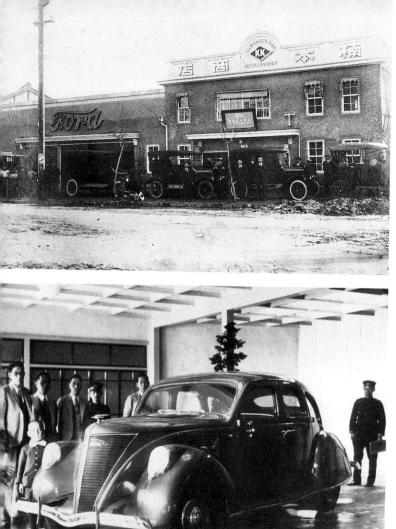

The Kusumoto Ford dealership in Seoul, Korea, 1931. The family lived on the second floor of the central building.

Sam Kusumoto, 9, stands next to a Lincoln Zephyr, sold to the Japanese governor of Korea. Others in this 1937 photo are salesmen and police officers.

1940 family portrait with Sam Kusumoto, 12, at center. Others, left to right: his mother, Fumie; grandmother, Yuki; brother, Koji; father, Enichiro; and grandfather, Kichitaro. Ribbons worn by boys commemorate Japan's 2,600th anniversary.

OPPOSITE: Sam Kusumoto boarding the SS President Wilson in Yokohama, February 1954, en route to America for the first time.

William J. Daly of the Kanematsu trading company at Minolta's six-by-six display at March 1954 Master Photo Dealers and Finishers Association show in Chicago. This was Minolta's debut in the American photo market.

TOP: *GIs brought quantities of the Minolta 35 camera back to America, though it was sold only in Japan.* ABOVE: *The Minolta 16, the "spy camera," was widely sold in America through the Sears Roebuck mail-order catalog.* LEFT: *The Autocord twin-lens reflex camera, distributed by FR Corporation.*

Augie, secretary at Kanematsu, poses with 1956 swept-wing DeSoto, one of three American cars Sam Kusumoto bought during his first four years in the United States.

OPPOSITE: *Larry Fink, president of FR Corporation, being greeted in 1956 on his arrival at Tokyo's Haneda International Airport by Minolta founder Kazuo Tashima and "Miss Tokyo." OVERLEAF: Sam Kusumoto and his bride, Kuniko, cut their wedding cake at the Osaka Grand Hotel, March 29, 1960.*

35-mm lens shutter camera developed with the mass market in America very much in mind. Technically, the Auto Wide had a behind-the-lens shutter in the center of the camera. This allowed for a simpler matching of points in relation to the exposure meter. For the camera enthusiast, the Auto Wide's big innovation was eliminating the necessity of reading meter numbers to get the correct exposure. The operation was still manual. The photographer turned the lens wheel to establish the correct setting but did not have to check the shutter speed or f-stop.

Whether it's automobile transmissions or cameras, Americans love products that promise to be automatic. The Auto Wide was designed with this in mind. The Uniomat, which had a built-in selenium meter, was introduced in 1960. It went even further in reaching out to the American passion for automatic ease. In the Uniomat, the shutter blade functioned as the diaphragm. The shutter opened halfway, admitting light, which automatically determined both the shutter speed and f-stop. A quarter of a century later, Minolta's engineers exploited to the maximum this drive toward automation with the highly computerized series of cameras appropriately called the Maxxum.

But even in the 1950s we recognized that customers in the world's biggest camera market wanted their cameras to be as automatic as possible. We pushed the technology of the time to its limits to meet that market demand. Making cameras for the American market also means being sensitive to camera and film format innovations from Kodak. Kodak continues to introduce new cameras primarily so it can sell film, just as Gillette makes razors so it can sell blades. You may sell a razor or a camera only once to a particular customer. But you can sell the same customer blades and film for a lifetime.

When Kodak introduces a new film format, Minolta must come up with cameras that can handle it or risk losing market share in America. Nikon, confident of its leadership with professional photographers, tends to ignore Kodak innovations aimed at the mass market. Canon and the other Japanese manufacturers sometimes follow Kodak's lead and sometimes don't. Minolta, so heavily dependent on the American market, was the only Japanese camera company to follow each of Kodak's leads into the Instamatic cameras in the 1960s, the 110 film format in the 1970s, and, unfortunately, into the disc camera format of the 1980s. The disc camera was a flop for both Minolta and Kodak. Nevertheless, to me it makes sense to follow Kodak's lead. It enjoys an 80 percent share of the American film market and 60 percent in Europe, but not everyone who buys Kodak film wants a Kodak camera.

Sometimes it's necessary to go even beyond Kodak to keep up with the other end of the American camera market—the professionals and the serious amateurs. For many years the standard measurement for film speed was the ASA (American Standards Association) number 100. Kodak then introduced its Super X film with an ASA of 200. Our engineers thought that was as far as they would need to go in terms of camera shutter speed. But American photo ingenuity doesn't end with Kodak. It extends into the darkrooms of professional photographers and serious amateurs.

Robert Capa's famous D-Day photographs, which appeared in the June 19, 1944, issue of *Life*, were an early example of what can be done. Capa waded ashore with GIs under German fire at dawn on the Normandy coast on June 6, shooting with available light and grabbing some of the war's most dramatic photos. But after he had taken his shots, Capa couldn't be certain what his prints would show. Developed in an ordinary manner, his shots, which were taken under difficult conditions with dim light and uncontrollable movements of both camera and subjects, might show nothing at all. Shutter speeds fast enough to freeze the movement might be too fast to allow enough light for proper exposure. The quiet technological drama that unfolded in Capa's darkroom back in London re-created the excitement of the landing itself. Sacrificing print quality and using a lengthy developing technique, Capa coaxed his powerful, grainy images from film to paper. Looking at those photos I can imagine the impact they must have had on Capa as those grim-faced soldiers took shape in his developing tray just as they had through the gray waves and mist and gunfire on Omaha Beach.

David Duncan during the Korean War, like Capa during World War II, took battlefield photography to new levels of dramatic intensity. Their work in *Life* magazine gave that publication an authority in photo images that set it apart. To me *Life* was as important an element in the American camera market as Kodak. Its photographers set standards that many serious amateurs aspired to and used techniques—including darkroom techniques—that thousands of camera enthusiasts imitated.

By the 1950s it wasn't unusual for professionals and at least some amateur enthusiasts to be kicking effective ASA film speed up to

1,000 and even 1,600. I had a hard time convincing our engineers that Minolta needed cameras with higher ASA speed indications when the fastest film on the market was only 200 or the 300 that Kodak brought in with its Tri-X film in 1957.

But this was another area in which I had KT's support. He wanted Minolta to be the General Motors of the photo industry, not in terms of size, but in the sense of covering the entire spectrum of photographic and other optical and electronic products. Minolta has long prided itself on having a full range of photo equipment products to offer its customers. From 1967 to 1975 Minolta had a full line of movie camera systems that recorded sound as well as images. These systems included everything from sophisticated and versatile cameras to directional microphones and a state-of-the-art projector. Our three silent movie cameras included the Autopack-8 D12, which could handle time-lapse photography, animation, dissolves, fade-ins, and other sophisticated motion picture techniques.

Television never quite fulfilled early predictions that it would kill the movie industry, but home video technology has effectively killed the home movie business. Minolta helped. In 1984 we designed and manufactured our first portable video camera. In 1986 we introduced a series of sophisticated video camcorders. Minolta also manufactures and markets some of the world's finest binoculars, industrial meters, and sophisticated optical-electronic equipment used in medical research and communications technology.

Our first venture into the business equipment industry, however, was very modest. In the 1950s, the Dutch company Van der Grinten was a large office equipment manufacturer. Minolta obtained a license to use Van der Grinten's principles to manufacture the Minolta diazo copier, utilizing a process previously used primarily for reproducing architectural blueprints. One of our Japanese competitors, Ricoh, started to make copiers at about the same time. Ricoh primarily manufactured less expensive cameras; and as the photo market became more sophisticated, the company fell behind, devoting more of its efforts to copiers. It soon became one of Japan's leading copier manufacturers. Minolta had just the opposite experience. Because of our success with cameras, we were slow to develop our business equipment capacity, though KT knew we must diversify in this direction. The diazo was never really successful as a general office copier. The copy quality was not good and, to be frank, it smelled bad. Most of our sales were in Japan with a few exports to Europe and Third World countries. It wasn't until 1964 when the Toyokawa business equipment plant opened that we moved into the copier market in a big way.

But overall in those days I was very proud of Minolta's technological achievements and the speed with which we could respond to market demands. Meanwhile, my personal problems, the presence of a rival on the job and the absence of a wife in my home, were being resolved by means typically Japanese.

12

Becoming Japanese

Though I had lived in America only four years, by the time KT brought me back to Osaka, I had forgotten a bit of what it means to be Japanese. The process of my reeducation was subtle, but effective.

It started with housing. Though it's tough to get a good apartment in New York these days, Americans have no idea of what a real housing shortage means. Osaka in 1958 still hadn't recovered from the leveling of the city during the war. But business had boomed, and the population was growing. Even today, space in general and housing in particular are among the shortages we suffer on our tight little islands. Consider the Japanese passion for golf. It's real, but we have little room for golf courses. The substitute for most people is vertical driving ranges: tall, green canvas backdrops and nets that tower over low-scale urban neighborhoods. Quality golf courses are so rare that memberships are traded like seats on the stock exchange, often at comparable prices. For the most part, Japanese don't have room to drive golf balls hundreds of feet on a horizontal plane. So they drive them up in the air. Even our pinball machines, known as pachinkos, are vertical rather than horizontal. That way, pachinkoparlor owners can pack more of them into a crowded storefront. Players operate them by pounding on handles on either side.

Both the golf ranges and the pachinko machines are used by many Japanese to vent the frustrations they experience on the job. Pretending that the golf ball or the handles of the pachinko represent your boss can give you an intense experience in venting repressed anger. And Japanese experience, and repress, many frustrations, not only on the job but in many aspects of our increasingly urban, crowded, and fast-paced life. Japan is a small country with a huge population. We can't afford giant egos or sprawling golf courses. We have to learn to contain our conflicts and live and work together peacefully in conditions so cramped they would drive an American crazy. One of the many misconceptions Americans have about Japan is that because our country has become prosperous, our people live well. We don't. The salary man like myself, even when his salary is fairly good, pays taxes and prices for basic commodities from housing to rice that are so high they would make an American gasp. In the last two years, living standards have improved, helped in no small part by increased imports at lower prices because of the greater strength of the Japanese yen. Rice continues to be expensive, however, because imports are banned, and the housing shortage goes on.

Even a man like KT, founder of a prosperous major company, lived modestly. He did have one indulgence—his Cadillac. For many years, KT always drove a Cadillac. He put up with all the disadvantages of driving a big American car in Japan—high fuel and insurance prices, narrow streets, difficulties in getting repairs and spare parts—for the joy of owning such a big and prestigious car. He was convinced that many more Japanese would drive American cars if only the Americans would adapt their wonderful automobiles to Japanese conditions. In Japan we follow the British way, not only with our parliament and royal family, but also by driving on the left. So naturally, in Japanese cars, as in the British, the driver's side and the steering wheel go on the right, just the opposite of cars made in America and on the Continent.

When Toyota and Honda want to sell cars in America, they don't insist on leaving the driver's side on the right. They adapt to American conditions and put the driver in the driver's seat—on the left, just as the British now do when they export Jaguars and Rolls-Royces to America. But American automobile manufacturers don't want to be bothered adapting for export. They send cars to Japan with the driver's seat on the wrong side and then complain that they can't crack the closed Japanese market. The Americans, like the Germans and the French, argue that there is a certain prestige or snob value involved among Japanese wealthy enough to afford a foreign car. Having the wheel on the wrong side may be a status symbol for a few. Until the mid-1960s, British cars with the wheel on the wrong side sold in the United States in limited numbers. But to reach a broader market in America, the British, like the Japanese, decided to adapt.

KT was stubborn, however. He wanted his Cadillac. It got to be a real problem when toll roads began to come in during the early 1970s. In Japan the toll booth, naturally, is on the right, where the driver is supposed to sit. But if KT were driving his Cadillac, he would be sitting on the left. He would have to get out of the car, run all the way around the huge Cadillac, pay the toll collector, and run back. KT had to find a way for his Cadillac to become Japanese.

Finally, he had a robotic device, a kind of mechanical arm, built that would reach across the seat with money to pay the toll collector. Not many Japanese would go to so much trouble just to drive an American car. But KT was convinced that American auto manufacturers would sell many more cars in Japan if only they would adapt for local conditions. I tell this story about KT and his Cadillac often, particularly when I'm giving a speech to an American audience on international trade and America's huge trade deficit with Japan. His story illustrates my view that the solution to the trade deficit lies not in reducing imports from countries like Japan, but in expanding American exports. You can't expand exports effectively, however, unless you're willing to adapt for local markets, a lesson I myself learned when I first came to the United States with excellent Minolta cameras that couldn't be used with the electronic flash attachments that had become popular in America.

The trouble KT took to adapt his Cadillac for Japanese toll roads makes a wonderful story with an excellent moral. By the time the toll roads became widespread, however, KT had a chauffeur, Mr. Ohtani, to drive his Cadillac. So KT had the robotic arm built to save trouble for the chauffeur, not for himself. It's still a good story and it still makes my point about adapting for export. But for storytelling purposes it works better if you're imagining KT himself, the head of a giant corporation, running around his car at every toll booth.

When I set out to try to tell the story of my life, which includes the history of the Japanese camera industry coming to America, I wanted to be as truthful and accurate as possible. Old letters, company records, and other written material have been important in this research. And, throughout my business career, I have kept a concise diary in Japanese of meetings and travel. Many people have been interviewed and manuscript drafts have been checked by researchers and friends who know parts of the story. All this helps to keep the record straight, but when I decided to start work on this book, one of my first instincts was to search for old photographs that lay in a trunk in my grandmother's old house. Since I was very young, working with the Minoltaflex camera borrowed from my uncle when I was growing up in Korea, I have kept a record of my life, of the places I've been and of the people I've met through the universal language of photography. To me the photograph is a magic touchstone, unlocking memory and bringing the past back in a rush of emotions and half-forgotten names and events. The photograph is my memoir, my visual diary. While this is personal, it is also typically Japanese, for as a people we love photography and cameras.

This is one aspect of being Japanese that I didn't lose while living in America. But there was much that I had forgotten, both about the ways we work and the way we live.

When I went apartment hunting in Osaka in 1958, for example, I occasionally did find vacancies that I could afford, but they were snapped up so quickly that it was tough to connect with one. The man who helped me find my apartment also gave me a lesson in Japanese ways. My housing mentor turned out to be the man who held the job I hoped to have one day—the head of our export department.

Mr. Sandow's approach was very Japanese. Befriending a rival makes it difficult for that rival to act against you. Much in Japan's tradition and history, from the legends of the samurai to our role in World War II, has given us an image as a warlike people. It's a good reputation to have, of course. Other people aren't likely to bully you. But the reality is more complex. When Japan was a land of small, feudal warlords with an emperor who had little power and no central government, there were frequent territorial wars. But we had a distinct warrior class, the samurai. No one else went to war. There were no mass armies and no massive battles. A defeated warlord was expected to commit hara-kiri and his family might do the same. The rest of the people went on about their business.

For most of our history, this has been the Japanese way. Right now, nearly everyone in Japan is more or less a pacifist, not only in foreign policy but also in everyday life. Unfortunately, because Japan is small in size and homogeneous in population, it is also a country easy to control through modern communications. Because of our prosperity and the democratic institutions now in place, Japan isn't likely to come under the sway of a military dictatorship. But if a charismatic dictator were to appear at the right time, he might be able to play on our samurai traditions, our respect for authority, and our nationalism to fire up any hostile spirits we ordinarily repress. Today we listen to many political voices and find the best way. But during World War II, when we heard only one voice, we followed—to war. No one speaks openly of these tendencies, but, even without acknowledging them, we seek to contain them. My quiet rival, Mr. Sandow, understood this. He knew our conflict could be damaging if it broke into the open. And so he moved to contain it by helping me find a place to live.

Mr. Sandow told me about a new concrete apartment building on the edge of town. He said many people had already applied but recommended that I try. He arranged an introduction to the renting agent. I knew there were already more than a hundred people on the waiting list for apartments in that building. Mr. Sandow had wisely suggested a gift, and a Parker pen turned out to be the key that unlocked the door. The made-in-the-USA Parker, like the Dunhill lighter, was then a symbol of great prestige in Japan. The agent was impressed by the pen, and I got my apartment quickly. It had a small reception area, a kitchen, a half-bath, and two rooms that, in typical Japanese fashion, could be converted from living rooms to bedrooms just by taking tatami mats and pillows from a closet. However, six families on each floor had to share a communal tub and shower, an arrangement that was fairly common until recent years. I wondered what Augie would have thought of that apartment. It was larger than most Japanese bachelors would ever dream of. By American standards, however, it wasn't much.

On the job I had many more opportunities to relearn what life was like in Japan. I sensed that many of my colleagues resented the rather direct ways I had brought with me from America. And so I began to present my ideas not as orders or even as suggestions, but as examples of the way things were done in America. Like a Parker pen, that made-in-America label on my ideas helped to unlock many reluctant doors. Slowly I began to learn not only the importance of consensus but also how to achieve it.

The Japanese capacity for consensus has been nurtured both by our tradition as a nation of farmers and by the way we live now in a society that is highly urbanized and very crowded. Unlike most Western nations, Japan has no tradition as a land of great hunters. The aggressive qualities of the hunter are not honored among us. We view the hunter as someone at war with nature, who lives by killing or trapping his quarry. By contrast, we view farmers as people who work with one another and with nature. It's a popular theory in Japan that Europeans are more independent and aggressive than we are because they were hunters before they developed agriculturally. One of the ancient names for Japan is Mizuho no Kuni, "Country of Rice Fields." Though farmers now make up only a small fraction of our population, we still cling to this image of ourselves. Farmers, unlike hunters, all tend to do the same things, working in harmony with each other and with the changing seasons of nature. But we value harmony not only because of outdated traditions but also because of present realities.

We live and work on top of each other. Americans outside of New York have no idea how jammed a subway can be at rush hour. And even New Yorkers can only guess what the Tokyo subway, with its uniformed "pushers," can be like. Driving in most parts of Japan can make a Los Angeles freeway or a crosstown street in Manhattan look like an open highway. Not only is our housing cramped, but our offices make maximum use of every possible square inch. Nearly everyone works in open areas, and four or five executives often share a single phone.

There are advantages to such working conditions. We are less isolated from each other than are executives in an American environment, including the one I work in when I'm in the United States. In Japan we have more of a chance to communicate. Answering each other's phones also gives us more opportunity to know what's going on outside our own narrow responsibilities. But it does make it more difficult to slam doors and sulk in private in moments of frustration. Harmony becomes not just a virtue but a necessity. We cultivate this harmony by socializing together after working hours more than most American managers do. Working in a private room with a private secretary, the American manager is relatively isolated from his peers. Reporting is mostly confined to a vertical chain of command—straight up to superiors. Japanese managers also communicate horizontally among their peers.

This greater camaraderie in the workplace is reinforced by the narrower salary differentials in Japanese companies. Yes, we do compete in terms of promotions and choice job assignments. But in the long run, salary differences are so slight that there is little resentment among those who are passed over. Though I've come to appreciate all this, back in 1958 I was still confronted with the fact that Mr. Sandow had the choice job assignment I wanted. And I was aware of the fact that when KT sent me to America, I had the choice assignment that my rival wanted.

Another conflict still brewing at Minolta pitted those who thought we should concentrate on our profitable domestic market against those who saw our still unprofitable foreign markets as the key to our future. This was KT's conflict, rather than mine, but needless to say I had a vested interest. Since sales planning included both domestic and international sales, I now had a foot in both camps. But I must admit that my heart, like KT's, belonged to the global market. Though today I am considered a success in my career, I'm not so sure I could have done as good a job if my work had been confined to Japan's highly competitive domestic market.

In the 1950s there were over forty Japanese camera companies battling for a share of a not very big market in a not very prosperous country. We used to say there was at least one Japanese camera company for every letter of the alphabet—Aires, Beauty, Canon, all the way to Zenza-Bronica—and for some letters more than one—Mamiya, Minolta, Miranda, Misuzu, Morita, et cetera. Today there are fewer than ten that really matter. This is fairly typical of the shakeout that has occurred in many Japanese industries, including electronics. When it comes to competing with Japanese companies in international trade today, Americans must realize that they are up against the very toughest, firms that have survived a domestic weeding-out process in which only the finest survived.

To survive in the Japanese camera industry, a firm had to have a strong foothold in the domestic market and at least some share of the export market. Without both, no matter how high the quality of its product, the quantity a firm could sell would not be high enough to keep its unit production costs down to the level necessary for it to be competitive in price. Many Japanese camera, electronics, and auto companies then in existence went out of business because they weren't strong in both domestic *and* foreign markets. American companies seeking to compete with Japanese firms today must heed this lesson. Their competitors have a long history of success both domestically and internationally.

I don't envy American companies trying to break into the Japanese market today, for I myself had a tough time breaking in when I returned to Japan more than thirty years ago. As I began working closely for the first time with our domestic salesmen, I was deeply impressed by the service they provided to their customers and the close personal ties they developed, not only with individual camera dealers but also with their families.

In Japan we make a distinction between the "wet side" and the "dry side" of business. The dry side includes those "strictly business" areas of product quality, price, parts availability, and service. The wet side involves the more personal touches. It is not unusual for a Minolta salesman to get involved in helping out with family funerals, making arrangements for weddings and other family ceremonies, bringing gifts at holidays, providing loans, helping out with shopping or being available as a chauffeur if the need arises, and in many other ways becoming the model friend of the family. An American can compete with that only by working with Japanese associates who understand this aspect of our business culture and are willing to devote the time it takes for success. When the American businessman is home having dinner with his own family, the Japanese businessman is often still out taking care of the wet side of his business relations. It makes doing business much more complicated than our foreign competitors realize. Our domestic competitors all do it, and sometimes the wet side can mean as much as product quality and price in determining who makes the sale. It is another one of those Japanese ways that no one really talks about, a trade secret we don't share with foreigners. No wonder foreigners find it so difficult to break into our domestic distribution system.

Old loyalties and a complexity that may have outlived its usefulness make Japan's distribution system another effective barrier against foreign competition. During the postwar recovery years, investment capital was so tight that it was almost impossible for a small retailer to get credit. The banks were more willing to make loans to the big domestic trading companies. And the trading companies then financed smaller distributors and retail stores. Even retailers that have since grown quite big are still loyal to distributors who have been their financial partners for decades. Manufacturers have also played a role in financing distribution, and complex networks have developed that include primary distributors, regional distributors, small local distributors, and then retail outlets. Margins tend to be small at each step, only about half the 20 percent markup common to distributors in the United States. But there are so many steps in the process that prices are high by the time the product gets to the consumer.

And retail competition is limited. Zoning laws can be used to block large stores from moving into most neighborhoods. A community consensus must be demonstrated before approval can be given, and often the owners of small existing stores exercise veto power over proposals to approve new stores coming in. There was a time when this multilayered system had some value in providing jobs. But in today's tight labor market, there's no longer any need for it. Changes are developing, though slowly. Some manufacturers now sell directly to the consumer. Discount chains and supermarkets have made their appearance. In time this "Americanization" of the distribution system may make it easier for American firms to break into the Japanese consumer market.

KT was such a dominant force in our company that those who favored our profitable domestic sales over our unprofitable foreign sales could not let that disagreement come into the open. Our income from operations in the United States, our biggest export market, was still limited. With the yen selling at 360 to the strong American dollar, doing business in the United States was costly. Therefore, our foreign operations still weren't making any profit. Until the mid-1960s, Minolta's domestic operations generated all of the company's profits. Understandably, this caused some resentment among those involved in domestic operations. As I learned more about the wet side, my admiration increased for those in the domestic camp. But in the final analysis, everyone had to be in KT's camp.

I also had to relearn the value of that great Japanese virtue— patience. I was young, full of energy and new ideas, and, in my Americanized way, not very willing to wait for results. I had become almost as impatient as an American manager tied to the pressures of the quarterly report, the time-study stopwatch, and the management-by-objectives scorecard. I needed to take a step back and rethink not only aspects of the Japanese way but also some of the lessons that many Japanese managers had learned from an American long neglected in his own country.

13

The Secret of Japan's Success

American managers continue to flock to Tokyo and Osaka, hoping to learn the business secrets many believe have given Japan a competitive edge over American products. This puzzles knowledgeable Japanese who realize the secrets of Japan's success are largely things we learned from America. The best example is quality control, a major factor in the postwar transition of Japan from a minor exporter of shoddy goods to a major exporter of quality products. Americans strive to learn the Japanese way of quality control. The Japanese shrug. We learned it from an American.

Dr. W. Edwards Deming has been a personal hero of mine and a national treasure in Japan for four decades. But it wasn't until January 1987 that we finally met over a Saturday evening dinner at the Cosmos Club near his home in Washington, D.C. What impressed me the most that evening was the hazelnut ice cream. Not only because it was so good, but because Dr. Deming took such a personal and passionate interest in its quality. He said that for years the Cosmos Club had served what many of its members considered the world's greatest dessert, its exclusive hazelnut ice cream. But then the supplier, a small Washington dairy, began having problems getting quality hazelnuts. Dr. Deming discovered the world's best hazelnuts could be found in the Black Sea region of Turkey. He arranged for a steady source and found a new dairy to follow the Cosmos Club's specifications. Hazelnut ice cream was soon back on the club's menu, better than ever. Though Dr. Deming let his guests choose their own entrées that evening, he insisted we have the hazelnut ice cream for dessert. I had to admit it was excellent, and I later realized that Dr. Deming had given me a down-to-earth example of his principle of continuous quality control.

Born in Wyoming in 1900, Dr. Deming is as old as our century and as up-to-date as the mid-1980s turnaround of the Ford Motor Company. In large part, Ford's improved fortunes resulted from its overdue adaptation of Dr. Deming's principles. He first visited Japan in 1947 to work for a brief period as a sampling consultant to the general headquarters of the supreme commander of the Allied powers, working with a statistical mission preparing for a 1951 census. Dr. Deming already had a solid reputation as a statistician in the United States. During the war years, he had begun teaching his methods of statistical quality control to executives and engineers at such firms as General Electric and the Hoover Corporation, and to graduate business administration students at New York University. In 1946 he was one of the founding members of the American Society for Quality Control.

But in the postwar years, another approach to scientific industrial management became popular in the United States. The so-called Taylor Method of time-and-motion studies, pioneered earlier in the century by Frederick Winslow Taylor, was well suited to stepping up assembly-line production, particularly where workers labored on a piece-rate basis, getting paid for the number of units they produced in a given time period. Meeting pent-up demand in the vast American consumer market put greater emphasis on quantity production than on quality products. Time-and-motion studies tended to push quantity production, with little concern for quality. At first, given the skills and pride of American workers, quality remained high. But as domestic demand increased, and the worldwide demand for American consumer products began to grow, both quality and worker morale began to slip.

Quality control came to mean inspection at the end of the assembly line. Deming's concepts of continuous quality control—from product design through procurement of materials and parts to every step of production, assembly, and marketing—were considered too time-consuming and costly. When he began talking about his ideas in Japan, business executives and product engineers assumed that Deming's approach must be one of the secrets of the great American success story. No one in Japan knew that Deming was ignored in America. So when Deming spoke, people in Japan listened.

But in the United States, the situation was very different. America pressed ahead, rapidly expanding its economy with assembly-line methods of quantity production. Japan began to take a different path. Listening to Dr. Deming, we began to rebuild for quality.

Shortly after the war, a group called the Union of Japanese Scientists and Engineers (known in English by the acronym JUSE) had organized to help in rebuilding our shattered industrial capacity. When Deming returned to Japan in 1950 to work with MacArthur's GHQ, he was invited by JUSE to conduct a week-long seminar for research workers, plant managers, and engineers. Deming consented and, in a sentence typical of his oratorical style, replied, "As for remuneration, I shall not desire any."

Though that first seminar was a success, Deming had learned from his sad experience in America that without the support of top management, his methods could not be put into effect. Through Keidanren, an association of top officials of industrial firms, he arranged a meeting with the presidents of Japan's leading industrial companies. As he said to me over dinner, "Twenty-one men invited. Twenty-one attended."

Other meetings followed, including an extended conference with fifty key industrial officials at a mountain resort near Hakone. In her excellent book *The Deming Management Method*, Mary Walton notes, "In addition to teaching statistical techniques to thousands of technical people, he had within a few weeks reached the management of most of Japan's large companies. Although some of those men would tell him years later that they had privately thought his optimism was crazy, at the time they had been willing to swallow their disbelief. In a sense, having lost all, they had nothing to lose. The Japanese embraced the Deming philosophy."

It is impossible to exaggerate the impact Dr. Deming had. In his book *The Reckoning*, which deals with Japan's apparent competitive edge over the American auto industry, David Halberstam wrote, "With the possible exception of Douglas MacArthur, he was the most famous American in Japan during the postwar years." That's true. But if those postwar Japanese industrialists had known how little influence Dr. Deming had in America, they might never have listened to him, much less adopted his complex charts, diagrams, and maxims for improving production. But they did listen. His ideas did work. And Japan was on its way to setting industrial standards that others, especially Americans, now seek to imitate.

By 1951, JUSE had established the Deming Prize, which has become Japan's most prestigious industrial award. The annual awards ceremony is carried by national television and receives extensive press coverage. Dr. Deming was ultimately "discovered" for Americans by a television producer. Clare Crawford-Mason, based in Washington and working on a proposed NBC-TV documentary, in 1979 began researching what soon looked like a very dull story in television terms on Japan's economic threat to America. Then someone told her about Dr. Deming, who lived in Washington and had done some work in Japan. Dr. Deming, outspokenly angry about the way he had been ignored in America, turned out to be highly telegenic. He had also just begun working with a major American firm, Nashua Corporation, the New Hampshire maker of paper for copiers.

I'm sorry to say that it wasn't Minolta but one of our competitors, Ricoh, that had recommended Dr. Deming to Nashua. Ricoh Company, Ltd., won the Deming Prize in 1975. I must admit that's something Minolta has never done, despite my admiration for Dr. Deming. Nashua, at that time, distributed Ricoh copiers in the United States. Crawford-Mason interviewed Nashua officials, who were enthusiastic about the improvements they had made since bringing on Dr. Deming as a consultant. She realized she had an exciting story, but it wasn't until June 24, 1980, that a fifteen-minute segment on Dr. Deming finally aired. Mary Walton refers to the program as "one of the most successful documentaries in television history." The title was "If Japan Can . . . Why Can't We?" Cecelia Kilian, Dr. Deming's secretary, described the results as "a nightmare. We were bombarded with calls. They had to see him tomorrow or yesterday or their whole company would collapse."

Dr. Deming was eighty-six when we met for the first time that evening at the Cosmos Club. My mission was to ask him to accept the annual award of the Japanese Chamber of Commerce of New York and to attend the chamber's annual award dinner. I worried as

I waited for him to arrive at the club that his advanced age might make it difficult for him to travel to New York and sit through a formal dinner that would last several hours. It turned out that I was right to be worried about his ability to attend but wrong about the reason.

The first thing that impressed me about Dr. Deming was his size. He is a big man, well over six feet, and he carries perhaps more weight than he should on an ample frame. He grew up in the Wyoming town of Cody, named for "Buffalo Bill" Cody, the cowboy-showman who was a friend of the family. There is little of the Wild West in his manner, though occasionally his temper rises when he discusses the shortcomings of American management. He enjoys life and loves Japan, good food, alcohol in moderation, the company of women, and hazelnut ice cream. He is a wonderful storyteller and I listened to him through dinner, very much in awe.

Having been honored so much in Japan but ignored so long in America, he was pleased at the prospect of the award dinner, both because the sponsoring organization was made up of Japanese businessmen and because the event would be held in New York with an audience that would include many American business leaders. Over the next nine months we encountered many problems in arranging that dinner and the award presentation. And we encountered the first problem head-on that night. Dr. Deming consulted his appointments calendar.

The chamber's dinner is always held in November. But Dr. Deming's calendar was almost totally booked for November, ten months in advance. He suggested the possibility of postponing his award until early the following year, when his schedule was a bit more open. I had recently been named secretary of the chamber and was vice-chairman for the November dinner, with James D. Robinson III, chairman and chief executive officer of American Express, serving as dinner chairman. I knew it would add to the chamber's prestige to have Dr. Deming as our award winner and was also amazed that a man of his age was scheduling appearances nearly two years in advance. But I also knew my colleagues at the chamber would not be happy with Dr. Deming's insistence on making an acceptance speech of thirty to forty-five minutes. The award winner is usually an American who has made an important contribution to Japan, and he is expected to make brief remarks. The keynote speaker is generally a major Japanese business leader, and he is the one who gets to talk the longest.

But Dr. Deming was adamant. "This is an important audience, and I have an important message to deliver. I need at least that long or it won't be worth my while to try to fit this in."

I hedged, falling back on the time-honored tactic of saying I would have to discuss this with my colleagues on the chamber's board of directors. The award to Dr. Deming had been my idea. As vice-chairman of that year's dinner program, I had not expected any problems, apart from Dr. Deming's ability to travel and survive a long dinner. Now I had to worry about the length of his speech and even more about his crowded schedule.

In addition to frequent trips to Japan and seminars in Montreal, London, and Sydney, Dr. Deming had meetings and lectures scheduled in Detroit with Ford and General Motors officials and engineers. He had a lecture coming up at the University of Wisconsin and a steady series of seminars with business groups and universities, criss-crossing the country and leaping oceans at a pace that would exhaust a much younger man. There was some hope, however. Dr. Deming keeps an apartment in Manhattan, where he conducts Monday after-noon lectures at New York University. But on each of the possible Mondays in November, he was scheduled to fly to Detroit early in the evening for meetings with auto industry leaders the following day.

"Perhaps we can work something out," I said with more hope than conviction. "But how can you keep up such a schedule?"

"I must," he said. "I went so many years without people in the United States knowing what I had to say. Now this is what I must be doing."

Thirty years after Japan, America finally began catching up with Dr. Deming. Donald E. Petersen, chairman of Ford Motor Company, describes himself as a Deming disciple and says, "We at Ford are committed to his principles, particularly to the ethic of continuous improvement and the involvement of all employees."

Ford was one of the first companies to recruit Dr. Deming after the NBC documentary. Deming was first called in to meet with Ford officials in the spring of 1981, and Ford was soon applying such Deming concepts as statistical quality control, long-term operating budgets, and close relations with suppliers to the development of "Team

Taurus." Ford created a team that crossed divisional lines ranging from research and development engineers to marketing experts who met together to develop a program to create and sell a car that could lift Ford out of a long period of decline. The award-winning car developed by that team sparked a turnaround that has made Ford the most profitable of the major American auto companies. In 1987, Ford began exporting the Taurus to Japan, where it has won top awards for quality and performance.

The team concept, under the name "simultaneous engineering," has also caught on at General Motors, where Dr. Deming has worked with both the Fiero and Cadillac divisions, and at Chrysler Corporation, where it's known as "product-driven design." The concept involves getting representatives from every area of the company—design, engineering, manufacturing, marketing, finance, and even suppliers—working together simultaneously rather than sequentially in developing a new product.

In our modest way, with a small group drawn from various departments and our mandate to coordinate our operations with the work of Minolta's research and development, production, sales, and advertising teams, the sales planning department I set up in 1959 moved Minolta toward the simultaneous engineering approach. Some American observers say Dr. Deming's techniques will never work in the United States. They contend that the cultural differences are too great: Japanese workers are more dedicated; loyalty to the company and the work ethic are far stronger; et cetera. But the fact is that the real secrets behind Japan's competitive edge originated in America. And, as Ford and other Deming clients have proved, the ideas that originated in America can work in America.

Meanwhile, Dr. Deming continues to lecture widely and often. Fordham University's Graduate School of Business has announced formation of a Center for Advanced Management Studies with a program largely based on Dr. Deming's ideas. Dr. Marta Mooney, who will head the program, says she hopes eventually to call the unit the Deming Center. Dr. Charles Collazzo, professor emeritus at Northeastern University in Boston, is seeking business and academic support for his recommendation to the Nobel Committee that Dr. Deming be given the Nobel Prize for economics. He certainly deserves it.

Based on my own more modest effort to have Dr. Deming honored by the Japanese Chamber of Commerce of New York, Dr. Collazzo may have a tough job on his hands. Dr. Deming's schedule might not allow him to get to Sweden for his acceptance speech. In fact, it turned out that he did not get to New York for the chamber's award dinner, but not for any of the reasons I might have anticipated.

At the last minute, a sore foot kept him away.

14

The Midnight President

Many factors combined during these years to create a golden era for the Japanese camera industry. Technology had a great deal to do with it. So did the free-trade policies that came to the fore, particularly the Kennedy round of tariff reductions during the 1960s. So did the low value of the yen in relation to other major currencies, which made Japanese products less expensive on world markets. So did the fact that Japan was still a poor country with few jobs and low labor costs. Many of these same factors combined to create a golden era for another Japanese industry—the hostess bar.

The two developments complemented each other nicely. International buyers flocked to Japan seeking high-quality bargains in textiles, electronics, cameras, and other products. Japan was forced to export to earn the foreign exchange it needed to pay for its fuel imports. We were anxious to sell and, as the reputation of our products improved, foreign buyers were anxious to come shopping.

Entertainment has always oiled the wheels of politics and commerce in Japan. The modern and somewhat Westernized equivalent of the traditional teahouse with its geishas in flowing kimonos is the

140

hostess bar. Though some hostess bars feature young ladies in traditional costume, Western dress prevails and yet the West has no real equivalent to such places.

The customers buy drinks at inflated prices for the young ladies who join them. Pleasant conversation and some dancing puts the men in a more relaxed and friendly mood for the tough business dealings that are in progress during the day. In Japan such get-togethers are essential to the smooth running of the business world.

Apart from entertaining customers, the bars are also the scene of after-hours meetings at which executives and employees can meet for informal discussions that often aren't possible during the disciplined atmosphere of the working day. This is the time for letting your hair down, doing some griping, getting some advice, and strengthening the contacts that can help you further your career. Very little entertaining goes on in the Japanese home. This is another of those areas in which the scarcity of space in Japan affects the way we live. The homes of even wealthy Japanese are generally so small and crowded that there just isn't room to have business associates stop over. And so Japanese businessmen tend to do their socializing outside the home. This can create domestic strains, but Japanese women are used to the system and for the most part accept it.

But for the American businessmen who came to Japan in those golden years, our way of life and of doing business was a revelation. There is no doubt that Japan in those days was very much a man's world. And men enjoyed it. Few jobs were open to women, and educational opportunities were limited. Even factory jobs were rare for women. Without doubt, the hostess bars provided the best jobs available for many young girls. In addition, many had lost fathers and potential husbands during the war. With no man to take care of them and few other jobs available, economic necessity made hostess jobs appealing. The most beautiful and intelligent girls competed for those jobs. Many became wealthy and famous, setting up their own places of business. For example, the Copacabana in Tokyo was a sophisticated nightclub that featured such top American entertainers as Frank Sinatra and Sammy Davis, Jr. Its owner, Madame Cherry, was world-famous. The late Jack Kreindler, then the owner of the "21" Club in New York City, once asked me if I knew his "good friend," Madame Cherry. He had visited the Copacabana in Tokyo and admired the way she ran her operation.

The big cabarets of that era, like the Fuji and the Metro, were multistoried fantasy lands and had over a thousand hostesses. I must admit these places were not very sophisticated. They usually had dance floors and showgirl revues. Loudspeakers would blare out commands to the girls like "Meet your customer at table number 10." If a girl sitting next to you got such a message, she would drop you in a minute, and with an abrupt apology rush off to her next assignment.

There were also smaller bars with neither music nor a show and maybe about ten hostesses. There were also distinctions based on geography. Generally, the hostess bars in the downtown areas were more refined. A girl working in such a place might have one or two "special friends," but she was not a prostitute. At the hostess bars in outlying areas, most of a hostess's income might have come from dates she made with customers. Another geographic distinction existed between the downtown bars in Tokyo, which tended to be the most elegant, sophisticated, and international, and those outside the capital. Even the finest bars in Osaka were not up to the standards of the best in Tokyo. In other cities and the provinces the distinctions were even more noticeable.

The traditional teahouse was in another category altogether, as were the geisha girls who worked in them. The geisha prides herself on her abilities at singing and dancing—arts in which she has been specially trained. There were three distinct types who performed together: singers, dancers, and musicians who play difficult classical instruments. The geishas mingled with customers between their performances. The teahouse itself was an elegant restaurant. Typically, the customers were businessmen who arrived for drinks and dinner at around six in the evening. They were usually entertaining important customers, and, after drinks, performances by the geishas, and dinner, stretching over a period of about four hours, they would move on to a more informal hostess bar.

Many of these distinctions still exist.

It is very difficult to explain to foreigners where sex does—and doesn't—enter the picture in the world of the hostess bars. Only the very wealthiest men could ever dream of being able to afford a geisha as a mistress, and there are no one-night stands or brief affairs with geishas. They are relatively well paid for their skills as entertainers in a classic tradition. The typical bar girl makes a relatively small salary and earns most of her money from the drinks she encourages her customers to buy. The hostess bars are not sex clubs, and virtually none of the girls are available for sex outside the clubs. A few, however, have developed outside relationships, some of which have involved wealthy, well-known customers. It is considered a form of upward social mobility for the girls and their families.

One hostess, for example, became the number two wife of former president Sukarno of Indonesia. The more successful girls often receive lavish presents and are taken by customers on trips to places like Paris, London, Hong Kong (a favorite for shopping), and Hawaii. Once during a trip to the United States I had a stopover in Honolulu. By the pool at the hotel I stayed at in Waikiki I ran into a major American camera distributor who was there with five bar girls he had brought with him from Japan.

"Sam, can you take a couple of these girls off my hands?" he asked.

I had to make my apologies. It was one thing to entertain American customers at the hostess bars in Osaka and Tokyo at Minolta's expense. But this was something else. KT would never have approved. I realized that the income of these girls was ten times greater than mine and that they were used to royal treatment by wealthy men, like my friend from America. Successful camera distributors in those days could afford to live like kings.

KT himself visited the hostess bars with American and European camera distributors and business equipment dealers. At that time, I was known as "The Midnight President of Minolta." People said that KT was the president until about ten-thirty at night. Then he would bow out and Kusumoto would take over.

My actual title was still the much more modest head of sales planning. Though that assignment gave me only an indirect role in exports, KT wanted me to be the host for our foreign visitors because of my overseas experience and my knowledge of English, which he still assumed was much better than it actually was. I had no objections, but also no illusions about the reactions of some of my more resentful co-workers. During the evenings, at least, my standard of living was far higher than that of many of my more senior colleagues. I was having a great time, but I knew I must be creating some ill will back at the office. No matter how late I was out, however, I made it a rule to always be in the office by eight-thirty in the morning. I did not want to set a bad example or add to the resentment others might feel. My privileged status also meant that I got less sleep and put in a longer working day than did most of my colleagues, but I had no complaints.

Rock 'n' roll was becoming popular in those days, and it seemed there was a new dance to learn every month. Since I graduated from my militaristic secondary school in Korea, dancing had been my only form of exercise. And in those days I was at my dancing best. I was in the clubs almost every night, popular and spending freely. For a young man who had grown up almost totally isolated from Japanese girls my own age, this was a heady experience. KT once told me it was cheaper for Minolta to send me to America and keep me stationed there with all my living expenses than to have me in Japan with the bills I ran up entertaining foreign camera distributors at the hostess bars.

I soon developed a network of English-speaking bar girls and used to organize "convoys" for our distributors and the girls to go sightseeing to places like Kyoto and Nara on Sundays. The girls never charged us for these outings and enjoyed them as much as the men did. Of course, they made plenty on our business at the bars. And Minolta and its foreign distributors made money together on the close business relationships that were oiled by our pleasant hours there. I used to joke that these girls were my "business partners," but with their furs and Paris trips and wealthy admirers, they were clearly the senior partners.

In the 1960s our efforts to show foreign buyers a good time were a real boon to our exports. We had to establish sales channels and learn how to deal in these unfamiliar markets. In the camera industry there was heavy competition, not only to show prospective buyers the superiority of our product but also to show how well we could treat foreign visitors. The Japanese theory was that visitors would enjoy such royal treatment so much that they would be anxious to come back and be entertained again in grand style. Of course, to do that, they would have to sell lots of our products back in their home countries. It was a very basic form of a marketing technique that we now call, in a more organized format, the dealer incentive trip. The hostess bars of Japan provided a novel extra form of incentive, perhaps making up for the fact that the distributors paid their own transportation costs.

KT was always very kind to our customers who visited from Europe and the United States. He made my job easy by so often being on the scene himself. The buyers loved having the president of Minolta acting as their host on these occasions. I often felt sorry for Mrs. Tashima, for I knew she was home waiting for him. Getting to Japan by propeller-driven plane was still a long and expensive ordeal. A round-trip air coach fare in 1960 equaled my annual salary. KT said that when people take the time and expense to visit us in Japan, they deserve to be treated like kings. He also believed in treating all buyers the same way.

"The big buyer is important," he said. "But so is the small buyer who may be from a small country with little buying power. But what he is spending is very big to him. I remember it was that way for me when I first went to Europe. We must never forget where we come from."

Getting to know our foreign customers was important in those days, for the Japanese and Japan's products were still suspect. Of course, our entertaining would not have made much difference to potential customers if we had not had innovative, quality products to offer at competitive prices. Though I came to appreciate this wet side of our business—perhaps more than I should—I also knew that the dry side was vital. During the day, we showed our visitors our research facilities, our factories, and prototypes of new products. And we talked prices and volume.

In the camera industry, until the early 1970s, we relied on a small number of wholesale distributors. It was easier to get to know each other than it is in today's more complex market, where we work directly with a large number of retail dealers. Today, the industry and the reputation of Japan's products have a momentum of their own. In addition, since the mid-1970s the changing economic and social circumstances of Japan have had their impact on the hostess bar. While the huge cabarets with over a thousand hostesses are gone, a few smaller clubs remain—some garish, a few very elegant. But in the more prosperous Japan of today, women have far more economic and educational opportunities. From factory jobs to fashion models, young girls have a greater choice, and relatively few want to work as bar hostesses. Younger Japanese men prefer to spend more time with their girl friends or wives. For foreign businessmen visiting Japan, the novelty has worn off. And cheaper air travel now makes it possible for our visitors to bring their wives.

Eventually, our visitors found it a real chore to try to keep their Japanese hosts happy by indulging in long hours of partying. Like us, they realized it was important to please the people they did business with. But after a while it got to be a bit of a strain.

They also had trouble coping with the presents that were show-

ered on them, particularly the farewell presents they were traditionally handed at the airport, which were—guess what—geisha
dolls. Most of their Japanese hosts had never been inside an airplane
and had no idea of the cramped quarters their visitors would have
to share with an oversized, glass-encased geisha.

As our business has grown, our business relationships have become too complex for the close ties developed over drinks and dancing
and the singsong chatter of pretty girls. I'm sure all these changes
are for the better, but I must admit that doing business isn't quite
as much fun.

15

A Marriage in Japan

My years in America had turned my head. When I first returned home, the appeal of Western women had made it difficult for me to feel attracted to Oriental charm. But the subtle process of my reeducation as a Japanese continued. One fringe benefit of my nights at the hostess bars had been to reattune me to the special attractions of Japanese women. However, when anyone spoke to me about settling down and getting married, I remained evasive.

The maligned tradition of the arranged marriage was being pursued on a variety of fronts, almost independent of my own will. With the big car I drove in New York, I had become the unofficial "greeter" for the Japanese business community and had become friendly with many influential people I picked up at the airport. Most had returned to Japan before me and were among the most determined of the various groups intent on finding me a wife. I must have looked at hundreds of photos of eligible young girls along with what we call "specs," or *tsurigaki*, which are almost like product specifications sheets for cameras or copiers, but with more emphasis on family and

147

educational background and interests than on what Americans call vital statistics. That was part of the problem.

When I first got back to Japan, few Japanese girls, no matter how pretty, seemed sexy enough for me. I considered myself a sophisticated man-of-the-world and just shrugged as I looked at all those photos of lovely young Japanese girls. I was still bewitched by Western women even though I knew how difficult it would be for a Western woman to adjust to life in Japan. There is no doubt some divine justice in the fact that the wonderful woman I finally met and married has, in the years since, herself become so enchanted by her life in America that she finds it difficult to imagine living again in Japan.

I had been back in Osaka about a year when I first heard of a young lady named Kuniko Sumomogi. She was related to the Ohto family who had owned the teahouse my grandfather had frequented in Korea. Mr. Ohto was our "unofficial" matchmaker. From her photo, I could tell Kuniko was very much my type. She was still in school at Hiroshima Jyogakuin College, a mission school near her home at Saijo. I noted that she had studied English and that her father taught English. Since I was convinced I would one day return to America, that intrigued me. Though Kuniko was a relative of the Ohto family, her family name, Sumomogi, sounds very strange to Japanese ears. My father, suspicious, hired a detective to investigate, a fairly common practice in Japan.

In America, people often hire detectives to collect evidence for divorce proceedings. In Japan, people are more likely to hire a detective in advance of a possible marriage. The only finding I remember from the detective's report was that the roof of the Sumomogi family's house was as strange as the family name and looked as though it might be a Chinese temple. When I later visited Kuniko's home, I saw that the style of architecture was common in that area. Apparently my father's detective focused his attention too narrowly. With a bit more investigation, my father found that the Sumomogis, despite their foreign-sounding name and strange roof, were pure Japanese and a well-established family in the Hiroshima-Saijo region.

Through the Ohtos we arranged for a well-chaperoned first date in Osaka. Mr. Ohto obtained theater tickets for a party of seven that included the Ohtos, my parents, Kuniko and her mother—and me. The show was a romantic comedy, like life, but I don't remember much about the details. After the theater, Kuniko and I had a chance to be alone. We went to a coffee shop and talked. A week later, I told Mr. Ohto I would like to "continue the conversation."

Our first meeting was very much in the tradition of the arranged marriage that Americans criticize; but the arranged marriage in Japan has changed completely since the war. In the past, a woman had to accept her family's choice of a husband whether she agreed with that choice or not. Kuniko could have rejected me. Happily, she didn't.

From the very first, I knew that I liked her. In Japanese we use the expression *miai*—"first glance." Kuniko took her time, and only much later, after we were married, did she tell me the thing that intrigued her the most about me was that when I proposed, I promised I would take her with me to live in the United States. Of course, she was joking.

Kuniko came to Osaka again and I took her to Kyoto, acting as her guide on a tour of the shrines. By this time, I had been to Kyoto often with our foreign visitors. I did my best to impress her with my knowledge, though I suspect she was more interested in what I had to say about my life in America than in what I had to say about Buddhist monasteries and Shinto shrines. Kuniko happened to be in Osaka on another visit in the fall of 1959 when I was entertaining my Canadian friends, Max Zell and Abe Feigerson of Anglo Photo. We had dinner together at a popular restaurant called Alaska, which featured Western food. I must admit that was unusual. Japanese businessmen are rarely accompanied by their fiancées or even their wives at business dinners. It was Kuniko's first exposure both to foreigners and to such non-Japanese delicacies as escargot. Though her English was then limited, it turned out to be a delightful evening. My friends were charmed by Kuniko and told me I was making "a good choice."

Of course, I agreed. In December I traveled to the Sumomogi family home, with its strange roof, in the town of Saijo, a rural community of ten thousand about twenty miles east of Hiroshima. I officially proposed. Kuniko and her family officially accepted. The marriage was set for March 29, 1960.

Marriage in Japan is very much a marriage of two families, as well as of two individuals. The Shinto ceremony reflects this. Key members of our families were formally introduced. The families sat opposite each other and exchanged cups of *sake*. Kuniko sat with her family, but after the ceremony I took her to sit with my family, creating the impression that the marriage would take her away from her family. In the Japanese ceremony, only the husband makes the vows. The bride merely follows what the husband says, an echo of the old tradition in which the bride had no say in her parents' arrangements for her marriage.

It was not unusual then—and not unusual even today—for a young bride to move in with her husband's parents. Few young Japanese couples can find or afford a place of their own. But we were lucky. I already had my own little apartment, well furnished and equipped. In Japan the two families share equally in the cost of the wedding, but in our case at least I handled all the arrangements, which is an easy and convenient process. I made only one stop. Weddings are often held at hotels, which handle all the details, including invitations, photography, flowers, wedding room, reception—everything including your choice of Shinto, Buddhist, or Christian priest. I simply went to the banquet manager of the Osaka Grand Hotel, then the newest in the city. Since neither of our families was devoutly religious, I did what most Japanese would do for a ceremony celebrating birth or marriage. I said we would have a Shinto wedding. For more somber occasions, such as a funeral, most Japanese choose a Buddhist ceremony. We are a flexible people. I told the banquet manager there would be about one hundred guests and he set a price for the hotel's "deluxe" wedding. That was all I had to do.

Our guests of honor included KT, of course, who I think was greatly relieved to see me settling down with a Japanese wife, as well as Mr. and Mrs. Kinji Moriyama and H. Kobayakawa, the former head of the Kanematsu trading company's New York office, who had returned to Japan as a member of the board of directors. Though Mr. Ohto deserves credit for bringing us together, the "official" matchmaker, who has an honored place at weddings, is customarily someone of high rank. At my father's request, this role was taken by Sanhichiro Tamaki, president of the Tanabe Chamber of Commerce, who also ran the *sake* brewery that kept my grandfather supplied even during wartime. Old schoolmates and other friends, including some of the Japanese I had met in New York, were there as well as friends and relatives of Kuniko's, including her American-born uncle, George Aratani, and his wife, Sakaye.

Even more than my family, with its Ford dealership, Kuniko's family had ties to the United States. Her mother's brother, George

Aratani, is a prominent businessman based in Los Angeles whom we have become close to since my return to the United States. Kuniko's father had visited California and been at Stanford University, which had impressed him very much. Years later he was pleased to hear that his granddaughter Eriko was going to attend Stanford. In Saijo before the war he had owned extensive rice lands. Under the postwar land reform, he had to sell off all but enough to sustain his family. The immediate family remains wealthy, and they are well educated and international in their outlook.

Kuniko's father had the amazing experience of having survived the atomic bombing of Hiroshima. He was in the city, talking to a friend who was killed instantly. But Kuniko's father was apparently shielded from the immediate impact of the blast by the wall of a building. He never suffered from radiation exposure. Kuniko and other members of the family were safe in Saijo.

Through the years, I have been impressed by the way Kuniko has blossomed into such an accomplished woman, particularly during the nearly twenty years that we have lived together in America. I was very happy and quite proud of my new young bride as we left the day after our wedding to fly to the Kyushu Islands in the south for our honeymoon. Kuniko was then very much a country girl, naïve and with little knowledge of the world outside her family and school, and of course, her dreams, especially her dreams of America. She had never flown before. In fact, for most Japanese, flying was still a rare and special event. The pilot of the Japan Air Lines plane came to our seat to congratulate us and present us with a certificate for our "Honeymoon Flight." We spent a week on Kyushu, visiting the hot springs, the volcano, and other sights. On our return, we spent a few days in Osaka, then went on to Tanabe for a traditional reception at an old-style Japanese teahouse. My grandfather, then too old to have traveled to Osaka, was there with my grandmother and over a hundred other guests, including Kuniko's parents. Mr. Tamaki, the "official" matchmaker at our wedding, was among the guests. Seeing Mr. Tamaki and my grandfather together, sipping their *sake*, was very moving and sad. It was the last big party my grandfather ever got to attend. Two years later, at the age of eighty-eight, he died.

With my new bride by my side in her kimono and obi, our new life just beginning, I watched my grandfather, sensing that his life soon would end. With the other guests we sat on tatami mats and exchanged cups of *sake*. I felt very Japanese that day, no longer the brash, Americanized young guy who had returned from New York the year before.

We settled into our married life, but my role as Minolta's midnight president did not change. Kuniko was both very naïve and very understanding about all the entertaining I had to do. She accepted it and always waited up to make me feel glad to be home at last. In fact, for Kuniko there was a certain satisfaction in knowing that her husband's responsibilities included entertaining important foreign customers. There was a good deal of competitiveness among the wives of younger executives. If a husband came home late, it was considered a sign that he was important. We also had the prestige of having our own apartment rather than living with parents or in an inexpensive dormitory provided for the families of younger executives. And I talked to Kuniko about what I was doing and how it would help make it possible for a second assignment in the United States.

Maybe five or six times a year I would get a chance to take Kuniko out with me to dinner with foreign distributors. Once, our Canadian dealers, Max Zell and Abe Feigerson, took us on a boat trip to the Kyushu Islands. This was before our younger daughter, Mariko, had been born. My mother looked after our first daughter, Eriko, then just a baby. At the time, such special treats were more than enough for Kuniko to be able to accept my late hours entertaining customers. But now that she has lived in America, I could never get away with that.

Had I spent the rest of my professional career working for Minolta in Osaka, Kuniko might never have had the opportunity to become the gifted woman she is today. She would have been tied to her home, even in the evening, waiting for her husband to come from the teahouses and hostess bars at one or two in the morning. Her daughters, now both graduates of American universities who have begun their business careers, would have grown up much the same way Kuniko had. They would have had better educational and job opportunities, but our society's traditional definitions of a woman's role still exist.

When I think of my wife and my daughters and of other Japanese women who have managed to break out of the traditional mold, including women of great public accomplishments like Mayumi Moriyama, I mourn a loss that few of my countrymen recognize. So many of our wives, daughters, mothers could have accomplished so much more and enriched the lives of their husbands, fathers, and sons so much more if their opportunities had not been so restricted. Our country has made great economic strides in recent decades. But I sometimes wonder how much more we might have done if one-half of our human resources—the women of Japan—had had more of an opportunity to participate fully in our economic, political, and social development.

When I was at Keio University, there were no girls among the students. In Japan today, depending on the school, about 20 to 40 percent of the students are young women. This is only one sign of the expanded opportunities that now exist for women. Up through the 1960s there was a sort of unwritten rule that when a young woman who had taken a job after school or college got married, she should resign from the company. Today that's changing, but most young girls, even if they don't quit working when they marry, do quit when the first baby is due. And very few return, primarily because of company hiring policies. There has even been some questioning of young women attending publicly financed colleges like Tokyo University since they don't stay in the job market long enough to justify the expense of their education.

On the other hand, there's been increasing recognition of the contribution women make in the business world. And companies also recognize the increasing importance of working women as consumers. Most single working women continue to live at home with their parents. Therefore, they have more disposable income than men and tend to be more avid shoppers and travelers.

But most Japanese men still do not accept women as equal partners in marriage or careers. Coming from an older generation, I'm not entirely free of these attitudes myself, and my wife and daughters sometimes tease me about it. Though my daughters visit Japan frequently, I doubt that either will settle there. For many reasons, my assignment in America has lasted far longer than that of most Japanese executives sent overseas. When we talk about the possibility of my being transferred to Japan, my wife smiles at me and says, "Well, I hope you will come back here to visit me often."

She says it as a joke. I hope.

16

Pitcher and Catcher

Patience paid off. The high drama often found in the stories of American business leaders, like Lee Iacocca's chronicle of his struggles with Henry Ford II, doesn't often show up in the real-life stories of Japanese executives. We're dull by comparison and tend to settle our differences by quiet compromise—or just by waiting. For two years I worked in sales planning while a senior official held the job that I could only dream of: head of international exports. I learned a lot in sales planning, which included my first exposure to the new office equipment side of our business. But it wasn't where my talents and experience could be used to their fullest.

One day in 1961, after two years of hard work and about a year after I had been safely married, I heard that Mr. Sandow, the head of the export division, was being transferred from Osaka headquarters to Minolta's Tokyo office. KT named me to replace him.

Soon after his move to Tokyo, I heard that Mr. Sandow left the firm. It is very unusual in Japan, particularly for a man of his years, to leave his company before retirement. He was never my friend or ally, but he was never really my enemy either. He had helped me find an apartment. As far as I know, he never did anything to undermine my position, and I did nothing to plot against him. Yet I regret that my move into his job may have troubled him enough for him to leave Minolta. Since we were not close, I have never known for sure what he did next, though I did hear a rumor that he had opened his own trading company. I hope he did well.

KT expanded the scope of the export department to include business equipment as well as cameras. I knew we needed to expand our Asian and European markets, which were then negligible. But the United States and Canada, as our biggest market, also demanded my attention. Ken Nakamura, who had taken over my job in New York, had been doing very well. We had worked together for two years after he was sent over by KT. We had lived together in Forest Hills, had chased girls together, and had cut our teeth on the photo business during those early years in New York. And now we were able to work together again as a team even though we were thousands of miles apart.

Having had the same job, I understood the vast market that Ken faced and the problems that confronted him. When I returned to the United States in 1969, Ken came back to Japan and took over part of my job as photo export manager. This system worked beautifully for Minolta. It meant we always had a man in Osaka who understood our biggest market and a man in New York who understood our corporate system in Osaka.

We called the arrangement our "pitcher and catcher" system. Ken and I were veterans who had worked together on the same problems for years and understood each other's signals. I credit this system with being the biggest reason for Minolta's success in exporting to North America. With all the current talk of global communications, twenty-four-hour-a-day international exchange markets, and satellite data transmission, the most important element in a successful communications hookup still comes down to the human beings at either end. The pitcher and catcher. The sender who knows what he's saying and the receiver who understands what he's reading.

Whether Ken is in Osaka and I am in New York or the other way around, we have been a terrific team. Whether we communicate by phone at strange hours, by telex, or, increasingly, by facsimile, it's our mutual understanding of the North American market and of Minolta's capabilities and corporate culture that makes the hookup work. A few other Japanese companies have had pitcher-catcher combinations like Ken and myself, but I know of none that has worked so effectively or endured so long. If anything, Ken and I have endured too long. Japanese often complain that Americans transfer executives too frequently for effective relationships to develop. But I know of only one other Japanese company that has kept a top official in an overseas post for more than twenty years. Fujio Mitarari, president of our most successful rival, Canon USA, lived in the United States continuously from 1967 to 1989. Ken Nakamura was in the United States for thirteen years, ten of them as president of Minolta Corporation. I have now held that post for twenty years.

I must admit that when Minolta first got into the office equipment industry, I didn't know much about the business. But most people at Minolta knew even less. By now I have twenty years' experience with copiers and more recent experience with newer products in our office equipment line, including our facsimile systems and the PCW series that combines several office functions in one unit.

In 1964 we introduced our compact, streamlined-looking Minoltina line of cameras, which were given their name by one of our British distributors, Charles Strasser. Most of the 35-mm cameras then on the market were fairly bulky. Manufacturers were more interested in packing as many complex features as possible into their 35-mm cameras than in compact, easier-to-handle packaging. Minolta produced both a popular-priced Minoltina-P and the Minoltina-S, with a bigger lens and built-in range finder. The Minoltinas were exceptionally well designed cameras that worked perfectly in every respect—except one. They didn't sell.

It turned out that 35-mm camera buyers just weren't ready for a camera so compact that it didn't look as if it could do all the things bulkier cameras could do. A decade later everyone wanted just such a camera and many did very well, including Minolta's own XD series. But the Minoltina turned out to be a great idea ahead of its time. We later called it our "Three O'Clock in the Morning Camera." We called the world at three A.M. to deliver it, but no one woke up.

In most cases, however, when Ken Nakamura and I called each other, the ideas we bounced back and forth paid off. Not just Minolta, but Japan itself benefits from having top executives in overseas posts for long periods. To much of the world, Japan and the Japanese are still something of a mystery. Sometimes knowing and getting to understand one individual can help us to understand a strange country better than textbooks, movies, college courses, or guided tours. But we have never had a "Mr. Japan" in the United States. Sony's chairman, Akio Morita, would have been ideal. He knows and understands America well. He is intelligent and outspoken and has a real sense of humor, which is unusual in a Japanese businessman. He enjoys a high degree of visibility in both Japan and the United States and also has the advantage of looking just right for the role of businessman-statesman. Mr. Morita has been a good "face" for Sony's top management. Top managers in most Japanese companies, including some like me who have lived in America for some time, are self-conscious about their English. Mr. Morita has no reason to be. He speaks fluent English and, I must admit, has worked much harder at it than I have. He is also warm and outgoing, and Americans who meet him, including print and broadcast journalists, respond to him well. His frequent presence in America and his understanding of the American market have been important elements in the acceptance of Sony products. If Japan had more like him, there might be less friction between our two countries.

It is an indication of how important the American market is to a Japanese firm that Mr. Morita, president of Sony, moved his family to New York in 1962 to make sure that his company got a solid foothold in the United States. Morita opened a showroom for Sony on Fifth Avenue and took an apartment farther uptown, opposite the Metropolitan Museum of Art. To help finance Sony's expansion in the United States, he also had two million shares of Sony stock offered as American Depository Receipts. Sony was the first Japanese company to offer its stock in the United States. Mr. Morita lived here for nearly two years. He still maintains an apartment in New York and spends about one-third of his time in America. But in recent years, he has been more of a frequent commuter than a long-term resident.

Most Japanese companies have no visibility—or "face" as we call it—in America. Americans know our products, but they don't know who the people are behind those products. When frictions develop, Americans have no one they can talk to, no one whom they know and trust. And so tensions grow and mutual suspicion increases.

Needless to say, because of a pattern of short-term overseas assignments, no American company in Japan has had anyone like Mr. Morita to give their company—and the United States—"face" in Japan. One American corporation, NCR, does have a reputation for having pitcher-catcher combinations. They must be doing something right, for their business machine sales make them the fifth-ranking U.S. company doing business in Japan.

Minolta's pitcher-catcher approach, if more widely adopted, could have a useful impact on international relations, as well as on foreign marketing. Ken Nakamura later had a similar relationship with Akio Miyabayashi, who had started working with us part-time when he was a student at New York University. After graduation, he became a full-time Minolta employee. In 1973, he was sent to Hamburg, Germany, as head of our European marketing operations, a position he held for many years as Minolta's exports flourished. As our European pitcher-catcher combination, he and Ken worked as well together as Ken and I did for the North American market.

Minolta Corporation also benefits from the fact that there are now many people in key positions with our parent company in Japan who have worked in the United States. This includes such areas as production, inspection, corporate relations, sales, and marketing. Their understanding of our operations in the United States makes our job much easier in the sometimes difficult task of coordinating the efforts of those in the field with the efforts of the people at headquarters. Rotation has its advantages. But so do long-term assignments, particularly for people in top spots, who are not only their company's key executives, but who should also be their company's— and their country's—most visible representatives.

The pitcher-catcher relationship I had with Ken wasn't the only one I enjoyed. For a period when I was head of exports for Minolta, I had a similar hookup with our man who was then in Europe, my own brother, Koji Kusumoto.

17

Adventures in Europe

My first trip to Europe convinced me that Minolta and the Japanese camera industry could never compete with the Germans. Traveling from the United States, I went to Europe in 1956, primarily to attend Photokina, the biannual photo industry trade show in Cologne, West Germany, that draws people from all over the world. Like the Hanover Fair, its business equipment industry counterpart, Photokina introduces many new products and provides opportunities for making important contacts. No company involved in the industry can afford not to be there.

That year the famous German manufacturer Ernst Leitz introduced its Leica M2, sister camera to the Leica M3. Both had a range finder's wide frame lines for 35-, 50-, and 90-mm lenses. The Leica M3, introduced in 1954, with is single-stroke film advance option, had shocked the camera industry and was considered one of the world's great cameras. The Leica M3 had made it possible for a single camera to handle a range of lenses from 35-mm to telephoto. Minolta had just begun to make its modest way in America, but when I saw that Leica I was sure we would never be able to catch up with the Germans.

As it turned out, the Leica M3 proved to be the highest point

159

reached by the German camera industry. In fact, the name of the model introduced two years later, the Leica M2, sounded like a numerical step backward. The Germans' rather stiff-backed reluctance to listen to the advice of marketing experts in the United States and other countries soon began to undermine their technological excellence. The Japanese not only caught up with the Germans but moved well ahead of them.

KT's youngest brother, Yoshizo, who held the important post of director of research and development for Minolta, had been in Europe with Tooru Tada, then our planning manager, buying German and Swiss machine tools for our factories. We had met in Switzerland and gone on to the Photokina trade show in Cologne. We then took a few days off for sightseeing with a friend from Kanematsu as our guide. We were on a highway near Eutin, a small town about fifty miles north of Hamburg, when our car flipped over on a curve. The rest of us were only shaken up, but Yoshizo suffered a severe neck injury. He was hospitalized, and we were all very worried about his condition.

When we got word to KT, he ordered me to forget about my other duties and stay with his brother. Once the German doctors convinced me that Yoshizo would eventually be okay, I realized that there was little I could do except enjoy an enforced but pleasant vacation. I stayed at a drab railroad-station hotel and, after spending the day at the hospital with Yoshizo, there wasn't much choice but to catch a train into Hamburg. I was still a bachelor in those days and passing some time in that port city wasn't exactly the worst fate a young man could face.

On that trip I had with me an American-made Zenith portable radio, one of the first of the transistors. The radio, about the size of a VCR videotape, had a rubberized backing that was adhesive. I had great fun riding the train to Hamburg with the radio in the pocket of my raincoat, playing music. The Germans in the train would wonder where the music was coming from. Once I had their attention, I would pull out the radio and stick it to the window. The Germans would be suitably impressed at what they described as this example of marvelous Japanese technology. I would smile—inscrutably. Since I was in such awe of what I had just seen in German camera technology at Photokina, I didn't mind letting the Germans think my impressive American radio transistor had been made in Japan.

I created similar interest with a television set I brought to Japan from America in 1958. Not more than one household in fifteen had television in Japan. Most television sets were bulky, but my black-and-white Philco could fit in a suitcase and was ideal for the narrow confines of a Japanese home. It would have made an excellent export to Japan, but as far as I know no one but me thought of that. It amuses—and saddens—me that American companies trying to export to Japan overlook the fact that export products must be adaptable to the target market. My skinny Philco TV was perfect, but bulky American refrigerators and heavy furniture won't fit in the traditional Japanese home and oversized American cars with the wheel on the wrong side aren't ideal for Japanese driving conditions. My TV caused quite a sensation among my friends and even among the customs inspectors when I entered the country. I was delayed not because of any problem, but because the inspectors were fascinated by the impressive American technology that could make so compact a television set that would be so ideal for the Japanese home. My Philco television that fascinated people in Japan and my Zenith radio that amazed the Germans show how well American technology can create export products—if only American management would take the trouble to pursue export markets.

Yoshizo soon was able to leave the hospital, but his neck was still in an uncomfortable cast. Flying east, the most direct route back to Japan, involved stopovers in such tropical cities as Singapore and Hong Kong, which KT decided would not be good for Yoshizo in his neck cast. He ordered me instead to take Yoshizo back through New York and to get the most comfortable accommodations possible. I had no problem with that. The Pan Am StratoCruiser of that era had sleeping cabins on its upper deck. Since I had to stick close to Yoshizo, I obtained one for each of us. Mr. Tada, who was traveling with us, had just an ordinary seat. I felt a bit guilty, but my cabin was truly luxurious and included a built-in icebox well stocked with champagne. I drank it all during the trip and wound up feeling more giddy than guilty. We were met at Idlewild airport by people from both Kanematsu and Minolta, including Ken Nakamura.

In his heavy neck brace, Yoshizo walked very straight and upright. I did not. Ken said it looked like the injured Yoshizo was escorting me. And, after a few days in New York, it was Ken who escorted KT's brother the rest of the way back to Japan. Yoshizo and I both recovered. Today, he is a director of the company and heads Minolta's domestic camera sales.

Five years later, when I took over the export department, I was still convinced that our technological shortcomings, compared with those of the Germans, would forever hold us back in Europe. KT told me to give the Asian market the highest priority, but I also had to do what I could to build up our market in Europe. From 1961, I traveled often to Europe, but what helped us most in our early struggle to gain a foothold there was the close relationship I had with our new man on the Continent.

My brother, Koji, had been destined for a medical career. My father had harbored the same dream for me; when I disappointed him, he focused on Koji. He enrolled Koji at Chiba University, which had a prestigious medical department. But in those days studying medicine in Japan still meant studying in German. In the prewar years, Japanese medical students often went to Germany for at least part of their studies. Students in most technical fields did the same, while the French educated our army officers and the British schooled Japan's naval officers and politicians. These European influences lingered even in the postwar years.

Chiba happened to be one of the few Japanese universities with a serious photo department. Since Koji found German difficult and shared my interest in photography, he switched majors without telling our parents. My father was furious when he found out, but by then it was too late. Koji had changed his career destiny. As his graduation neared, I let Koji know I didn't like the idea of his possibly going to work for a competing camera company. So he joined Minolta, starting in our domestic sales department in 1957, not long before Minolta made its first effort to establish a European operation. A gentleman named Mr. Hiroshima, a fairly common family name in Japan, had a desk at the Kanematsu office in Hamburg, representing Minolta in Europe.

In part because Koji had studied German, KT decided to send him to Hamburg in September 1960. Koji's German was even worse than my English had been in 1954, and trying to crack the closed markets of Europe was a much tougher assignment than working in the relatively open atmosphere of the United States. But once again, after I moved into exports in 1961, Minolta had a pitcher-catcher team linking the home office and the field. Ken Nakamura, our man in New York, had become *like* a brother to me. Koji, our man in Hamburg, *was* my brother.

Since our early childhood days, playing together among the auto parts and towering piles of tires in the Ford agency in Seoul, Koji and I have always been close. With only four years difference in age and as the only two children in our family, we developed ties that have endured even though as adults we have nearly always lived continents apart. We worked well together and also benefited from the fact that the Japan Camera Industry Association (JCIA) began to take an active interest in promoting exports to Europe.

Trade restrictions weren't the only reason the European market was even tougher to crack than the United States. Europeans are slower to change than Americans when it comes to new ideas and new products. This may have been particularly true of the Germans, but it seemed that each European country shared in this conservatism and also presented specific difficulties of its own. For example, the British were especially sensitive to price. Cameras made in East Germany, hardly a major factor on the international market, were very popular in Britain. The East Germans were willing to undersell everyone else in an effort to get a foot in the door. West German cameras continued to dominate the rest of Europe. The French, who are not great camera enthusiasts and did not have a significant camera industry, were the most protectionist of all the Western European countries. But a high degree of protectionism, like conservative individual buying habits, was common to all European countries.

Recognizing this, the JCIA began inviting groups of European government officials, journalists, camera dealers, and distributors to Japan to tour our factories, meet our engineers, and study our products. At the same time the government lobbied against Europe's high tariffs and low quotas. Several years of hard work went into this industry-wide campaign, which dovetailed with Minolta's efforts to establish a European marketing network. I often hosted our European visitors. Though the Europeans were generally more conservative than our American visitors, they also enjoyed the Japanese way of combining business with the pleasures of the hostess bars.

I traveled frequently to Europe during the 1960s and saw more of my brother than I had during any period since we had left Korea. Europeans still had great respect for the United States' economic clout, which accounted for about 45 percent of the gross national product of the entire world. The Europeans wanted to know how the Americans did it. American fan and trade photo publications were widely read by European distributors, so many were aware of what Minolta had been up to in the United States, including our advertising campaigns. We spent about 10 to 15 percent of our sales volume on advertising, about double the usual industry average of 7 percent in foreign markets at the time. My marketing background in America, plus Minolta's willingness to spend money to develop a new market, meant that my ideas carried weight among the European dealers. But my American experience did mislead me in one respect. I wasn't prepared for the compact size of Europe compared to the vastness of the United States.

During one of those early trips I arranged with a Mr. Beaukreur, the Minolta distributor based in Brussels, to visit the major cities in several European countries. I allowed three days for each, as I would if visiting, say, Chicago, San Francisco, and Los Angeles. But after our first day in Brussels, Mr. Beaukreur drove me to Cophenhagen. That took all of half a day. Another brief trip took us to Amsterdam. I was left with six days on my itinerary and nothing much to do. Seeing Paris had always been a dream of mine, and so I made an unscheduled visit to the City of Lights. But I was really there as a tourist and so I never got the feel of the city, as I had in New York.

It wasn't until 1969, when many trade restrictions were lifted, that we began to develop much of a market in France. But elsewhere, things began picking up. In 1965 Tim Nishimura, who is now an executive vice-president for Minolta in the United States, opened Minolta's first full-fledged office in Europe. That Hamburg office, which later moved to Ahrensburg, has since spawned a European network of subsidiaries in Switzerland, the United Kingdom, Holland, Austria, Belgium, Sweden—and even France. Minolta's exports doubled or tripled every year from 1965 to 1975. By 1971 Minolta's exports exceeded our domestic sales for the first time since the early postwar era, when the American military PXs took nearly all of our production. That same year, again for the first time, Japan's camera production exceeded Germany's. The following year, an even more important event, symbolically at least, occurred when Minolta agreed to a technical cooperation pact that had been sought by the great German camera firm Ernst Leitz.

Frankly, I was as shocked as I had been eighteen years before when Leitz astounded the photo industry with the introduction of the Leica M3. Then I had thought Minolta could never catch up with the Germans. Now Leitz officials, impressed by a visit to Minolta's factories in Japan, asked us to take over part of their production and to share some technology. The first result of that agreement, jointly designed and produced by Leitz and Minolta, came out in 1973. Minolta marketed it as the Leitz Minolta CL, and Leitz sold it as the Leica CL. At the time Leitz had difficulty finding skilled workers. The tight job market in Germany pushed labor costs up while quality production faltered. Our agreement has worked well for both companies.

18

Minolta's Space Program

Minolta entered the space age on February 20, 1962. We didn't know it was happening, but the first American to orbit the earth, John Glenn, made us very famous that day. America's National Aeronautics and Space Administration (NASA) hadn't made any provision for a camera on Glenn's spacecraft, *Friendship 7*, but Glenn wanted one. A few days before the flight, he went to a drugstore near the launch site at Cape Canaveral. He bought seven cameras, including an Ansco Autoset, which was actually a Minolta Hi-Matic.

Minolta was the original equipment manufacturer (OEM) for the camera that GAF (General Aniline Film) Corporation sold in the United States as the Ansco Autoset. It was identical to the Hi-Matic except for the name. The Hi-Matic, a 35-mm range finder camera with a built-in selenium meter, had just been introduced in the United States, where it was marketed under the Ansco name. Glenn returned to the wood-frame, barrackslike apartment he shared with his family and spread his seven cameras out on the bed. He compared the cameras, feature by feature, and finally selected the Hi-Matic, primarily because he thought it could be adapted for easy operation even when wearing an astronaut's heavy, protective gloves. NASA technicians drilled holes to make the camera lighter and equipped it with a special handle. The Hi-Matic had the advantage of programmed autoexposure, making it the simplest, most reliable camera then on the market. Like the earlier Uniomat, it operated with a shutter blade that worked as a diaphragm. By the time the NASA engineers had adapted the camera to meet Glenn's requirements, that Hi-Matic looked virtually nothing like the handsomely designed camera that Minolta's Tatsuo Kobayashi had proudly created. But the inner workings were the same except that the camera was set permanently at infinity. The Hi-Matic got the job done. Photographs that Glenn took from *Friendship 7* were published all over the world and with them, in many cases, the story about the camera he had used. Today, that modified Hi-Matic is in the Smithsonian Air and Space Museum in Washington, D.C.—but still without the Minolta name.

The first news stories identified the camera as an Ansco. Since the GAF people in the United States knew it had been made by Minolta, they called the Minolta Corporation office in New York to let them know what had happened. When Minolta's New York office cabled the news to us in Osaka, we were stunned. Minolta publicized the story, which soon went around the world, identifying Minolta as the manufacturer. The news caused a sensation in Japan.

With its traditional fear of Russia and its postwar admiration for America, Japan had been shaken when Russia ushered in the space age with *Sputnik* in October 1957, and Yuri Gagarin became the first man in space in April 1961. The following month, Admiral Alan B. Shepard, Jr., became the first American in space, but in a much more limited flight. It was widely perceived that the Russians were well ahead of the Americans in space, which was frightening to the Japanese, who depended on America for military security.

The Japanese media followed developments in the rival space programs intently. When the news broke that the Americans were pulling ahead of the Russians and that the first camera in space had been made in Japan, Minolta attracted an incredible amount of attention. Our telephones rang constantly. Congratulatory cables poured in from Minolta distributors all over the world. Minolta's stock on the Tokyo exchange nearly doubled in less than a week. No one had thought Japan would ever be able to stick its nose into the space race between the two superpowers. Now, all of a sudden, there was Minolta, just a small camera company compared with Japan's real industrial giants, playing a role in America's first manned space flight. It may well have been the biggest event in the history of Minolta.

After John Glenn's flight, a grateful Japanese government invited Mr. and Mrs. Glenn to visit Tokyo, and Minolta extended that invitation to include our headquarters in Osaka. The visit was arranged for the spring of the following year, 1963, and the five days that the Glenns spent with us turned out to be one of the most exciting times of my life. KT assigned me to be their guide. It was the beginning of a friendship for my wife and myself that has lasted for a quarter of a century with two of the warmest, friendliest, and most impressive people I have ever known. The Glenns were accompanied on that trip by their daughter, Lynn, and son, Dave. It was very much a family visit and we have retained a family friendship.

The task of driving us around fell to the highly respected Mr. Ohtani, then the driver for our export department, who was later promoted to be KT's chauffeur—and the beneficiary of the robotic arm KT had built for his Cadillac. He was as thrilled as I was, particularly when we visited Kyoto and the police provided a motorcade escort. As we drove through Kyoto, Glenn spotted a junior high school band practicing in a field. He asked to stop and led us onto the field. Glenn's visit was highly publicized, and the press followed us wherever we went. So there was no need for me to introduce him to the director of the band. Glenn asked to take the baton and lead the band in the march they were playing. It would have made a great moment for one of his later senatorial campaigns, and his Japanese "constituents" reacted with as much enthusiasm as the voters in Ohio would have. As we were leaving, the band struck up the United States Marine Corps hymn. They hit a few wrong notes but, if anything, that made the moment even more moving.

The Glenns also gave me an excuse to make a trip to the Takarazuka Theater to see its famous all-girl troupe perform, an event that made up for my disappointment when a railroad strike in 1959 kept me from a special performance that I had bought a ticket for. The troupe, of course, had been alerted to the fact that we were coming and were very excited at the chance to meet John Glenn. At the end of the performance, we were all called onstage and introduced. Minolta has every reason to be grateful to John Glenn for taking our camera into space, but I'm also grateful to him for taking me onstage at the Takarazuka.

The Glenns had let us know in advance that they wanted to stay in typical Japanese accommodations during their visit to Osaka. So I had arranged a tatami room for them at the Miyako Hotel. Basically, this means that guests sleep on a tatami mat rather than on a Western-style bed with Western pillows and a full mattress. KT wanted to grant his guests their wishes, but he did insist that I go to the hotel to make sure the room would be comfortable enough for our friends from America. I decided it was and the Glenns agreed.

At the Minolta plant at Sakai, outside Osaka, Glenn planted the seedling of a phoenix tree that has since grown to be taller than I am. KT led the plant tour, showing the Glenns every step in the making of a camera. I introduced John to Tatsuo Kobayashi, inventor of the Hi-Matic, the Uniomat, and other innovative cameras of that era. Since the Hi-Matic had been manufactured at our plant at Toyokawa, we had the manager and two workers from Toyokawa come to meet the Glenns. The officials of the city of Sakai were proud to have John Glenn as a visitor and arranged for a troop of uniformed Boy Scouts to line the road to the factory. This must have impressed John, for I have often heard him tell the story. His fellow astronauts must have heard the story often, too, for when we get together they often kid him about it.

After his retirement from the space program, Glenn visited Osaka twice while in Japan in his capacity as president of Royal Crown, the cola manufacturer. KT, my wife, and I joined him for dinner, and our contacts have continued since I returned to the United States.

Senator Glenn is so well known that there is little I could say about him that would be new. But his wife, Annie, is equally remarkable, though she has been much less in the public eye. She has a speech impediment that makes her rather shy. Coupled with her striking appearance and dignified bearing, her shyness has caused some people to make the mistake of considering her aloof or even snobbish. Nothing could be further from the truth. She is down-to-earth, kind, and considerate to others. Without ever seeking acclaim for it, she devotes herself to helping others with speech impediments and those who are lucky enough to get to know her find her to be a wonderful woman.

I have only seen her show anger once. That was a few years ago when the Glenns were our guides on a tour of Cape Canaveral. We discovered that the gantry from which John Glenn's *Friendship 7* spacecraft had been launched has fallen into a rather sad state of disrepair. Our visit took place in the period after the tragic loss of the space shuttle *Challenger* and its crew. There was again serious concern about the state of the American space program. As we stood on that windswept, decaying concrete platform where so much history had been written, Mrs. Glenn controlled her anger. But a glance at her eyes told me that, however briefly, anger was there. And sorrow.

The others who were with us that day, including Alan Shepard, who heads the Mercury 7 Foundation, Edward Buckbee, director of the United States Space Camp, and John Glenn's friend and business partner, Henri Landwirth, shared a combination of sorrow, anxiety, and hope as we viewed neglected icons of the space program's history and the giant assembly building where the next space shuttle, *Discovery*, was being prepared. At the space camp in Huntsville, Alabama, I had handled the instruments of a simulated space shuttle, and at Cape Canaveral I was instructed by Shepard and Glenn in what it took to prepare an actual shuttle for launching. It was like walking in the company of gods.

The Minolta camera brand name, first used in 1933, had become so well known as a result of Glenn's use of the Hi-Matic that KT decided in 1962 that the time had come to change the name of the company from Chiyoda Kogaku Seiko to Minolta Camera Company, Ltd.

Minolta was back in space, with considerably more foreknowledge and planning, with the Apollo moon program in 1968 and 1969. This time Minolta's contribution wasn't a camera but a light meter. The Minolta Space Meter, specially designed for NASA, was first used by the *Apollo 8* astronauts Frank Borman, James A. Lovell, and William A. Anders when they made the first flight to the moon. The Minolta Space Meter was also there when Neil Armstrong and Edwin E. Aldrin became the first men to walk on the surface of the moon. The camera that shot those famous moon photographs was a Swedish-made Hasselblad. That put our light meter in very good company, for the Hasselblad is one of the world's great cameras.

Minolta light meters are used almost universally among professionals, perhaps in part because of the reputation they developed within the industry as a result of the use of the Minolta Space Meter on the Apollo flights. Minolta's Auto-Spot II is a direct descendant of the prototype Space Meter developed for NASA. It provides automatic pinpoint accuracy as the photographer sights through a single-lens reflex viewfinder. The Auto-Spot II is also the world's most precise exposure meter with focusing capability, and it is only one of our light measuring devices that professionals swear by. Our Space Meter was also used on the historic linkup of the American *Apollo 18* and the Russian *Soyuz 19* spacecraft in 1975. The international publicity given to Minolta's role in the American space program caused many people to pay more serious attention to Japanese technology. We still had to struggle in those days to overcome the image of Japanese manufactured goods as shoddy "toys."

The year that John Glenn took the Hi-Matic into space, 1962, was also the year that Minolta made its first venture into the data retrieval field with the introduction of the Minolta 401S microfilm reader-printer. Appropriately enough, when we celebrated the twenty-fifth anniversary of both events at Minolta Corporation in the United States, we did it with the help of the Mercury 7 Foundation. The foundation—which provides university scholarships in science and technology, and to which Minolta Corporation has contributed—was established by six of the seven original Mercury space program astronauts and Mrs. Betty Grissom, widow of Virgil I. Grissom.

In 1987, to celebrate the anniversaries, three of the original astronauts participated in a ceremony at our New Jersey headquarters. At Ramsey, Alan Shepard, Donald "Deke" Slayton, and Scott Carpenter planted a dogwood tree, echoing John Glenn's planting of a phoenix tree at our Sakai plant nearly a quarter of a century before. The three astronauts also joined our micrographics dealers on a dinner cruise around Manhattan Island, visited our micrographics booth at the AIIM (Association of Image and Information Management) show at New York's Jacob Javits Convention Center, and had lunch with our headquarters employees at our business equipment training and in-house television production studio at Blauvelt, New York.

Our association with the astronauts led to our involvement with the United States Space Camps at Huntsville and Cape Canaveral. Minolta has replaced Polaroid as the official camera for the camps, and we are exploring the possibility of additional involvement. The space camps are wonderful places where youngsters—and adults—can learn not the knot-tying and fire-making skills of the traditional camper, but the skills used by modern astronauts.

During our 1987 meetings with the astronauts, I told them about

Minolta's latest venture into space as co-manufacturer of the world's most sophisticated planetarium. Infinium is a joint venture bringing together Minolta's wizardry with optics and the computer programming magic of Mitsubishi's Electronic Company. Infinium, introduced at the Tsukaba Science Fair in 1985, represents a great leap forward for both companies and a major advance in the planetarium field. KT's vision propelled Minolta into manufacturing planetariums back in 1958, not just out of a quest for profit or product diversification, but because he feared that young people in Japan would lose touch with the heavens. As a young man, KT had been fascinated by the starry skies the naked eye could easily see. In that preindustrial era, it was possible to study astronomy seriously with nothing more than a simple telescope. On cloudless nights, the sky was alive with stars that could set the mind dreaming. But by the late 1950s the bright lights of our big cities and the pallor of industrial pollution had combined to block out the distant formations that had guided and inspired mankind since we first learned to stand and lift our heads toward the mysterious night sky. KT resolved to use modern industrial technology to restore to as many viewers as possible the skies that industrial development had shrouded. Minolta has since become the world's leading producer of high-quality and affordable planetariums. There are more than 120 planetariums made by Minolta in the United States alone, including highly sophisticated models that are used in the study of astronomy at the United States Air Force Academy, the University of Arizona's Center of Astronomy, and the Kitt Peak National Observatory.

But Infinium is in a class by itself. All previous planetariums display the universe only from the perspective of Earth. Infinium liberates viewers from Planet Earth to let them view the universe from any point in the universe. They can also view the universe from any point in time. For example, viewers can see how the firmament looked at the time of the birth of Christ, a popular planetarium Christmas show that usually requires shutting down operations for two weeks for reprogramming. Infinium's computers can reprogram such changes in a few minutes. Viewers can also see how the universe looked when the constellation that for centuries has been known as the Southern Cross was visible in the Northern Hemisphere. They can even view the universe from the perspective of a comet or an astronaut on a space voyage, including a prospective space voyage not yet undertaken. When I've described this capability of Infinium to Alan Shepard, John Glenn, and other friends from the Mercury 7 Foundation, I've watched their eyes light up with a fascination equal to my own. Infinium may turn out to be the best thing to happen to Minolta's space program since John Glenn discovered the Hi-Matic in a Florida drugstore.

19

Our Co-Prosperity Sphere

Europe and outer space are both pretty tough markets to crack. Asia is even tougher. Tight trade restrictions are the rule, and even today most countries in the area are relatively poor. When I hear American business and political leaders complain about Asian trade restrictions, I have to agree. It was even worse back in the early 1960s when I first tried. But there are ways to get the job done. It helps to be patient to a degree that is often difficult for non-Orientals. It also helps to have a friend in Hong Kong.

I made my first trip to Hong Kong in May 1960 soon after my marriage. Hong Kong is certainly the most important of the handful of free trade zones that keep the wheels of international commerce turning in parts of the world where trade is difficult. Though Americans complain bitterly about Japan's supposedly restrictive trade policies, we actually rank with the United States itself as one of the world's more open markets. Most other Asian countries are another story. Tough trade restrictions make it difficult to export to countries like the Philippines, Indonesia, Taiwan, People's Republic of China, and Korea. But Hong Kong is an open showcase for international

174

products. Well-to-do people from all over Asia, when they visit Hong Kong, wind up buying the latest fashions, watches, cameras, and a wide array of electronic products. Such visitors are usually important people in their own countries—government officials, business leaders, and so forth. To have any chance at all in other Asian markets it is important to become well known in Hong Kong. The products brought home by wealthy visitors to Hong Kong may set trends and create demand in a variety of Asian countries. Such grass-roots domestic demand may eventually help a company crack a country's trade barriers. This may seem like a rather roundabout approach, but as I said, it sometimes takes Asian patience to conquer Asian markets.

Minolta until the 1960s had been represented in Hong Kong by a small and not very active agency. KT sent me there to find a new agency that could increase our sales and, perhaps even more important, our visibility in that international showcase. When I got there, I found that Minolta was already better known than we suspected. Nearly all the colony's business leaders read English. The American fan and trade photo magazines were well known among Hong Kong photo dealers and consumers. *Modern Photography*, *Popular Photography*, *Photo Trade News*, and *Photo Dealers* all circulated widely along with some British photo magazines. Even though our cameras weren't readily available, the attention Minolta had been getting in the United States had stirred up interest in Hong Kong. As I started visiting camera dealers, word spread fast through the tight little business community. By my second day in Hong Kong I started getting invitations to lunch and dinner from people wanting to be Minolta's agent. I don't think I have ever been wined and dined so well.

On the other hand, to keep costs down, I stayed at a small, second-grade hotel in Kowloon, the tourist section of Hong Kong. Late one evening I returned to my hotel and stopped at the desk for my key. The lady behind the desk told me I had checked out. I started to argue with her when a Chinese gentleman came up and asked if I was Mr. Kusumoto. Still confused, I said I was.

He told me that I deserved to be staying in a much better hotel so he had checked me into the Ambassador, which is still one of Hong Kong's best, and had moved all my things there. His company was paying for everything, and he wanted to talk to me about representing Minolta. I was shocked, but at that point I had no choice. I was to discover that all this was very much in the Hong Kong style. The business atmosphere is highly charged, competitive, and very aggressive.

Business goes on around the clock, including twenty-four-hour tailor shops that custom-make suits. I ordered two suits at such a shop and, when I returned to pick them up the next day, the owner told me they had already been paid for. I never did find out who had bought my suits for me, but from then on I was aware that various people were following me wherever I went. I was approached by many companies, both British and Chinese, wanting to represent Minolta. All looked good. But by this time I felt I had had enough experience dealing with distributors in America to be able to set Minolta up without being tied to a trading company or a distributor handling competing camera companies. Hong Kong is so small, with only about sixty camera dealers, that I didn't think we would need a big company to handle our distribution. We would only need a few salesmen and some boys to make the deliveries. This would keep distribution costs low and leave more money for advertising, which I believed would be important to get the maximum value out of Hong Kong as an Asian showcase for our products.

In those days there was no tunnel connecting Kowloon and Hong Kong so I commuted by the Star Ferry. I was impressed by the many advertisements I saw at the piers and decided to find out who controlled them. I visited the Dentsu advertising agency's Hong Kong office and was told that a man named George Ho controlled the pier advertising and much else through his firm, the Goddard Company. He also owned a commercial radio station, which is unusual in a British colony, where public broadcasting is the tradition. I was told that he was also the distributor for Chrysler air conditioners, Carnation milk, Hitachi electronic products, but no camera equipment.

Dentsu arranged a meeting. From the very first, I liked George Ho and sensed that Minolta had found the friend it needed in Hong Kong. Later I realized that at least one reason I took to him so quickly was that he is very Americanized. He and his wife, who had actually been born in America, had been educated at the University of California at Los Angeles. Unlike most Hong Kong Chinese, whose English is inflected with clipped British accents, George sounded more like I do. But it was more than just our Oriental-American accents. We also thought alike, again in ways influenced by our respect for the United States. His views on distribution in Hong Kong and on the importance of advertising confirmed my impressions, and I quickly decided that he should be our agent. But I must admit I was afraid to make my decision public while I was still in Hong Kong.

Business tactics are so aggressive there that I wasn't sure what might happen. Today, I'm sure my fears were exaggerated, but I actually thought I might be kidnapped or shot. I told George Ho, confidentially, that he would be our agent. I told everyone else that I hadn't made up my mind yet and would have to think about it back in Japan. George respected my wishes for secrecy and suggested it would be better if he didn't see me off at the airport as he would ordinarily do with a business associate. But I certainly wasn't lonely at the airport and soon realized that the only real danger I faced was being killed with kindness.

More than fifty people showed up to see me off and shower me with gifts. Even after I cleared customs and was heading for the plane, someone threw a package over the rail to me, shouting, "Here, Mr. Kusumoto, this is for you."

This was my first trip abroad after my marriage. My wife naturally was pleased to see all the gifts I brought back and thought that would happen every time I traveled. But nothing like that ever happened again.

George Ho turned out to be the ideal representative for us in Hong Kong. Not all my moves in the Asian market were so smart, however. When Japan occupied New Guinea during World War II, the naval and air base at Rabaul became one of the most important outposts for our military in the Pacific. Because of its strategic location, we heard almost daily radio reports of heroic combat missions and great battles engaged in by Japanese forces based at Rabaul. It became a famous symbol of Japan's resistance as MacArthur began his island-hopping advance. MacArthur bypassed it, but that only increased its reputation as an invincible stronghold. Hearing those stories as a boy convinced me that Rabaul must be a very important place, an impression that naïvely stayed with me when I became Minolta's top man in international trade. So soon after my coup in Hong Kong, I sent one of my assistants, Shizuo Nakajima, to Rabaul. Within a week, I received a cable that I have never forgotten.

"I've arrived in Rabaul," said Shizuo. "I should have brought shoes rather than cameras. People here walk the streets barefoot. I could sell lots of shoes, but I don't see any chance to sell cameras."

He returned, still complaining that I had sent him to such a backwater. All I could say in my defense was that I had been brainwashed by all that wartime propaganda.

Hong Kong, meanwhile, continued to work well for us. Minolta's name and the quality of our cameras gradually became known in other parts of Asia. The international shoppers who spent so much money in that free-trade zone played a role for Minolta almost like that of the American GIs who bought our cameras at the military PXs in Japan and brought them back to America.

Such zones have an importance that not many people appreciate. Everyone likes to pick up duty-free bargains, but the free-trade zones are more than just a convenience for shoppers. If your product is a winner in that market, it's proof that your product is good and that your prices are competitive. The most important zones—Aden for the Middle East, Panama for Latin America, the Canary Islands for Europe, and, of course, Hong Kong for Asia—give international manufacturers a window through which their products can be seen by shoppers from countries whose tariffs, quotas, and other restrictions may tend to keep competitive imports out. The free-trade zones are an effective way of demonstrating the advantages of freer international trade.

American business and political leaders frequently criticize their trading partners, including Japan, accusing them of unfairly restricting imports and subsidizing exports. The Americans proclaim themselves advocates of free trade and call for a "level playing field" so products from all countries can compete fairly. Yet it saddens me that there is so little American corporate presence in the free-trade zones, which are our closest approach to a level playing field in international trade. Even in Panama, with its close ties to the United States, the neon signs alone offer convincing evidence that the Japanese traders are much more active than the Americans. Canon, one of Minolta's most aggressive competitors, maintains a permanent office in Panama. Yet American companies tend to ignore the trade potential inherent there and in the other free-trade zones. It's another reflection of the puzzling lack of interest in exports shown by so many American companies. On the other hand, you can find many American importers on buying trips in the zones, particularly in Hong Kong. Minolta and other Japanese camera and electronics companies invest heavily in advertising and promotions in the free-trade zones. Our success in Hong Kong was spurred by the publicity surrounding John Glenn's use of the Hi-Matic, which we promoted heavily.

Fresh on the heels of that success, our international visibility got another big boost in 1964, when the Summer Olympics were held in Tokyo. Japan, just beginning to come into its own as a postwar economic power, took new pride in its achievements and wanted to show the world its progress. Construction included new sports facilities and hotels, expansion of the Tokyo subway network, the start of a nationwide system of super-highways, and a new railway, the Shinkansen, which follows a heavy but amazingly punctual schedule between Tokyo and Osaka, with "bullet" speeds of over one hundred miles an hour. Not to be outdone, the Japan Camera Industry Association (JCIA) built a camera center at Olympic Village to provide developing and parts and repair services for the athletes and the press corps. In addition to its own staff, JCIA urged the various camera companies to assign multilingual employees to help run the center. Since Koji knew both English and German, he was brought in by Minolta.

While working at the center, he met a young girl from JCIA named Yasuko, who spoke both English and Spanish. In that exciting atmosphere, the two young people fell in love. The parents of both eventually agreed to the marriage, and Koji and Yasuko were married the next year. The Olympics had played the role of "unofficial" matchmaker; the official matchmakers were KT's brother Yoshizo and Yoshizo's wife, Teruko. Other prominent guests at the wedding ceremony included Mr. and Mrs. Kinji Moriyama. I understand that it was an impressive ceremony at the Okura Hotel in Tokyo. I can't testify to that personally, however, because my duties as Minolta's director of exports required that I be in Europe for a sales meeting. Though we take our family ties seriously in Japan, business comes first.

Koji, like me, seems to reproduce only daughters. My wife and I have two. Koji and Yasuko have three. Our father often complained that his sons had not given him any grandsons. Unless something we don't expect happens soon, the family name will die out with us. Of course, Koji or I might adopt a son as our grandfather did, give him the Kusumoto family name, and marry him off to one of our daughters—and hope for grandsons.

In 1964 Minolta moved into the business equipment industry in a major way with the opening of our copier manufacturing plant at Toyokawa and production of the Minoltafax 41, the world's first copier with reduction capabilities. It was also one of the first copiers to use an electrostatic process developed by the American firm RCA. We obtained rights under a license arrangement. The machine sold well in Japan and, though we never sold it under our own name, it provided us with our first entry into the vast American business equipment market. It turned out to be particularly popular in America because it could reduce legal documents, which are 8½ by 14 inches, to standard letter size, 8½ by 11 inches. The Minoltafax 41 was also a well-designed machine and, in 1966, won the United States Visual Communication Congress Award.

An even more important introduction occurred in 1966 with the Minolta SR-T 101. This was our first single-lens reflex camera with through-the-lens metering. That first SR-T camera also introduced Minolta's patented Contrast Light Compensator for improved exposure of shots that are backlit. The SR-T series proved to be a Minolta classic—easy to use, durable, and competitively priced. We produced them continuously for fifteen years, and they have been one of the most popular cameras in our history. Sales soared, particularly to our export markets. In 1968 Minolta won the important Ministry of International Trade and Industry award for its outstanding contribution to exports. Since I headed our export department at that time, I took some pride in the MITI award, though I know many others—from KT to those responsible for the SR-T 101—had more to do with it than I did.

Koji returned to Japan from Europe in 1970, and the following year became general manager of our first Asian subsidiary, Minolta Hong Kong, Ltd., working closely with George Ho, as I had done in getting us started there.

From that Hong Kong base, our reputation spread quickly. By 1972 we were ready to open a sales office in Singapore. The following year Minolta took the even bigger step of opening our first overseas manufacturing plant and began producing business equipment products at a modern factory in Kuala Lumpur, Malaysia. When American firms begin manufacturing or sourcing overseas, they are sometimes accused of "exporting jobs." In Japan today we don't see it that way. The pressures often cited to justify Japan's military expansionism fifty years ago still exist. But today we believe we have found a more positive way of creating a vaster co-prosperity sphere with our neighbors than our military leaders envisioned during the war years. In fact, the co-prosperity sphere we've developed is global. By creating manufacturing jobs for Malaysians, we're helping them develop a more robust economy and become a better market for our products.

It's an approach that Henry Ford understood when he insisted on paying auto workers enough so they could become buyers of the cars they made. And it's an approach that America understood in the postwar years when it helped the devastated countries of Europe and Asia rebuild their economies and become better markets for American products.

Though Minolta made an early beginning with our plant in Malaysia, we have since moved more conservatively than some of our competitors and firms in other industries, particularly the auto industry. But we do have another copier plant in West Germany; we now also assemble cameras at our plant in Malaysia, and in the United States, at Goshen, New York, we have a highly automated plant producing toner for copiers.

In 1969, on rather sudden notice, I returned to the United States to deal with problems very different from the problems I had faced years before. I have lived and worked in America ever since. In these twenty years I've come to recognize that Japan and the United States are so mutually interdependent that the problems of one can't be resolved without solving the problems of the other. I could say the same about Minolta and its biggest market and about my own problems as a man bridging all that divides the two countries I love.

It didn't happen overnight, but when my family moved to America, our lives—and our world—were destined to change in ways we could not have imagined.

V

DRAWN TO
THE MAGNET

1969–1989

20

Starting a Second Life

Even as I left the United States to return to Japan in 1958, I knew the allure of America one day would pull me back. When it happened, the call came suddenly.

Under its first president, Ken Nakamura, Minolta Corporation had become so successful that it had outgrown the structures we had set up to launch that growth. This was true both in our well-established camera business and even in our relatively new but promising business equipment operations. The relationship we had established with FR Corporation back in 1955 had served us well in getting started in the American market. But by 1967 Ken Nakamura realized that depending on FR to handle our distribution no longer worked in the face of growing competition from other Japanese camera companies.

Minolta's early success created interest in Japanese photo equipment, and major distributors began signing up with our competitors. We were particularly concerned about Yashica, which had picked up three major distributors in 1957 and was doing quite well. Canon distributed through Bell & Howell, and Pentax through Honeywell, both major American firms. Ken decided that a small firm like FR just didn't have the resources Minolta needed to stay competitive in the huge American market, and he did not renew our agreement with them. Instead he reached out to much larger distributors, including Raygram, Hornstein, Wesco, and, a few months later, Intercontinental, the largest of all. The arrangements didn't last long. At that time, both Raygram and Intercontinental also handled Yashica. Within a few months, Intercontinental dropped Minolta and unloaded a huge inventory of our cameras in a "closeout sale" to the giant department store, R. H. Macy's, at heavily discounted prices.

What was soon called "Minolta's Macy Dump" created a sensation in the industry. That event convinced Ken Nakamura that depending on third-party distributors was not in our best interests. We decided to become our own distributors with our own sales force selling directly to retail outlets. Ken proceeded to drop all our distributors and to establish direct relations with retailers. Minolta was the first Japanese camera company to distribute directly to retail outlets, establishing another precedent that our competitors all followed— once we proved such a strategy could succeed. But success did not come easily. Our decision to terminate our contracts with our remaining distributors led to bitter court disputes.

Americans are in love with their lawyers. And American lawyers love their lawsuits. I recognize the importance of litigation in maintaining order in the marketplace. I have great respect for the American judicial system, and for the American lawyers and law firms Minolta has worked with over the years. But the American passion for litigation still mystifies me. In a *Wall Street Journal* article a few years ago, reporter John B. Fialka suggested that one way to ease the American trade deficit with Japan would be to export excess American lawyers. He noted that there is one lawyer for every 355 Americans and only one lawyer for every 9,000 Japanese. By contrast, Japan, with half the population of the United States, has an equal number of engineers. The law is a vital profession. But lawyers don't produce anything. Engineers do. The preponderance of lawyers in the United States must reflect something deeply embedded in the national character. Disputes that in Japan might well be settled by negotiation, compromise, and consensus tend to lead to nasty lawsuits in America.

Minolta Corporation faced another legal problem with its copier business. Graphic Communications of New Jersey was our American distributor for the Minoltafax 41 reduction copier, which they sold

under the name Graphic 200. We later decided to distribute a reduction copier directly to American office equipment dealers. About
80 percent of the components in this copier, called the Minolta 1714,
were new. But Graphics Communications sued, claiming our direct
marketing of the 1714 violated our agreements with them over the
Minoltafax 41.

KT wanted to settle the lawsuits so we could get on with the
business of selling cameras and copiers. He also thought the time
was ripe for Ken Nakamura and me to switch jobs. Ken had been in
America for fourteen years, ten of them as president of Minolta
Corporation, then an unprecedented stay for a Japanese executive.
KT also felt that having a new face on the scene might help us to
resolve the lawsuits peacefully.

The strategy worked. I returned to the United States in March
1969, and Ken and I overlapped for about three months. Most of that
time we were tied up with the court cases. Minolta was able to reach
out-of-court settlements. For roughly half a million dollars, I concluded buy-out arrangements with our three camera distributors. In
March 1970, we began to distribute directly to photo equipment dealers. The suit with Graphic Communications also was resolved in our
favor, and we began direct distribution of the Minolta 1714.

Distributing directly also had the advantage of bringing us a step
closer to our customers. Feedback from our customers, both dealers
and consumers, is vital to our survival. Though we keep up heavy
programs of consumer research and frequently survey our dealers,
having our own sales force in direct contact with business equipment
dealers and photo retailers gives us another channel of communications directly from the source, rather than filtered through a distributor.

As I started my second tour in America, I realized that my
business responsibilities had doubled. I was again starting from
scratch, though on a much higher level than in 1954. I had to create
sales organizations for both cameras and copiers. It was very much
like starting a whole new company. And, no longer a carefree bachelor, I now had a family to provide for and settle in a strange new
land. I began to realize how strange it would be for my family even
before we left Japan.

"Daddy, are we already in America?" asked Mariko, our younger
daughter, who was only four years old. We weren't yet in America,
but I could understand her confusion. We had been living in a three-

bedroom house my parents had bought for us between Kyoto and Osaka. Since we would be starting fresh in America, we had shipped our furniture to my parents' home in Tanabe. For a few days before we left Osaka, we stayed in a then-new and very modern hotel, the Shinhankyu. Mariko thought anything so grand must be in America.

We flew by way of Hawaii, where we spent an extra day because my family loved it so much. It was Kuniko's first time outside Japan. I could sense her excitement. Our next stop was Los Angeles, where we stayed with Kuniko's uncle, George Aratani, whom I had met at our wedding in Osaka. Though we are related by marriage, rather than by blood, I identify strongly with George. Like me, he was born in a foreign country—not Korea, but the United States. Like me, he is a graduate of Keio University. Again like me, he had to be brought back to Japan to become Japanese before returning to the United States and becoming a successful businessman. George, in fact, is both much more American and much more successful than I. As an entrepreneur his interests include the high-fidelity sound system company Kenwood; the fine-China firm Mikasa; and orange groves, originally developed by his father, and other real estate holdings. He and his wife, Sakaye, who was also born in America, live in the Hollywood hills outside Los Angeles and also have a home in Palm Springs.

They met and married in a concentration camp. Though they were both native-born American citizens, like all other people of Japanese descent who were in the United States and Canada when World War II broke out, they were packed off to the camps. Today, both are active in philanthropic work among American-born Japanese in California. George has been honored in Japan with the Emperor's Third Order of the Sacred Treasure, and Los Angeles Mayor Thomas Bradley has honored him with a "George Aratani Day" celebration. George has played a major role in the development of Los Angeles's "Japan Town," including the first big building to go up there, the Kajima Building. It bears the name of Japan's largest construction firm, of which George is a director. Mrs. Aratani, an active supporter of a nursing home for elderly Japanese in Los Angeles, was honored with the emperor's medal even before her husband, a very unusual event.

If you spoke to George in English over the phone, you would have no idea that he is of pure Japanese heritage. Which may be one reason why his father shipped him back to Japan to attend secondary school and college. It is easy to forget your heritage in the American melting pot.

Kuniko and our two daughters stayed with George's family in Los Angeles while I went on to New York to set up our new high-rise apartment. When they joined me in April to settle into Skyline Tower, off Main Street in the Flushing section of Queens, it was clear that for Kuniko and the children, even more than for me, this was to be the start of a second life. The first year wasn't easy for Kuniko. She missed her family and complained often that she wanted to go home. I have since learned that this is a common pattern for Japanese wives when they first come to the United States. But at the time, I was worried about Kuniko's happiness.

Our most immediate task was to get Eriko started in elementary school. She was seven and spoke no English. Kuniko did not know how to drive, spoke little English, and was still shy in this alien land that had fascinated her so much from a distance. I took Eriko to P.S. 120 in Flushing to apply for admission. I expected it would take a week or more, as it would in Japan. Eriko was admitted that same day, and the school clerk suggested that I attend a class with Eriko. I did. I warned the teacher that Eriko spoke no English. "That's okay," the teacher said and went on teaching her first-grade class as usual. I later learned that in New York it isn't unusual, particularly in the lower grades, to have children who don't speak English. The teachers make the necessary extra effort. I must say I'm grateful for the American education my daughters have had, and especially to those teachers who helped them so much during their first years. I sat through that class, realizing that Eriko understood not one word. But I noticed that she was smiling as she looked around. She seemed happy and some instinct told me it would work out fine.

I know it would not be so easy for an American in a Japanese school. The family would have to invest in teaching the child Japanese before an application to an expensive private Japanese school would even be considered. In most cases, the child would have to go to one of the special foreign schools. But this is America, I thought, where everything is possible. In the democratic American way, Eriko was accepted immediately in a free public school.

The Japanese community in New York, though nothing like what it is today, had grown considerably since I had first been in America. There were no more than two hundred of us then, and we all knew each other. By 1969, there were several hundred in Flushing alone. Eriko discovered she had a Japanese classmate, who spoke both languages and was very helpful to her. But since Eriko didn't understand her homework, I did it for her and did my best to explain it. I also bought her every educational toy I could find, including one I remember well that had pictures of different animals. You pushed a button under the picture of a cat, for example, and a recorded voice would say "cat." I played with her by the hour, and Kuniko and little Mariko, who would start kindergarten the next year, joined in. Slowly, we became a modestly bilingual family, and Eriko began riding the school bus by herself to P.S. 120.

That summer Eriko went to a day camp, where again no special provision was made for foreign children. She soaked up English by osmosis and necessity. By the time the new school term started in September, the Americanization of Eriko was well under way. She was soon in the school chorus, and I remember how proud I was when we were invited to a "parents' night" at which they sang. I noticed that the friendly man who showed us to our seats busied himself adjusting lights and windows. I assumed he was a clerical or custodial employee and was later surprised to find out that he was the principal. At such an event in Japan, the principal might make a dignified speech that would last at most a minute, then sit looking stern through the rest of the evening. He would not be friendly, but he would have the respect of students and parents. Though teachers in Japan may be a bit more relaxed than they were in my time, the principal still remains aloof. He embodies dignity and fear of authority. I may be old-fashioned, but in this respect I think the Japanese way may be better. Fear of authority keeps Japanese students in line, at least until college. In the lower grades, even if we were very sick, we would never think of missing a day. And no one was ever disruptive in class.

The best system may be somewhere between what schools were in Japan in my day and what American schools are like today. But I must say, based on my daughters' education, there's a lot to be said for American public schools. I realize the quality of education, even in the same public school system, can vary from one neighborhood to another. Relatively wealthy neighborhoods get better public services of all kinds, including education. But in my own personal experience, and in Minolta's outreach programs, I have had some involvement with schools, ranging from a small private college, Ramapo, near Minolta headquarters in a well-to-do suburban area of New Jersey to a special program in Harlem that's designed to keep teen-age mothers in school. I know American schools in some communities face problems that include inadequate funding and an inefficient educational bureaucracy. A troubling breakdown in the American family structure also has had a negative effect on children in schools. But in general I have been impressed by the quality of American education and the dedication of American educators. Both my daughters spent all of their elementary and secondary school years in public schools, first in New York City and then in Fort Lee, New Jersey, where we have lived since 1973. Both went on to excellent universities. They also had the educational benefit of life in America with its great cultural and ethnic diversity, its economic strength, and its trend-setting world leadership in so many fields, ranging from the pure sciences to popular music.

Their mother has also benefited from this exposure to life in America. From the first she enjoyed the fact that I was home much more often in the evening to be with her and our two girls. Men-only business dinners are rare in America, and we were invited out much more often as a couple. By the time we moved to Fort Lee, Kuniko's English had improved greatly. She learned to drive and eventually we bought a second car. In Japan her best friend had been that old Philco television set I had brought from America. Now she has become an expert mah-jongg, tennis, and golf player and participates in international bridge tournaments. She is very active in the American-Japanese Women's Club and other organizations. It shocks me that when we go to functions at Japan Society, she usually knows more people than I do. But she always introduces me very graciously.

Since we joined the Apple Ridge Country Club near Minolta's headquarters, she has had even more opportunities to enjoy life in America. In Japan it would be unheard of for a housewife to play golf, except for a tiny handful of wealthy women and a few professional players. When Kuniko compares her life here with her life in Japan, I remind her that then we had two very small children at home. She agrees but insists that it is not just our family life-style that is different. It is also the style of life of America. I can't argue with that. Americans live better and enjoy life more than most other people.

Kuniko and I have tried to keep our daughters from being totally Americanized. When we first arrived, there was no full-time foreign school for Japanese students. But we did enroll the girls in a special Saturday school that concentrated on the Japanese language. Neither liked it, compared with their American schools, but they did well and are grateful now to know both languages. Eriko, by the time she graduated from this school, was number one in her class despite the fact that most of the other students had lived far longer in Japan than she had.

Both girls did well at Fort Lee High School. When it came time to choose a college, each selected a school in California, still within the continental United States but otherwise as far from their parents as possible. Eriko's first choice was Stanford. Three years later, Mariko went to Occidental, a smaller but highly esteemed school near Los Angeles.

I had first heard of Stanford from Kuniko's father, who had been there during a trip to California before the war. I had visited the campus myself during a 1970 trip to Palo Alto. I was as impressed as Kuniko's father had been. I must confess that it wasn't just the school's academic reputation but also the sheer size and beauty of the campus, which includes its own private lake and yacht club. As I watched students strolling and biking across the lovely campus under bright, sunny skies, I told myself that this wasn't a college at all. It was paradise. I thought back to my own college days, trying to take notes while wearing gloves in classrooms with bombed-out windows. If I were younger, I thought, this is where I would want to go to college. I had no idea that within a few years my older daughter would live out her father's dream.

Kuniko has always been a strict parent and was not at all pleased at the thought of Eriko going away to college. I kept talking to her, saying how lucky we were to have a daughter able to go to such a fine school, how pleased Eriko's grandfather would be, and how much more free time Kuniko herself would have with one daughter away at college and the other busy with her high school activities. Finally, Kuniko agreed. But not until we overcame more misgivings about the co-ed living arrangements at some of Stanford's dormitories.

Eriko wanted to live in one of the mixed dorms. Frankly, I was as shocked as Kuniko at first. When I had gone to college in Japan, boys and girls didn't even attend the same schools, much less live in the same buildings. But I had confidence in Eriko and convinced her very conservative mother to agree to a first-year trial in a co-ed dorm. We made the same decision when it was Mariko's turn to start college, and, when I visited their campuses, I never got the feeling that there was any funny business going on. The boys and girls seemed to mix so naturally that I came away again regretting that my own college years had been so monastic.

We never had any reason to regret our decision. Both girls did well, and Eriko, an honors student, went on to do a year's graduate work in biology. What we didn't think of, however, was that during college many students develop contacts and friendships, some of which will last a lifetime. And that very few of the boys our daughters would be meeting at their California colleges would be Japanese. It was several years before we had to confront our feelings about this. When the time came, my own reaction was one that I could not have anticipated. I wasn't worried about nationality. I was worried about the divorce rate in America.

21

The Cheese in the Mousetrap

No one likes to pay bills but I remember how impressed I was when we received our first phone and utilities bills after we moved into our Flushing apartment. I showed them to Kuniko and said, "Look, in America the phone bill comes from New York Bell, a company named for Alexander Graham Bell, the American who invented the telephone. And the electric bill comes from Consolidated Edison. That's named for the American who invented the light bulb and other electric appliances. It shows how far ahead the Americans are in technology." Kuniko nodded, but I don't think she was as impressed as I was. We still had to pay the bills.

I hear a lot about Japanese technology beating out American products in international markets—and in the American market as well. But I have lived in the United States too long to believe that. I've flown in American airplanes. I drive an American car. I wear American-made clothes and live in a high-rise apartment built by American construction workers. Most important of all, I have to compete against American companies like IBM, Xerox, and Kodak. Believe me, if American technology were so bad, I wouldn't have so much trouble competing. And I have had trouble. Imagine coming to America, the home of Kodak and Xerox, to try to sell cameras and copiers.

Yes, Minolta has some pretty good products, but not, in many cases, any better than our American competitors. The past twenty years that I have lived and worked in America have convinced me that poor technology and poor workmanship haven't been America's problems. American firms have continued to invent, design, and produce the better mousetrap. But marketing, what I call the cheese in the mousetrap, has been a weak point. For most American companies, the problem has been bad marketing decisions, rather than poor manufacturing capabilities. Consider the case of the Hoover vacuum cleaner.

Soon after we settled in New York in 1969, my wife and I bought a Hoover. It was virtually unchanged from the model I had bought when I rented a room in a private home in New York fifteen years before. At first, with my usual admiration for all things American, I took this to be a good sign. I told Kuniko American technology was so superior there had been no need to change the vacuum cleaner in all these years. It wasn't technological or production shortcomings that had held Hoover back. It was a marketing decision. Hoover had a vast and growing American market to supply. It had little effective domestic competition and, for many years, even less foreign competition. From a marketing point of view, there was no real need to modernize the product. Certainly Hoover could have updated and improved its products, and since then it has. But I began to wonder about the eventual impact of such marketing decisions on America's technological and production capabilities. By the end of the 1970s it was clear that in such major industries as steel and autos, short-sighted marketing decisions had held back the modernization of America's manufacturing capabilities. The failure to adapt quickly to the need for fuel-efficient autos after the 1973 oil crisis and the failure to modernize production facilities in both the steel and auto industries left the United States vulnerable to foreign competition.

On the other hand, in most respects American technology continued to overwhelm me—and the world. Take Xerox, for example. For several years, Minolta had been trying to break into a copier market that was dominated by Xerox with its strong technology and marketing know-how. Between 1959, when it introduced the world's first successful plain paper copier, the 914, and 1968 Xerox had grown from virtually nothing to a company that reached a billion dollars in international sales, which is about half of what Minolta does today. No company has ever grown so rapidly. The name Xerox is derived from the Greek word for "dry writing." Most copiers then on the market used a liquid development process that produced wet, messy copies. Using Xerox's dry toner process gave dry copies on plain paper, which meant you could make notes on your copies, something you couldn't do on wet or coated paper. It also meant a big reduction in paper costs. But Minolta and a few other Japanese companies realized that Xerox did have a couple of weak spots.

First, it ignored the lower end of the market. Most of Xerox's machines were designed to handle heavy copy volumes. They competed against equipment ranging from mimeographs and Ditto machines to more sophisticated duplicators and photostatic copiers. Several Japanese firms thought they could break into the American copier market by competing against something much simpler—carbon paper.

Most of Xerox's machines were too big and too expensive to do a cost-effective job of reproducing something as basic as one file copy of a two-page letter. Sets of carbon paper were commonly used for five or six copies for filing and distribution to several people. Making corrections by eraser was a laborious process. A copier that could take one easily corrected original and inexpensively and quickly make a few copies could find a market that Xerox had ignored.

Xerox had another vulnerable point. It rented, rather than sold, its machines. Costs to end-users—and profits to Xerox—were high. And no matter how much they paid out in rent, fees per copy, supplies, and service costs, customers never owned the machine. I must emphasize that these vulnerabilities were based on marketing decisions, not technological shortcomings. Xerox certainly could have sold as well as rented its machines and has since done so. In addition, Xerox no longer ignores the middle and low ends of the market. It rounded out its product line with smaller copiers made in Japan by Fuji Xerox. But, during the 1970s, its domination of the vast American market led Xerox to ignore the market niches that the Japanese made their own.

In Japan, KT was one of the first to realize that the camera market was nearing a point of maturity at which growth would begin to slow down. To keep expanding, companies like Minolta would have to diversify. Optics and electronics, the two key technologies then used in cameras, were also basic to copier technology. We believed we could create a low-cost machine that, at a relatively low price, could be sold outright rather than rented. The move made sense, but at first we had only a vague notion of what we were doing.

Minolta wasn't alone in starting out shakily in the copier field. Several American firms also recognized that Xerox might be vulnerable at the lower end of the market, and at first they did a better job of trying to fill the gap than any of the Japanese firms. The most successful was APĒCO (American Photocopy Equipment Company).

The APĒCO machines were inexpensive, in the two-to-three-thousand-dollar range, but rather flimsy. Per-copy costs were a modest three cents, but copy quality was poor. APĒCO, however, more than any other firm, knew how to find a market. From the end of World War II until the ascent of Xerox, APĒCO was the most successful copier company in the world. Its eventual decline turned out to be a boon for Minolta and many other companies in the business equipment industry, not because there was one less competitor but because so many APĒCO-trained sales and marketing dynamos were available for new careers. Today you can find APĒCO alumni throughout the industry.

APĒCO thrived because of its sophisticated marketing and sales training programs. Its sales managers were the first to bring the "puppy dog" sales approach to the copier industry. Rather than expecting the customer to come to a sales showroom, as Xerox did, an APĒCO salesman would demonstrate the copier in the customer's office and then leave it for a trial period. The idea is that once you have the "cute little puppy" for a few days, you can't resist buying it. APĒCO also led the way in selling copiers to independent business equipment dealers rather than to end-users, pioneering the approach later taken by Minolta and the other Japanese manufacturers.

Xerox's impact on copier technology and the impact of Japanese competition on Xerox have drawn considerable attention in the media, in popular and scholarly books, in business schools, and even in political debates on international trade. But the APĒCO story, and the importance of marketing as opposed to technology, has been largely ignored. Undoubtedly, Japanese competition hurt Xerox. The lead paragraph in a *Wall Street Journal* story in 1981 told how an apparel store in Salisbury, Maryland, after using Xerox for ten years, had bought three Minolta copiers for the price of one Xerox. The article quoted the store manager as saying, "We didn't need all that speed. Besides, the Minolta's reproduction is clearer and its per-copy cost is about half that of Xerox." As Gary Jacobson and John Hillkirk note in their book, *Xerox: American Samurai*, "From 1976 to 1982, Xerox's share of worldwide copier revenues dropped by half, from 82 to 41 percent. Japanese companies, led by Canon, Minolta, Ricoh and Sharp, were mostly responsible." That book, which extensively quotes Al Kusada, Minolta's vice-president for business equipment in the American market, tells how the Japanese manufacturers cut into Xerox's market share and how Xerox staged its comeback. Xerox remained profitable and, in the early 1980s, began to improve both its product line and its manufacturing and distribution procedures. In recent years Xerox, which has also used Dr. Deming as a consultant, has regained considerable market share against the Japanese manufacturers. It was really the smaller American firms, like APĒCO, that suffered the most from Japanese competition.

Minolta's first effort to break into the copier market—selling the Minoltafax 41 through Graphic Communications—was fairly typical of the approach taken by other Japanese camera companies. Konishiroku, for example, began providing copiers that Royal, a Litton Industries subsidiary, sold under its name. Savin, an American firm, ran into union problems at its Bronx plant and began a long and successful period of marketing under its name copiers made in Japan by Riken Kogaku. Xerox had created a market demand for copiers that far exceeded the supply. It seemed that every company in America felt it could not survive without copiers. As Minolta and the other companies moved in, successful business equipment dealers became millionaires in a matter of months. Salesmen from American firms like Xerox and Savin made enough money to set themselves up as independent dealers, often handling Japanese products. Sales were great, sales projections were staggering, and credit was easy. It seemed that anyone could make money in the copier business, even with sloppy management.

Demand was so great that success required little more than a reasonable inventory of products and some basic sales skills. It also became difficult to find and keep qualified sales personnel for business equipment. The photo industry was fairly mature by that time, and compensation was pretty well standardized for each level of employment. But the copier business was brand-new and booming. I interviewed many young sales managers who were asking three times as much as what we were paying for comparable jobs in our photo division. As we moved from working through a small number of distributors to selling directly to a large number of dealers and retail outlets in both photo and business equipment, I had a tough time creating two separate sales forces.

In business equipment, the toughest area, the decline in the fortunes of APĒCO came just in time for us. I could never name all of the people who learned their trade at APĒCO who have also played an important role in Minolta's business equipment division. Ken Leon was perhaps our first hire from APĒCO, where he had been a major accounts manager. Ken, like John Glenn, was a Marine Corps veteran, and I thought he would be the ideal man to set up our copier sales force. Charlie Panarella, the man I selected to create our photo sales force, had a similar type of personality. Like Ken Leon, he was outgoing, aggressive, and tough. He came to us from GAF-Ansco, where, again like Ken Leon, he had been a major accounts manager. Camera sales soared and Panarella set up a nationwide system with distribution, service, and training centers near Chicago, Atlanta, and Los Angeles and a sales office in Dallas. Both Panarella and Leon did an excellent job in getting us started with our own direct sales staff, but neither stayed with us very long. Two of the men that Charlie developed, however, Jim de Merlier and Bob Lathrop, are still with us and have become the mainstays of our photo marketing and sales operations. They are also the first Americans to have become Minolta vice-presidents.

Ken Fukae, whom I had recruited in the 1950s, and John Poppen, whom I hired away from Royal in 1975, became long-term top men in our business equipment division. John, who had been president of Royal's Canadian operation, had a knack for hiring good people, and I gave him the freedom to build his own staff. Throughout my career at Minolta I have always been lucky enough to have bosses who have given me a reasonable amount of freedom to make my own decisions—and even on occasion my own mistakes. It seems to me that it's human nature to do our best when we are given full responsibility for the job assigned to us. Too often, shared responsibility gives us a chance to shirk our duties. KT was my role model in this approach to management. I give 100 percent authority to the people I trust, but I always want to be kept informed. If I see something moving in the wrong direction, I step in to keep our people from making what may turn out to be a great mistake. But I don't try to control all our day-to-day operations. Americans seem to appreciate this approach more than Japanese do. Many Japanese prefer the security of letting the boss make all the decisions.

The most successful Japanese companies operating in America follow Minolta's approach of letting their managers on the scene make most of their own decisions. Others have to check with the home office even on the smallest matters, which is the usual pattern in Japan. Like other Japanese managers given senior responsibility in an American subsidiary, I find adjustments have to be made for the more independent spirit of the Americans who work for us. The managerial style that I have evolved for the most part has worked quite well. Most of the people I have trusted have functioned as I thought they would. From time to time, however, this approach has backfired with managers to whom I have given too much authority. A few just couldn't handle the responsibility. They became too anxious, too nervous to be able to function effectively. But most often when American managers go off track it's because they become too ambitious.

I sometimes suspect that within every American corporate executive there's an entrepreneur struggling to get out. This spirit is a necessary ingredient in the makeup of the successful corporate official. It is also a vital ingredient in the dynamic nature of the American business world. Without it, the new ventures, the exciting innovations that so often have fueled business growth in the United States, would be sharply limited. That drive for independence has helped to make America the great country that it is. But when the entrepreneurial spirit gets too strong in a corporate manager, it's difficult for him to continue being a good company man, a good team player. As a manager's confidence develops through success in the corporation, the urge to get rich overnight sometimes proves overwhelming. Over the years Minolta has lost some very good people, some of whom left to set up businesses of their own. This certainly happened in the business equipment industry with successful sales managers who went on to set up their own dealerships. There have also been some whom we had to fire because they could no longer work effectively within the corporate framework. But for the manager who prefers the corporate setting, the Japanese style can provide a better atmosphere than many American companies. In Japanese companies, loyalty works both ways. We seldom fire anyone, and layoffs are rare. In many American companies, top management expects undying loyalty from its employees, but in some cases management's loyalty to employees is only as strong as yesterday's job performance or last month's profits. Of necessity, in running Minolta Corporation I have had to blend the best of the Japanese system of loyalty with the best of the American preference for independence and responsibility. It has worked well, helping us to find and keep people with the necessary balance of initiative and staying power.

We soon developed the nucleus of a good sales force for both our camera and copier lines. There was only one problem. Though our camera line was strong, we didn't have a really first-class copier. The 1714 series did fairly well, particularly because of its reduction capabilities. But many firms by then had comparable units. And for three or four years our new product efforts were flops. We had started to sell directly to dealers but had signed up just thirteen. All were doing well, and we also had some success selling directly to banks, insurance firms, and other large corporations in the New York area. But to get national reach, we needed the kind of product that would appeal to more dealers. I was beginning to despair, but I soon found out that help was on the way.

22

Minolta 101:
Cameras to Copiers

Two products and an address tell a lot about the growth of Minolta Corporation since the mid-1960s. Having introduced the original SR-T 101 single-lens reflex (SLR) camera with a through-the-lens exposure meter in 1966, we continued to produce cameras in the series until 1981. They became Minolta Corporation's best-sellers. When I returned to America we were selling about three hundred SLR cameras a month. KT told me it was his dream that one day Minolta might sell a thousand a month. We reached that goal by 1973 and were soon selling three to five thousand a month, replacing Nikon as number one in the SLR market in the United States.

The SR-T 101, expensive for that time at about $260, was a solidly constructed and well-balanced camera that felt good to handle. The modern term is *ergonomics*, but in those days we used the phrase *human engineering* to describe products that were designed with the reactions of the end-user in mind. The SR-T 101 had all the semiautomatic features then so popular in America. Many people who bought a camera in the SR-T series a decade or two ago still use it today. In my own opinion it was the best of the old-fashioned, me-

202

chanically operated cameras. I kept telling the home office in Japan that we needed a copier as good as the SR-T 101 if we were going to have much impact on the American business equipment market.

The SR-T 101 had helped us to expand our American operations to the point where we could afford to consider building our own corporate headquarters. When I first returned to the United States in 1969, however, Minolta rented space at 200 Park Avenue South at East Seventeenth Street where our windows overlooked Manhattan's then rather seedy Union Square Park and its famous but now vanished S. Klein department store.

The city I'd loved so much in the 1950s had entered a period of sad decline. The Vietnam War was at its peak and, in New York at least, a sense of disillusionment had set in. The city retained its old vibrancy, but the streets seemed dirtier and more snarled by traffic even though New York had lost both population and jobs. The city faced severe financial problems and had begun to cut back on basic services. About the only good news New Yorkers had that year came from their sports teams. The Jets won the Super Bowl, the Mets won the World Series, and, the following winter, the Knicks beat the Los Angeles Lakers for the professional basketball title. The Mets' victory was considered so important that it was credited with helping Mayor John Lindsay, whose popularity had declined with the fortunes of the city, to win reelection. Since I'm not a sports fan, however, I couldn't much share in the enthusiasm. Our apartment building in Flushing, then the tallest in the area, gave us a sweeping view of the city from La Guardia airport to the Manhattan skyline. But as I looked out on that panorama I felt a strong nostalgia for the New York I had known fifteen years before.

The move out of Kanematsu and into our own offices was only one of the changes Ken Nakamura had made while I was in Japan. He had also obtained warehouse and additional office space in Long Island City. What was more important, he'd changed our advertising strategy and, in the process, moved to a new agency.

My old mentor Jesse Wilkes corrected me in a conversation a few years ago when I referred to his agency as "small." "It was the biggest ad agency in the photo industry," Jesse said proudly.

And it was. But Jesse concentrated almost exclusively on the fan and trade photo publications, with an occasional ad in *Life* and *Playboy*. But by the mid-1960s Minolta was selling also to department stores as well as specialty photo stores. To target their customers, we needed to reach out more broadly to consumer publications, including *Time, Newsweek*, and *Sports Illustrated.* Our move into the business equipment field called for an entirely different approach to advertising. This involved not only different media, but also more extensive direct mail and cooperative advertising with dealers, a process we had begun earlier with our camera distributors. Ken had therefore shifted our advertising to E. T. Howard, a midsized firm that could provide a wider range of services. It wasn't long before we had to make another change to a much larger agency.

As our business grew, I realized we needed a new location. The problem wasn't so much office space as it was our distribution needs. We were trying to supply a nationwide sales network with products that now included relatively bulky copiers as well as compact cameras. Both our warehouses in Long Island City and our downtown Manhattan offices gave us nightmares in terms of transportation. We had to deal with freight elevators that moved even more slowly than trucks stalled by traffic on the city's congested streets. Our Manhattan offices did have one advantage. They were close to my favorite Italian restaurant, Paul and Jimmy's, which was then on Irving Place near Seventeenth Street. Minolta people who were with us then tell me the waiters didn't bother to ask me what I wanted because it was always linguine and clam sauce. I think they exaggerate, but I did order it often.

Steady increases in rents and taxes and the steady decline in city services also encouraged me to move. We considered sites everywhere from the Midwest, because it's ideal for nationwide distribution, to California, because of its proximity to Japan. But I was reluctant to leave New York because of the city's importance as a financial, informational, and media center. The best creative advertising talent has always been concentrated in New York, and I realized how important advertising would be for a company so little known in so vast a market.

The New York area also has a strong concentration of corporate headquarters and, as we moved into the business equipment industry, that gave us another reason for sticking close to the city. I started hunting, first on Long Island. But I soon realized that Long Island's transportation problems were getting to be as bad as New York's. I next scouted around in New Jersey and found an ideal spot in a commercial park that was being developed in northern Bergen

County. In those days the area was still largely rural but roads were good and access to New York was easy. With the financial nest egg we had earned from our SR-T 101 camera sales, we bought the land in 1973 and in May 1974 moved into our handsome new building in its campuslike setting in Ramsey, New Jersey.

On one of my trips back to Japan I tried to persuade my parents to visit America. I was particularly anxious to convince my father to come, for he had long dreamed of the great country that had produced men like Henry Ford and technology that he considered the finest in the world. But it didn't work out that way. My mother, Fumie, jumped at the opportunity, but my father, in his conservative way, backed off. Despite his admiration for technology, he feared flying and did not enjoy travel in general. There might also have been something deeper at work. My father's dream of America was so pure that he might have sensed that the reality could never match it. As hard as I tried, I could never convince him to come to America. I flew to the States with my mother February 2, 1973. It was her first trip out of Japan since returning from Korea, and her first flight in a plane. She stayed with us for three months and had the time of her life. Of course, I took her to see Minolta's new American head-quarters, which was then being built. I'm not sure if my mother has ever quite understood what I do for a living or why I think it's so important. But seeing our new building going up gave her something visible to latch on to. She told me she was very proud to see what her son was doing.

Fumie, of course, enjoyed being able to spend so much time with her young granddaughters, but she also enjoyed the trips we took her on. "I knew it was going to be big," she said one day, "but America is so beautiful." We drove up through New England to Montreal, Toronto, and Niagara Falls. But, best of all from my mother's point of view, was the trip to Washington, D.C., at the time of the cherry blossom festival. She declared it more beautiful in Washington, where the trees were sturdier and the blossoms fuller, than in Japan. "The soil must be richer in America," she said. "No wonder it's such a wealthy country." Fumie speaks no English and, as we traveled, I thought how sad it was that my father was not with her, using his command of the language to enrich her understanding of the people and places she visited. We flew with her to Los Angeles and, after visiting with Kuniko's relatives, the Aratanis, she flew back to Japan by herself, a little old lady in her sixties, unafraid of the giant silver bird that would carry her back home, and filled with stories of the magic land she had visited.

Meanwhile, at our construction site, the new Minolta building went up rapidly. The road that winds through our little campus is called Williams Drive. I asked town officials for permission to establish our address as 101 Williams Drive in honor of the SR-T 101. That remains our address to this day, and I still think of our building as the house that the 101 built.

KT came over for the official opening, which turned out to be a gala—and important—event. We had a gaily decorated tent on our parking lot, a dance band, and flags with the Japanese symbol for the month of May, the carp, which also means samurai spirit. Though uniforms are not popular among American workers, that day all the secretaries wore white blouses and dark skirts. KT joined me in the *kagamiwari* ceremony, putting on a Japanese *happi* coat while I used a wooden mallet to smash open a keg of *sake* and then poured cups for each guest. KT and our other guests from Japan teased me about the elegance of our new headquarters, saying we had moved into Karwizawa, a famous resort outside Tokyo that had been developed by wealthy foreigners in the 1920s. Other guests, including our dealers, our competitors, and journalists from the trade and consumer media, were also impressed. We were the first Japanese photo and business equipment company to build our own headquarters in the United States, a fact that attracted considerable attention and was taken as a symbol of the success of our decision to go into direct distribution. We were also the first Japanese company to set up headquarters in northern Bergen County. Many companies have since followed our lead, giving the county one of the highest concentrations of corporate headquarters in the country.

It was an important day for us, especially since I already knew that our lucky number—101—had come up again. By the mid-1970s my pitcher-catcher ties with Osaka included not only Ken Nakamura in charge of photo exports, but also Koji, who had been placed in charge of copier exports. KT, Koji, and others had heard our appeals for an outstanding copier for the American market. At about the time we moved into our new building at 101 Williams Drive, Minolta in Japan began producing the EG 101, an electrographic copier using the photodrum produced by the Varian Corporation in California.

Like the SR-T 101, the EG 101 turned out to be an enormously successful product right from the start.

What made the EG 101 so special was that for the first time there was an inexpensive copier that could offer the low-volume user most of the advantages of plain-paper copiers at a fraction of the cost. The secret was in the charged-transfer, latent-image method, which for the first time combined a photoconductor drum and a lightly coated paper. The drum was given a smaller electric charge than was needed in the electrostatic process. The drum was then exposed to the image to be copied, which was transferred to the paper in the form of a latent image. Because the charge was relatively light, the paper had to be treated with less than half the coating used in other methods. The paper had the feel of the ordinary bond paper you could use with a Xerox. You could make notes on it and get good halftone reproductions of photos and artwork.

We used a reproduction of the *Mona Lisa* in our test chart for demonstrations and in our advertising and direct mail, challenging people to distinguish the Minolta copy from the black-and-white original photo. The ads also used the term *bondlike paper* to distinguish it from both coated paper and the plain paper used in copiers that were so much more expensive. At a time when plain-paper copiers ranged from $25,000 to $100,000, we were able to offer the EG 101 at under $3,000 retail.

Dealer and consumer response was unbelievable. In terms of profitability, the EG 101 had an added advantage. Consumers could buy plain paper anywhere, but the specially treated paper needed for the EG 101 could be obtained only from Minolta and its authorized dealers. Dealers soon discovered they could make even more money on the paper than they could on the machines. The EG 101 put Minolta on the map in the business equipment industry and played a major role in changing the nature of the industry.

Though we also sold directly to customers, we realized we could never build the national sales network we needed without the help of independent American dealers who knew their local markets and how to sell in those markets. With the EG 101 we had a product that could make independent dealers extremely wealthy. Our dealer network expanded by leaps and bounds. By following the APĒCO pattern of heavy reliance on independent dealers, but with a far better product than any available to APĒCO, we were changing the way copiers would be sold.

Until this time, the dominant trade show in the industry had been BEMA, the Business Equipment *Manufacturers* Association, a show sponsored by manufacturers and aimed at attracting business equipment buyers. The industry's dominant association and trade show has since become NOMDA, the National Office Machine *Dealers* Association, sponsored by the dealers for their own members to attend, with the manufacturers paying for space to demonstrate their products. The dealers have moved from a secondary to a major role in the industry, an historic change that Minolta and the EG 101 had a lot to do with.

In June 1974, a few months after we opened our new building, I returned to Japan and was named to the board of directors of our parent company, Minolta Camera Company, Ltd. I considered it a mark of recognition not of me personally, but of the growing importance of Minolta's market in America. In the early 1970s we had to create what was virtually a brand-new company, but we were so successful that the other Japanese camera and copier companies soon followed our lead and went into direct distribution to retailers and dealers. By 1975, Minolta's exports accounted for 80 percent of our sales. And nearly half of our worldwide exports went to the United States and Canada.

Though our address in America comes from the SR-T 101 camera, Minolta Corporation also owes much of its success in those years to the EG 101 copier. Those two products, and our decision to go to direct distribution, gave Minolta Corporation the chance to have a much bigger and more profitable operation in North America. However, those two products also had a problem.

They were too good. And they almost caused our downfall.

23

America, the Beautiful

Minolta Corporation, in both the photo and business equipment industries, has the reputation of having excellent dealer relations. If that reputation is at all deserved, it's because we realize that without our American dealers we are nothing. We can never know the United States and its countless local markets the way our dealers do. We now have over five thousand photo dealers all across the United States and Canada and more than five hundred copier, officer automation, and micrographic dealers. Because of their smaller number, relations with our business equipment dealers are closer, almost like those of a family, than they can be with our vast number of photo dealers. But in both industries many close personal ties have developed, and we consistently make every legally permissible effort to help our dealers succeed. Our dealer incentive trips, our participation in trade shows, our dealer training programs, our sell-through dealer support, and our after-sales dealer service support all earn high marks.

Thanks to the SR-T 101 and the groundwork laid by Ken Nakamura, we were able to hold our first photo dealer incentive trip—to Germany, Italy, and France—in 1971, two years after I returned to the United States to pioneer direct distribution to dealers. We had about 400 people on that first trip, but the trip that will always stand out in my mind is the one we made in 1973 aboard the cruise ship *Sea Venture*. We had 780 people, dealers and their wives, with us on a cruise that took us to several Caribbean islands. The *Sea Venture*, renamed *Pacific Princess*, later provided the setting for the television series "The Love Boat." It is a luxurious ship with swimming pools, two nightclubs, theaters, and more bars than I could count. Rough seas hit us coming out of New York and some of our guests were seasick. But that soon passed, and the rest of the cruise was wonderful.

That was the first time we hired celebrities to entertain our dealers. The dealers, many of whom were Jewish, loved the comedian Myron Cohen, most of whose jokes are about being Jewish. They were equally enthusiastic about the singer Helen O'Connell, whose biggest hit had been "Amapola" way back in the 1940s. The song had been nearly as popular in Japan as it had been in the United States, and I was excited that Minolta had been able to hire the artist who made that famous record. She was still a very beautiful woman in 1973 and still a great performer thirteen years later when she sang with the "Four Girls Four" group of big-band singers for our business equipment dealer party at a NOMDA convention in Las Vegas.

The cruise lasted ten days, which gave many of our guests a chance to get to know our celebrity entertainers. It also gave me a chance to get to know dealers who until then were only names on paper or voices at the other end of a phone line. My wife and I were very busy, visiting as many cabins as possible and socializing at the many events scheduled throughout the trip. Though we met many new people, there were also old friends on board, including Eddie Ritz. When I headed Minolta's export department, he was one of the few dealers big enough to be able to afford visits to Japan. His Washington-based Ritz Cameras is one of the biggest retail photo chain operations in the United States, with outlets covering most of the country with the notable exception of New York.

There have been many memorable trips with photo, business equipment, and micrographics dealers since that "Love Boat" cruise. We've been to Ireland, Rome, Rio, Paris, Monte Carlo, Yugoslavia, Munich, Greece, Portugal, Spain, Bermuda, Hawaii, Acapulco, and Japan. In 1979, so many photo dealers made their quotas that we had to schedule two trips to Hong Kong to handle all those who qualified.

But that cruise on the *Sea Venture* still stands out in my mind. One warm evening my wife and I stood on the ship's bridge with the captain, listening to the laughter and music from the decks below, gazing at the stars that stretched to the horizon. My thoughts swept back to the first sea voyage I had taken, traveling third class deep in the bowels of the *President Wilson* with my two suitcases of cameras that I would try to sell in America. Less than twenty years later I stood on the bridge of a much bigger and more luxurious ship, which Minolta could afford to charter for nearly eight hundred guests.

The phrase *only in America* kept running through my mind. I told Kuniko how grateful I was to the dealers who were on that ship, the most successful of the more than six thousand large and small photo dealers we had then. I also wrote to KT and my parents, trying to explain how I felt. "Minolta should give thanks," I told them, "to the bighearted and open-minded people of America." As I stood on the bridge that night, I thought that twenty years ago we had nothing, and now I almost felt as though I were the captain of a great ship, sailing smoothly through untroubled waters on a starry night. But while I was dreaming, our competitors weren't sleeping.

The first shock came from Canon in 1976 when it introduced the AE-1, the first camera with an electronically controlled exposure system. Previous automatic-exposure cameras required the photographer either to set the lens aperture, which controls the brightness of the image striking the film, to get an automatically determined shutter speed (lens priority) or to set the shutter speed to get an automatic aperture setting (shutter priority). The AE-1 automatically set an appropriate aperture/shutter speed. Its point-and-shoot simplicity appealed to the American market with its passion for automation. By relying heavily on electronics, Canon was able to reduce the number of mechanical parts. This made the AE-1 smaller, lighter, and easier to use than previous cameras, and it reduced the potential for mechanical breakdowns and trips to the repair shop. It also enabled Canon to price the AE-1 at about 25 percent below competing cameras with more moving parts.

For years I had been dreaming of a product that would have enough mass appeal to justify television advertising. Now Canon had the product. The AE-1 was cheap enough to sell to the vast target audience that can only be reached by television. Though lens-shutter compact cameras had mass appeal, they were priced too low to promote in a medium as expensive as television. Canon, with a more sophisticated single-lens reflex camera, priced just right for both mass appeal and promotion by television, had all the ingredients for a major marketing breakthrough. They did not miss the opportunity.

Canon had great confidence in the appeal of the AE-1 and took the bold step of becoming the first Japanese camera company to advertise heavily on television. That decision, even more than the camera itself, was the key to Canon's great success with the AE-1. It launched its ad campaign with tennis star John Newcombe, spending $1.5 million on network television coverage of the 1976 Olympics in Montreal. Very quickly, Canon replaced Minolta as number one in the SLR camera market.

About a year after Canon introduced the AE-1, my dream of advertising on television came true. The Minolta XG had the same advantages as the AE-1. Ken Nakamura had been working with a young account executive, Al Shapiro, at our agency, E. T. Howard. Al not only knew the advertising business but also understood photo marketing. At that time he was extremely helpful to us as an adviser in many areas, including product development and modification for the American market. He knew the American photo market better than our own Minolta people and had the respect of key Minolta officials back in Japan. E. T. Howard, however, had no television capabilities. We realized we needed a bigger agency and moved with Al Shapiro to Bozell & Jacobs, an agency that was to play a major role in our growth over the next several years.

Minolta, however, like the rest of the photo industry, was in the position of playing catch-up to Canon and the AE-1. Minolta introduced two first-rate cameras in 1977. The XG-2 was unique in its electronic "touch switch" operating button, which used the latent electric current in the human finger to signal the circuitry. A more important breakthrough, the XD-7, packed a variety of technological innovations into a lightweight, compact, and highly versatile camera. The world's first multimode exposure camera, the XD-7, can be used in aperture priority, shutter priority, or manual mode. It can also override an incorrect setting determined by the photographer in difficult lighting situations. The XD-7 was the first in a new generation of "smart" cameras. As other companies like Olympus and Asahi

Pentax jumped in with comparable automatic-exposure cameras and television advertising, the overall size of the SLR market increased, over a four-year period, from 700,000 cameras a year to more than two million. Nevertheless, Canon had—and held—the lead. It took nearly ten years and another technological breakthrough to regain the market share we had lost to Canon.

We also fell behind in the copier field by resting on our laurels. The EG 101 did very well but we stayed with the electrographic process and "bondlike" paper too long, while other companies moved into relatively inexpensive, midvolume plain-paper copiers. During the late 1970s, we introduced two more electrographic machines. The EG 201 was a console model, bigger and designed for higher copy volumes than the 101. The EG 301 was a significant technological breakthrough. It was the world's first copier to use focused fiber optics in the imaging process, which produced outstanding copy quality. Fiber optics also enabled us to reduce the size, manufacturing cost, and number of movable, mechanical parts.

We remained profitable, though shortsighted, by sticking to coated paper while other Japanese firms struggled valiantly, though without much success, to challenge Xerox on its home ground, the plain-paper copier market. The first successful Japanese-made plain-paper copier, sold in the United States as the Savin 750, was introduced by Ricoh in 1975, the same year it won Japan's Deming Prize for total quality control. Ricoh took advantage of the prize to give the 750 worldwide publicity. Copy quality was fairly good, and it broke down less often and was easier and cheaper to repair than the big Xerox copiers. Savin advertising challenged Xerox by name, which was still unusual in those days.

The energy crisis had hit America in 1973, and Savin salesmen compared the energy-saving advantages of a Japanese-made copier with the advantages, well recognized by then, of energy-saving Japanese automobiles. They also stressed the cost advantage of buying a quality copier for what it would cost to lease a Xerox for just one year.

Minolta tried to develop a plain-paper copier in the early 1970s. But with the promising EG 101 coming to market, the effort never amounted to much and the machine was never sold. We introduced our first plain-paper copier, the EP 510, in 1978. It produced a beautiful, jet-black image, the best copy quality then available. We pushed very hard, and at first it sold well. The machines functioned well in moderate use; but when they were worked hard, or underutilized, they jammed often. We realized that climate and central heating were part of our problem in America. In Europe and Japan, humidity is high. And in winter, homes and offices are not heated as intensely as they are in America. I had first discovered this with the cameras I brought to the United States in the 1950s. Copier drums and plain paper are also sensitive to variations in heat and humidity. Because it used coated paper, we had few problems with the EG 101. But in parts of the United States, like Nevada, that are very dry, and in offices dried out by central heating, we encountered all kinds of strange problems with our plain-paper copiers. At first we were mystified and sent engineers to the scene to make on-the-spot tests.

Once we identified the problems, we designed special testing rooms back in Japan to simulate conditions in the United States. We discovered it wasn't enough to adjust our products for the American market. The United States is so huge and varied that we have to adjust for various markets within the United States. What works well in southern Nevada may not work well in southern Florida, which is warm but humid, or in Alaska, which is cold and dry.

In 1979, we introduced our first successful plain-paper copier, the EP 310. The EP 310 was a compact copier with a moving top that could handle both legal- and letter-size originals. It sold well, and Minolta hung in as a contender in the business equipment field with a series of copiers that met with varying degrees of success. Several had reduction or enlargement capabilities and some had both. We were moving toward a technological breakthrough that would again make us a major player in the business equipment market.

The Beta series of zoom-lens copiers, the world's first with a wide range of precise reduction and enlargement ratios that can be set by the operator simply by pressing a button, gave Minolta a significant technological edge over the rest of the industry during the mid-1980s. All previous reduction and enlargement copiers had only a limited number of preset ratios. Our zoom-lens copiers were also the first capable of automatically determining what paper size should be used based on the reduction or enlargement ratio, or, in a different operating mode, what reduction/enlargement ratio should be used based on the paper size selected by the operator.

Sales soared to the point where in 1983 and 1984 our business equipment revenues for the first time accounted for more than half our income. Projections made at the time called for business equipment to account for 70 percent of our revenues by 1990. It might have happened, but in 1985 a camera called the Maxxum came along and changed all that, putting Minolta once again ahead of Canon as number one in the American and world SLR camera markets.

The seesaw competitive battles in the American market that foreign firms wage against each other and, in our case, against major American firms like Xerox, have created one of the economic miracles of the last half of the twentieth century. The continuing importance of the vast American market makes it the most important battleground for global success. No multinational company can succeed if it fails in America.

Except for free-trade zones like Hong Kong and Panama, America continues to be the world's most open country in terms of both trade policy and consumer attitudes. For a businessman like myself, this is one of the great beauties of life in America, and it sets a standard that other countries, including Japan, would do well to equal. Competition in the United States is as close to being fair and equal as we are likely to see in any major market.

As a result, consumers in America—and that includes all of us who live here—are far better off in most respects than consumers anywhere else. The size and wealth of the American market, coupled with America's relatively open trade policies, give American consumers a greater range of choice and a greater degree of price competitiveness than are available to consumers in any other country. It amuses me that even in times like these, when the American dollar is very weak, some Americans still travel to Europe, duty-free islands in the Caribbean, or even to Hong Kong in search of bargains.

The best bargains—and the most stylish fashions—can be found in New York, in other major American cities, and in shopping malls across the country. Right now, for example, you can buy what many experts have said is the world's finest camera, the Minolta Maxxum, for less money in midtown Manhattan than you can in Osaka. Japanese living in California can buy better Japanese-style rice for less money than they could if they were living in Japan. Italian shoes, Spanish leather, jade from southeast Asia, Parisian fashions, and French perfumes can usually be bought in the United States at higher levels of quality and in greater variety than they can in their countries of origin. It is not a question of dumping by foreign competitors. The rice I referred to, for example, is grown in America. But foreign producers must compete successfully in America to prosper internationally. This fierce competition gives American consumers advantages enjoyed by consumers in no other country. To paraphrase the song, from the mountains to the prairies, to the oceans white with foam, God has blessed America.

24

Lighting Up Times Square

The Great White Way started going dark in the 1960s. The wonderful old theaters—the Capitol, Loew's State, the Criterion, the Rivoli, the Paramount, all in Times Square, and the Roxy on Sixth Avenue—shut down or were converted. And the fabulous signs disappeared. When I first came to New York those signs included a ten-story-high, multicolored fantasy advertising Wrigley's gum; the block-long Bond sign with its flowing waterfall flanked by giant statues of a man and a woman; towering bottles calling attention to Pepsi-Cola and Heinz ketchup; a TWA display that included a huge replica of an airplane with wings stretching out over Seventh Avenue; and, as I have mentioned, my own favorite, the Camel cigarette sign with a man blowing smoke rings of pure New York City steam heat out over Broadway. There were many more, of course, but one by one they started going out, replaced, in some cases, by huge but static billboards, or by nothing at all.

The fading lights of Broadway were a dark reflection of the general deterioration of the city in those years. The energy crisis caused by the oil embargo of 1973 accelerated the trend as campaigns were launched to conserve energy—including the energy of bright lights. That was the year I made my final decision to move Minolta out of New York. But I never felt quite right about turning my back on the city that had meant so much to me during my first years in America. By the early 1980s the lights began coming on again along Broadway, and in almost every case the sponsor of the new neon signs was a Japanese company. The story of how that happened has never been told before.

In my conversations with other Japanese businessmen at the Nippon Club and the Japanese Chamber of Commerce of New York, we discovered that many of us shared similar career paths and a strong, nostalgic attachment to New York City as we had first known it. We had come to the city as young men, most often in the 1950s, and were here again for a second or third tour of duty. Several of us now headed our firms' American subsidiaries, but none of us had much money when we had first been in New York. We had all spent many evenings in the Times Square area, going to movies or, since we were poor, simply enjoying the spectacle of bright lights and crowded streets. In those days, flying into New York at night, you could see a bluish glow spreading over the city from its neon heart in midtown Manhattan. In those days, Tokyo looked pallid from the air, covered with a pale yellowish light. Japan was still so poor that lights were turned off an hour or two each evening, and there were few advertising signs.

By the 1970s, the night sky over Tokyo looked bluer than New York. My Japanese colleagues in New York and I all knew that while Times Square was going dark, the Ginza in Tokyo and downtown parts of other cities in Japan had turned into a festive blaze of neon. We all considered the giant neon signs a good medium for advertising and believed that Times Square, like the Ginza, was a great location with heavy concentrations of traffic at all hours of the day and night. In addition, all our companies were now doing very well thanks to the relative openness of the American market and the buying power of American consumers. We realized we owed a debt to the generosity of the United States and of New York City, and we agreed that one way we could repay at least part of that debt would be by putting the lights back on Broadway. It seemed to me to be important both for New York City and for the United States to say that the lights are on again in the capital city of the world, that Times Square is not a dark and dreary place abandoned to muggers and derelicts.

My colleagues and I made a gentlemen's agreement to light up Times Square. Minolta moved its photo advertising business to William Esty in 1981, and the agency immediately began looking for a prime location. We didn't find the spot we wanted until 1983. By then several Japanese companies, including Sony, Canon, and Panasonic, and one American company, Coca-Cola, had all put up big new signs. The location we found was ideal: the northern façade of 1 Times Square, facing the X-shaped island formed by the crossing of Broadway and Seventh Avenue. Traffic on both streets runs south, toward the building, which looks out over the open area that stretches from Forty-third Street to Forty-seventh Street with sightlines beyond.

Built in 1904 by Adolph Ochs to provide new facilities, including basement printing presses, for his *New York Times*, the building has a proud history. Christened Times Tower with opening ceremonies on New Year's Eve, the building gave its name to the area. Since 1908, it has also been the site of the famous New Year's Eve ball drop. The moving headlines that wrap around the building with up-to-the-minute news bulletins are another long-standing tradition. The *Times* sold the building in 1961, and it has changed hands several times since. The most significant sale came in 1963, when Allied Chemical bought the building, stripped away its stone and terra-cotta exterior, and reskinned it with slabs of marble and gray glass. The animated Spectacolor sign, available to a multitude of advertisers, went up in 1982 on the lower floors of the building, which is shaped like a very tall piece of cake.

Even in its run-down state, Times Square is still the crossroads of the world. Surveys show that 1.5 million adults walk and drive through it every day, and that 71 percent "always" or "sometimes" look at 1 Times Square with its signs and running zipper of newspaper headlines. Each year 17 million visitors from out of town and overseas still make it a point to get to Times Square at least once. Despite the area's appearance in recent years, 45 percent of the adults who pass through Times Square have annual incomes of over $25,000. When I heard that the space above Spectacolor was being made available for the first time, I acted quickly.

I telexed Osaka, saying that Minolta Corporation had an opportunity to have a sign in Times Square. Since this was an international crossroads, visited by people from all over the world, including Europe and Japan, I believed that our parent company should also be part of this venture. I understand that when the telex arrived some of the younger people in our export and public relations departments called the sign "Sam's Sentimental Folly." To be frank, I am sentimental about our sign, but it was also a sound business decision. Our board of directors agreed to pay part of the cost. The sign, soaring the equivalent of sixteen stories, is not the biggest or the brightest on Times Square. That distinction belongs to Fuji. But it does have the dominant position. Its designers created a cascading effect in the letters that spell out our product lines—cameras, copiers, video— above the blue-and-white Minolta logo.

In addition to the hundreds of thousands who see the sign itself each day, it appears frequently on television news and weather reports, has been seen in several movies, shows up often in newspaper photographs, and has been sent all over the world on a popular Times Square postcard. More than a million people jam the square each year on New Year's Eve, watching the ball drop just above our sign, an event televised to an international audience of 200 million, the largest audience ever to watch any single event. We will never be able to measure fully the visibility Minolta gains through the sign. But to me—this is the sentimental part—the sign is even more important because helping to brighten up New York is one small way of saying thank you to the city I love so much and that has meant so much to Minolta through our years of struggle and growth.

We lit the sign for the first time on March 3, 1983. The lighting coincided with the dropping of the ball from the 1 Times Square tower. This was the only time the ball had ever been dropped other than on New Year's Eve, and we attracted considerable media coverage. Hugh Hefner, publisher of *Playboy*, arranged for its Playgirl of the Year, Shannon Tweed, to help me throw the switch. Shannon, who towered over me, was also appearing in a television series at the time, and the cameramen were as interested in her as they were in our sign. In my remarks that evening at a reception in the penthouse of the Hilton Hotel, I tried to give our guests some sense of the feelings I have both for the city and for the United States. Through the huge windows of the penthouse, we had a wonderful view of Times Square. A light rain was falling, and the wet streets below reflected the blue-and-white lights of our sign. To me it was a very beautiful sight.

Later that month, on March 25 in Las Vegas, KT was inducted into the Hall of Fame of the Photo Marketing Association, which has nearly nine thousand members in seventy-five countries. In July 1982, he had stepped down as president of Minolta Camera Company, Ltd. His oldest son, Henry, took over as president and KT moved into the newly created position of chairman of the board. Reluctantly, KT, in bad health, had begun to wind down his career.

KT became only the third Japanese named to the PMA Hall of Fame. The first had been my friend Kinji Moriyama, founder and chairman of the Japan Camera Inspection Institute and the Japan Camera Information and Service Center in New York. The long-term chairman of Canon, Inc., Takeshi Mitarai, was the second. As I watched KT being installed, I had no idea that three years later I would be the next Japanese to become a member.

My deepest pleasure at the time of KT's award was the fact that for the first time he had brought his wife, Mutsuko, with him on a trip to the United States, something I had been urging him to do for years. Even in 1978, when he was named Man of the Year by the Photo Manufacturers and Distributors Association, KT had come to the United States without Mutsuko. Being the old-fashioned entrepreneur that he was, KT believed that a business trip was solely for business. Only twice had he ever taken his wife on a business trip within Japan and this was Mutsuko's first trip abroad. But the PMA Hall of Fame is the highest honor our industry can bestow, and KT considered this trip very special. The newspaper *Nippon Keizai Shimbun*, regarded as the *Wall Street Journal* of Japan, published KT's autobiography in a series of twenty-six installments in June 1983. KT began the story of his life by describing the day he became a member of the PMA Hall of Fame. Then, in a flashback, he told the story of the rest of his life. Though he has won many other honors, including the Emperor's Second Order of the Treasury, his PMA honor is the only one he mentions in his autobiography.

After the PMA ceremonies, they came on to New York, including Henry and KT's favorite granddaughter, Naoko, for press interviews and, of course, a visit to Times Square to see our sign, which impressed KT very much.

The Tashimas stayed in the same Hilton Hotel penthouse suite we had used for our party the night the Minolta Times Square sign was lit for the first time. Minolta Corporation gave a reception honoring the Tashimas, but, even though I was paying for it, I wasn't able to attend. We were involved in a legal case with a dealer in Saint Louis whom we had discontinued for what the courts eventually agreed were valid reasons.

Not everyone was as pleased with our sign as KT and I. One magazine headline announced "Japanese Invade Times Square," and a newspaper editorial took us to task for "commercializing" the New Year's Eve tradition of the ball drop. Fortunately, these appear to have been minority viewpoints. It wasn't as if we were driving the Americans out. The American advertisers had already deserted Times Square, leaving it dark, before the Japanese "invasion." Now Coca-Cola, Kodak, Burger King, and other American firms are back in Times Square with dazzling signs that sell more than products. They sell the image of an America that has regained its confidence and reaffirmed its leadership on the world stage.

Japan's invasion of America—and of Times Square—has been matched by an American invasion of Japan—and the Ginza. The so-called 3-S Policy—sports, sex, and screen—introduced to Japan by General MacArthur's GHQ in the postwar years has had a profound effect on Japanese popular culture to this day. In fact, it's part of a worldwide phenomenon. Except in the more puritanical Communist, Islamic, and Third World nations, sports, sex, and American movies enjoy strong international popularity. American television, including the commercials, and popular American music might be added to the list. The use of American screen stars as advertising symbols is actually more common in Japan than in the United States. There are many examples. To me, the most interesting has been the late James Dean. Dean made relatively few movies in his life—*Giant*, *Rebel Without a Cause*, and, his most popular movie in Japan, *East of Eden*. As the misunderstood son in *East of Eden*, Dean became a folk hero among young people in Japan. He died young in an automobile accident, which added to his heroic stature in Japan, where drama and literature glorify tragic deaths.

With some good advice from a Japanese-American advertising agency, McCann-Erickson-Hakuhodo, James Dean became the symbol in a campaign that established Levi Strauss as a major force in the Japanese blue jeans market. In most of its export and overseas manufacturing operations, Levi Strauss has used the slogan "Original American Jeans." But in Japan, Levi Strauss decided to appeal to the buyers' emotions, targeting the young customers who make up the jeans market. James Dean became the symbol, and "Heroes Wear Levis" became the slogan.

Candice Bergen was the only American movie star used by Minolta in Japan. In addition to her screen reputation, she is a highly regarded professional photographer and is considered in Japan to be an exceptionally beautiful and sophisticated member of American high society. She was our advertising spokeswoman in 1978–1979 for our XD series of SLR cameras. Our television commercials featured Ms. Bergen taking photographs from a helicopter over the Las Vegas desert. The commercials relied on visual images to convey the message. There was just one bit of dialogue, spoken by Ms. Bergen in English—"Minolta is my style." The fact that the phrase was spoken in English gave it added appeal to the upscale audience we wanted to reach.

We have worked extensively with professional photographers in the United States, but not as advertising spokespersons. Celebrity photographers may not draw as much publicity as movie stars, but a well-executed public relations campaign can pay dividends. For example, during 1983, when the photojournalist Harry Benson was named Magazine Photographer of the Year, we arranged an extensive publicity tour. Linking practicing professionals with Minolta photo products increases consumer awareness of the quality and reliability of our equipment.

Minolta made perhaps its most successful use of a celebrity spokesman when we introduced our Beta series of zoom-lens copiers in 1983. They revolutionized copier technology and set a standard that the rest of the industry had to struggle to equal. After we introduced the first in the series, the EP 450Z, copier sales soared. This enabled us to increase our advertising budgets and even hire a very expensive spokesman, Tony Randall. Shortly before, Jack Klugman began what has by now become a fairly long association with Canon, advertising their small, personal copiers. Barbara Love, then advertising manager for our business equipment division, came up with the idea of hiring Randall, Klugman's co-star on "The Odd Couple." We drew considerable free publicity based on media and public interest in the pairing of Randall and Klugman on the still popular television series. The running joke on the show contrasts the passion for neatness of Felix Unger, as played by Randall, against the sloppiness of his roommate, Oscar, played by Klugman.

Randall's first commercial for Minolta was for the EP 650Z, a zoom-lens copier that can handle fairly high monthly volumes. Features include an automatic document feeder and collator, which gave

Randall a chance to praise it as a "neat copier." The closing line, which Randall wrote himself, went, "So you see, I'm not really a neat freak, but then I'm not a slob like . . ."

At a well-attended press conference to introduce both the EP 650Z and the commercial, Randall entertained the media with remarks on the fact that he is *not* the character he plays. He praised his co-star Jack Klugman, with whom he had just completed a tour of Australia in the play *The Odd Couple*, but insisted that far from being a real-life Felix Unger, he himself was a slob. Tony has since traveled with us on a business equipment dealer cruise to Mexico and to trade shows. From all accounts, he really isn't a neat freak. I've been told that his hotel room looks like a tornado hit within minutes after his arrival—and stays that way till he leaves. The free publicity stirred up by the "Odd Couple" of Klugman and Randall promoting rival copier lines gave Minolta nearly as much exposure as our paid advertising did. More than one television interview with Tony actually showed the commercial as a news clip.

Public relations can be an effective marketing tool, but it is not widely appreciated in Japan. I'm very keen on it, and in the years that I've worked in the United States I've learned that it can be particularly effective when tied to an advertising campaign. Well-integrated advertising and public relations efforts, like our Tony Randall campaign, can double the impression a company makes on its target audience.

Those two great stars, Tony Randall and Jack Klugman, will probably never escape the success of their roles in "The Odd Couple." Both have won wide acclaim for many other performances but, as the series continues in syndication on local stations across the country, the public continues to identify them as "The Odd Couple." Minolta has a similar problem.

Minolta is still thought of by most people only as a camera company, even though our business equipment sales in 1983 and 1984 exceeded our camera sales. This is a result of the heavy volume of consumer advertising we do to support our cameras in the mass media, particularly on television. The volume of our camera advertising dwarfs our business equipment advertising, and in advertising you get exactly what you pay for.

Bozell & Jacobs was still our advertising and public relations agency for business equipment when we introduced our Tony Randall campaign, but it was William Esty, the agency to which we had switched our photo advertising, that created our advertising tag line "Only From the Mind of Minolta." The Tony Randall campaign was the first time we used that tag for anything other than our photo line. Ever since, we have been using it for all our products. One of the main reasons we selected the Esty agency was the effective creative presentation they made built around that "Mind of Minolta" theme. Its first use was with the introduction of our X-700, a 35-mm single-lens reflex camera. The X-700 was an excellent camera, good enough to win the prestigious European Camera of the Year award in 1982, a fact we used in our advertising campaign. The Esty campaign demonstrated the power of creativity, with a variety of television, print, radio, direct mail, and point-of-sales display materials that helped the X-700 become one of our best-sellers of all time. Since 1983 we've continued to use "Only From the Mind of Minolta" as the tag line for all our products. This has helped us to build a more consistent image of Minolta as a producer of quality products in several fields.

The following year, we found another way to integrate our product promotions. Niagara Falls gets nearly as much tourist traffic as Times Square, seventeen million people a year, and for several years I had been envious of the visibility Panasonic enjoyed from the six-hundred-foot tower that bore its name on the Canadian side of the falls. In 1984, I heard from Minolta's Canadian subsidiary that Panasonic was giving up its lease on the tower. I moved quickly with Kaz Umeda, who was then Minolta's Canadian representative and has since become vice-president of our photo division in the United States. Together we picked up the lease and on May 23 we officially dedicated what is now known as the Minolta Tower. The tower, clearly visible from both sides of the falls, is topped by a huge Minolta sign above a six-story display area accessible by an elevator that runs up the tower's shaft. A variety of displays brings Minolta's full product line together in a museum-quality exhibition.

The international perspective of the tower, which looks out over Canada and the United States, has special meaning for me. Doing business across borders has been the story of my life, and making potential customers aware of Minolta's full range of quality products has been a major challenge in my professional career. The necessarily narrow focus of product advertising can convey a correspondingly narrow idea of what Minolta is all about. The Minolta Tower at Niagara Falls brings it all together.

Minolta advertises heavily on sports programs and, particularly in our camera commercials, we often use sports backgrounds. Buyers of expensive photo equipment and purchasing agents for business equipment tend to be men. And sports events appeal primarily to a male audience. Bruce Jenner, the track and field star, was one of the first sports heroes associated with Minolta. We featured him in several commercials for our XG-E cameras in 1979–1980. He spoke at sales meetings and became the focus of public relations efforts that increased Minolta's exposure. Through the years we've continued our involvement with sports. In 1988 we brought not just one but three sports heroes with us on our business equipment dealer incentive trip to Bermuda. All held seminars and led tournaments in their specialty: Arthur Ashe, tennis; Billy Casper, golf; and the America's Cup hero Dennis Conner.

Another event in which Minolta has been a long-term sponsor is the Miss Universe contest. Every year the finalists visit our New Jersey offices and meet with our employees, and in 1984 the winner, Miss Sweden, went to Photokina in West Germany as Minolta's guest. Beautiful women and photography go well together. And, again to reach that predominantly male audience that buys cameras, we continue to advertise frequently in magazines like *Playboy* and *Penthouse*.

It may be good for brand recognition—and a lot of fun—for an advertiser to have a well-known celebrity endorsing his products on network television. But when you have a product that breaks new ground in technology and offers important advantages to the consumer, you don't necessarily want to be identified with a pretty girl or a sports hero or a screen star. You may be better off letting your product speak for itself.

My education in learning how to market to Americans, which began with such early mentors as Bill Daly and Jesse Wilkes in the 1950s, has continued but, in more recent years, possibly no one has had more influence on my thinking than the Texan who has made a store in Dallas a worldwide symbol of luxury and elegance. The store, of course, is Neiman Marcus, and the man who made it famous, Stanley Marcus, is one of many reasons why Texas has had almost as much impact on my life as Times Square.

25

Texas and Me

Texas has always held a special place in my dream of America. It must have started with the cowboy movies I saw sandwiched in among the musicals, which were my favorites. Texas was surely part of me by the time I sailed for America aboard the SS *President Wilson* in my oversized Stetson fedora. But, unlike New York City, which pretty much confirmed the image I had of it when I first arrived, the Texas I have come to know and love is wildly different from the place created in my youthful imagination. Though Texas still has its John Wayne cowboys and oil field rough-necks, it's also the world of corporate boardrooms, the National Aeronautics and Space Administration center in Houston, major defense contractors and military installations, Neiman Marcus, the Dallas Symphony—and significant political power. It is also the world of Stanley Marcus and Liener Temerlin.

Marcus for many years was chairman of the Neiman Marcus specialty store chain. Its flagship store in Dallas and its famous catalog brought a new dimension of expensive elegance to retail merchandising. Perhaps no American since my early mentor Joseph Ehrenreich, who died suddenly of a heart attack in 1971, has had as much direct impact on my business philosophy as Stanley Marcus. I had read his books even before we met through Temerlin, who is chairman of Bozell & Jacobs, the agency to which we moved our advertising and public relations business in 1977. Based in Dallas, where the agency handles American Airlines, among other major clients, Liener Temerlin moves confidently in the Texas business, political, and cultural establishment. He and his wife, Karla, have been gracious hosts to me on several occasions and through him I've come to know a bit about the Texas that's reflected neither in the 1950 cowboy movie *Dallas* with Gary Cooper nor in the current television series of that name with Larry Hagman.

What has impressed me most about Marcus is his affection— perhaps I should say his passion—for high-quality products. One evening during dinner at the Temerlins' I asked him what had made him so successful. He said that when he gets excited by a first-rate new product, his affection carries all the way through store management to the salespeople and that this inevitably moves the customer. He believes anyone engaged in sales has to have that kind of emotion and find ways to communicate it to the people who work for him and to his customers. If you don't understand this, or don't know how to express your excitement to others, you are disqualified for sales.

I knew at once that he was absolutely right about this, but, until I heard him express it, I had never been able to formulate the idea. I began studying our most successful sales managers and dealers from what I think of as the Marcus perspective. All of them have that ability to become passionately fired up about truly superior products. Most of what's been written about the success of Japan as an exporting country has been told from the point of view of manufacturers and entrepreneurs. But I think of myself as a salesman and of my mission in bringing Minolta to the "New World" as the quest of a salesman with quality products to beat a path to his customer's door. The weight of those two suitcases of cameras I carried on my first trip to America is with me still. When I think of it, I can feel the straps cutting into my hands. But since those conversations with Stanley Marcus, I have realized that for the salesman emotion is even more important than hard work. Westerners have the belief that Orientals are incapable of emotion. No one who has ever heard me give one of my speeches on a topic that moves me—such as my gratitude to America, my feelings about my family and KT—could ever believe that about me. I sometimes have to blink away tears. But even Japanese who may be more inscrutable than I experience emotions more deeply than is obvious to the observer who doesn't know how to listen to silence. But what I learned from Stanley Marcus has been the importance of being able to put this emotion in words and convey it to others. Speaking at Minolta sales meetings and to dealer groups, I often quote him. I find that when I cite him as my authority when discussing the importance of emotion in business, I'm much more effective than when I try to convey similar ideas on my own. He has given me a clearer way to see something that I felt in my heart but could not explain, even to myself.

By 1984, Minolta was expanding rapidly and profitably, particularly in its micrographics and business equipment divisions. In 1982 we had introduced the world's first plain-paper reader-printer, the RP 505, and the following year the world's first zoom-lens copier, the EP 450Z. Such truly innovative products, properly marketed, have the best chance of success. Though competitors may follow with comparable products that may combine improved quality with lower prices, the innovator will nearly always maintain his advantage because of public perception of his technological leadership.

This has certainly been true of Minolta in the 1980s, and, thanks to Pope John Paul II and Japan's greatest all-round baseball player, Shigeo Nagashima, it inspired KT to think about exporting Japanese culture as well as Japanese products. In KT's mind, it was a subtle way of talking about creativity. Japan has still not escaped its reputation as a skilled copier of other people's innovations, perhaps with improved quality and lower prices, but certainly not with any originality. With the help of the Tokyo Giants' third baseman and subsequent manager, KT found a way to modify that perception.

Nagashima, in addition to being an outstanding baseball player, is also a public-spirited figure. In 1982, he had been invited to visit the Vatican by the pope and had been impressed by the treasures of the Vatican museum. Nagashima, a highly cultured man as well as an outstanding athlete, knew that Japan had comparable treasures that the West had never seen. On his return to Japan, he began to look for ways to promote his idea of introducing the rest of the world to Japan's hidden cultural heritage. Through Minolta's Japanese advertising agency, Dentsu, he met KT and, in the course of their discussions, the idea of a world tour of traditional Japanese art began to evolve.

Tensions over trade, defense, and other political issues were growing between the United States and Japan, and KT believed the time was ripe for Minolta to make a gesture toward bridging the gap. With the cooperation of Yoshinobu Tokugawa, a descendant of the Tokugawa shogun and director of the Tokugawa Art Museum in Nagoya, Minolta Camera Company sponsored an exhibition of nearly three hundred artworks from the Tokugawa shogun age (1600–1867), ranging from the swords, armor, and saddles of the samurai to exquisite tea-ceremony bowls and scroll paintings.

The exhibit opened in Los Angeles and then went on an eighteen-month tour that included Dallas, Munich, Paris, and Tokyo. James Clavell's novel *Shogun* and the television miniseries based on it had created widespread public interest in the shogun era and the founder of the Tokugawa dynasty, Tokugawa Ieyasu. In the early years of the seventeenth century, he unified Japan under his rule, ending over a century of feudal warfare. In addition to their great military and political power, the Tokugawa shoguns were also patrons of the arts, a role largely taken over in today's Japan by modern corporations. The shogun, however, kept Japan sealed off from the outside world. Today's corporate leaders believe in international economic and cultural exchange.

The shogun exhibit was the biggest collection of traditional art ever seen outside Japan, a fact that particularly impressed our Texas hosts, who are always interested in the biggest—as well as the best. Yoshinobu Tokugawa accompanied the show to the United States, along with KT and his eldest son, Henry, and their wives, and was with us for the Dallas opening on March 17, 1984. Liener Temerlin had been helpful in bringing the exhibit to the Dallas Museum, and he and his wife hosted a reception for several hundred people at their rambling home, which houses an impressive collection of art from around the world. This was a new world for me, the camera salesman from Japan socializing with people like Robert Crandall, chairman of American Airlines; H. Ross Perot, founder of Electronic Data Systems Corporation; the Dallas-based developer Trammell Crow; and James D. Robinson III, chairman and CEO of American Express. I must admit I was a bit star-struck, but this was the first time that Minolta in America had circulated with so many corporate leaders at one time.

At a dinner given by the trustees of the Dallas Museum, KT and his wife, Mutsuko, who was making her second trip outside Japan, shared a table with Kuniko and me and Mr. and Mrs. Ross Perot. Ken Follett's book *On the Wings of Eagles,* about the successful rescue mission Perot directed to free two of his employees who had been taken prisoner by Islamic radicals in Iran in 1979, had become a best-seller in Japan. Ned Moro, Minolta Camera Company's director of corporate communications, who is another veteran of Minolta's American training ground, had come over for the shogun exhibit and brought with him a copy of the book. I borrowed it and stayed up most of the night, reading the book from cover to cover.

The conversation at dinner was lively, focusing on Japanese and American technological innovations, world trade, and, of course, Japanese art. About a year later Perot invited my wife and me to attend the Winston Churchill Foundation award dinner being given in his honor in Dallas. The foundation gives occasional awards to individuals who have done outstanding work in the tradition of the former British prime minister. Perot was cited for his Iran rescue mission as well as for his work on behalf of American prisoners of war in Vietnam.

Prince Charles presented the award before an international audience that included First Lady Nancy Reagan and Churchill's daughter Lady Soames. Our table at dinner included Katharine Graham, chairman of the board of the Washington Post Corporation; Graham Whitehead, president of Jaguar Cars, Inc.; John Teets, chairman of Greyhound Corporation; and Merv Adelson, the Lorimar, Inc., chairman, who is married to Barbara Walters. My wife and I were also invited to a smaller reception at Perot's home, at which I had a chance to see this down-to-earth man in a more relaxed atmosphere. Despite his fame, he doesn't stand on ceremony. With his unpretentious ways he reminds me of Japanese businessmen like KT who do without the fancy trappings of success.

The impression Perot made also reminded me of Mike Mansfield, America's ambassador to Japan from 1977 to 1989. I met Mansfield when I served as Liener Temerlin's guide during one of his visits to Tokyo, in June 1981. This was the first time I had seen the inside of the American embassy building, which had been General MacArthur's residence during his six years as the Allied supreme commander in Japan. Mansfield's way was the direct opposite of MacArthur's imperial presence. After introductions, he asked if we would like tea or coffee. Liener and I both asked for coffee. Mansfield left the room and in a few minutes returned carrying a tray with our refreshments. I must admit I had never expected to be served coffee by an American ambassador. Perot, like Mansfield, despite his wealth and fame, has a homey, relaxed way that makes his company a real joy. Mansfield is from another of the western states, Montana, and I appreciate the "down home" ways of people from that area.

Perhaps the most fun we ever had in Texas was on a trip in May 1984, when we gave thirty of our top Japanese photo dealers a chance to see a blend of the old myth of Texas and the modern reality. The Japanese photo industry has sponsored many incentive trips to the United States for its domestic dealers, but usually to such well-worn destinations for Japanese tourists as Los Angeles, San Francisco, Las Vegas, and New York. I wanted something different for our Minolta dealers. Through the years I had been to Dallas frequently and often been a guest at the Temerlins' home, where I'd met their lovely daughter, Dana. Dana, who was then working in the public relations division of Bozell & Jacobs, represents the Japanese ideal of a beautiful Texas woman—full-figured, with long, blond hair and a warm, friendly smile. With the help of the Temerlins and particularly Dana, we arranged for what turned out to be a very successful Japanese dealer trip to Dallas.

It was a far cry from the usual tourist visit. Though Stanley Marcus was out of town, he arranged for a private tour of his fabulous store. Guests at a reception held at the Temerlins' home included former mayor A. Starke Taylor, who presented all of the dealers with scrolls proclaiming them honorary citizens of Dallas. The dealers' stay in Dallas overlapped with the shogun exhibit, and the museum arranged a special tour for them. They had a chance to study artworks that, up until that time, had been seen by few people in Japan. We also enjoyed a specially arranged exhibition of folk dancing, a horse show, and, the highlight of the trip, a hayride to a typical Texas ranch and a cowboy-style barbecue. We took the dealers to a western outfitter in Dallas and had them all decked out in cowboy style complete with boots, big wide belts, and ten-gallon hats. Our convoy of hay wagons, drawn by big tractors, made quite a sight as we moved along the highway to the ranch. The sight of more than thirty Japanese cowboys, perched on top of rocking hay wagons, amused the Texan motorists who passed us, blowing their horns, waving and shouting their greetings with a friendliness typical of the openhearted people of Texas. Of course, we waved back with our big hats and our bandanas.

The group from Japan was headed by our chief of domestic photo sales, KT's brother, Yoshizo, who had suffered that severe neck injury when we were traveling together in Europe in 1956. This time, I'm happy to say, there were no accidents. None of our Japanese cowboys fell off the hay wagons.

Dana, of course, made a big hit with our dealers. A month later, she came to Japan. In her stylish cowgirl outfit, she traveled all over the country presenting to each of the dealers who had been on the trip his personal album of photos from Texas. She was an even bigger hit the second time around.

Bob Crandall, the American Airlines chairman, recently reminded me of another of those Texas evenings that testify to the relaxed life-style of Americans in the western states. The Neiman Marcus Fortnight is an annual promotion of special events held at the flagship store in Dallas. Stanley Marcus himself had been responsible for the discovery of Hanae Mori, who is now Japan's most famous fashion designer. In October 1981, the Fortnight celebrations included a special Japan evening honoring Ms. Mori. Kuniko and I were among those invited to a gala party that took over the entire store. Several of us enjoyed ourselves so much dancing and socializing that we never took time to sample the lavish spread of Japanese food. By eleven-thirty, when the party was breaking up, we realized we were very hungry. Bob Crandall had invited Kuniko and me, and Liener, Karla, and Dana Temerlin, to his home for an after-the-party drink. But we were so hungry that on the way we all stopped at a McDonald's, where we bought several bags of hamburgers and french fries. All the men were in tuxedos and the women in full-length evening gowns, except for Kuniko who wore a traditional Japanese kimono. As we were leaving, the store manager said, "Y'all come back, but next time there's no need to get so dressed up."

In April 1987, Perot's son, Ross Perot, Jr., was with us, along with about two hundred other Texas business leaders, when we opened Minolta's business equipment showroom and training center at Trammell Crow's impressive office automation showcase, Infomart, in Dallas. There Minolta joined such high-visibility information system vendors as Xerox, GTE, Southwestern Bell, NCR, Texas Instruments, and IBM. Once thought of primarily as a supplier of cameras and low- to mid-volume copiers, Minolta by this time had moved strongly into office automation and such highly sophisticated document imaging systems as the Minolta Integrated Information Management System, which links micrographic and digital technologies to capture, store, and retrieve document-based information. Infomart is a stylish environment for showcasing the information system products that will dominate Minolta's product line as we move into the twenty-first century. My speech at the opening ceremonies gave me an opportunity to try out some of my ideas about how the United States can improve its trade balance not by restricting imports, but by expanding nontraditional exports, particularly in such high-tech areas as financial and informational services.

In recent years, as a Japanese businessman selling to a country that has developed an apparently huge trade deficit with Japan, I have been concerned with the necessity for improving trade relations between our two countries. In 1983 I had been interviewed for a television news program in Oklahoma City. The producers led into my interview with filmed scenes of angry American auto workers smashing brand-new Japanese cars with sledgehammers. More recently we've seen photos of political leaders smashing Japanese electronic products on the steps of the Capitol in Washington. Such images reflect the tensions that have developed between the two countries I love so much. The people of America continue to show great openness in accepting a wide variety of products from Japan, but some feel this "invasion" takes jobs away from American workers, that Japan competes unfairly in this country and restricts American imports and investments in Japan. The full story of Japanese-American trade relations is complex. I would be the first to admit that there are problems, including an anti-American backlash in Japan. But our problems can't be solved with sledgehammers—or with increased restrictions on international trade.

There is a limit to what any private citizen can do in the face of what appears to be a massive trade imbalance, unstable foreign-currency exchange rates, and the sudden reversal of the United States from playing a role as the world's biggest creditor nation to becoming the nation with the largest international debt. My own approach has been to speak out whenever possible with the voice of reason, to try to serve as a bridge of understanding between two highly interdependent nations and to offer suggestions for possible ways to improve relations. I used the opening of our business equipment showroom at Infomart in an effort to try to convey some of my ideas to an audience of influential American business leaders. The timing was interesting.

I delivered my speech on the eve of the imposition by the United

States of increased tariffs on a wide range of Japanese electronic goods. The tariffs, which did not directly affect Minolta, signaled American frustration at a trade deficit that continued despite years of hard-nosed negotiations and international currency manipulation designed to expand American exports and reduce imports. The immediate trigger had been charges that the Japanese semiconductor industry was dumping microchips on the world market at unprofitably low prices in an effort to destroy competition. The reality was infinitely more complex, and in my speech I detailed reasons why. However, the real problem wasn't microchips at all.

The real problem lies in the fact that both Japan and the United States have become postindustrial societies. Both nations are no longer dependent on manufacturing industries for economic growth. In the United States, manufacturing has accounted for less than 22 percent of the gross national product since the 1950s. The service sector now accounts for at least 70 percent of gross national product, 80 percent of all jobs, and 90 percent of all new jobs, according to government figures. In Japan, since 1965 the percentage of service jobs has been increasing three times as fast as it has in the United States. The difference is that to a large extent Japan recognizes this change to a postindustrial economy. The United States doesn't.

Another part of the problem is that neither country any longer has a purely national economy. For example, a strategic decision by IBM had played a key role in the surge of microchip imports from Japan. IBM, already the world's largest chip maker, decided to import huge volumes of memory chips from Japan rather than invest in new plants to meet the demand created by IBM's growing but unpredictable market for its personal computers. One plant that helped meet the demand is located in Miho, Japan. The plant is operated by Japan's most profitable microchip producer, a company named Texas Instruments. Based in Dallas but operating globally, TI produces all the 64K random-access memory computer chips for its worldwide operations in Japan. TI and the Japanese producers, responding to world demand, turned out huge volumes of chips, which enabled them to reduce unit production costs and drive the price down from eight dollars to about fifty cents. Since memory chips account for one-third of the cost of making personal computers, the inexpensive chips from Japan allowed IBM and other American firms to lower personal-computer costs and expand the market 30 percent annually. As a result, firms headquartered in America held about 70

percent of the world computer market. Overall, American firms produced $188 billion in electronic goods in 1986, more than double the
output not just of Japan, but of all of Asia. American companies
dominate the world electronics market because they follow a global
operational approach consistent with the increasing integration of
world information technology.

Nor is this phenomenon limited to electronics. General Motors,
Ford, and Chrysler all continue to expand their imports of both parts
and finished automobiles from Europe and Japan. American retailers
depend almost entirely on Asia for imports of 35-mm cameras and
video camcorders. Overall, more than 25 percent of America's imports
from Japan result from the production and marketing policies of
American firms, according to research compiled by Kenichi Ohmae,
manager of the Tokyo office of the international consulting firm
McKinsey and Company. This places rather severe restrictions on
trade policy and causes rather severe frustrations among American
policy makers. To have really limited microchip imports from Japan,
for example, would have severely hurt such American buyers of
microchips as IBM and such American producers of microchips as
Texas Instruments. Therefore, the tariffs that went into effect the
day after my speech in Dallas covered a wide range of electronic
products but had very little direct effect on the Japanese semiconductor industry that had been accused of dumping microchips on the
world market.

The equally important point I tried to make to my audience of
Texas business leaders hinges on the fact that the more advanced
countries of Western Europe, as well as the United States and Japan,
are already developing postindustrial economies based on high-tech
informational and financial services. Auto makers like Toyota, Nissan, and General Motors already derive as big a portion of their profits
from the financial side of their operations as they do from manufacturing. Such firms are not in business to make autos. They are in
business to make money. In fact, Toyota's determination to establish
itself in financial services is so strong that it has drawn criticism from
the Japanese banking establishment. But Toyota, looking into the
twenty-first century, sees the limits of growth for auto manufacturing
in Japan. Toyota, Nissan, and GM are not about to close down their
factories, but the factory is becoming less important.

Minolta is another example. Fifteen years ago, about two-thirds
of our Japanese employees worked in manufacturing. Today only

about 40 percent of Minolta's six thousand employees in Japan are involved in manufacturing. And the vast majority of our employees aren't in Japan at all. We have about nine thousand employees abroad. Very few of them are Japanese, and only about eight hundred, in Malaysia, West Germany, and the United States, work in factories. Minolta has good reason to be proud of its highly efficient factories and manufacturing systems. But today we are even prouder of our research facilities. We design and develop the cameras and business equipment of the future. But, more than in the past, we use high-tech communications systems to orchestrate a manufacturing process that depends more heavily on outside suppliers. It's like being the conductor of a great symphony orchestra, bringing together the work of many musicians through the communications magic of our baton. At Minolta, we realize that our world has changed, and that to survive we must adapt.

Japan also has learned to adapt, not only to the cultural, traditional, and economic realities of our export markets but also to changing technologies, changing market conditions, changing economic forces. This is a lesson America has not yet mastered as it struggles to come to terms with its new role as a postindustrial society in a global economy. In my speeches on international trade, I try not only to analyze the problems accurately but also to offer suggestions for improvement. My bias should be obvious. As a man who makes his living selling Japanese products to Americans, naturally I'm not in favor of restricting imports. In my view, that's never good for business. On the other hand, expanding exports, including expanding American exports to Japan and the rest of the world, is always good for business, and vital for a healthy world economy.

The question is what products America can export competitively and how it can successfully penetrate international markets. I have many ideas on the subject, but the one I stressed that evening in Dallas recommends what I believe would be the world's first foreign-trade zone designed exclusively for the export of services. Many so-called free-trade or enterprise zones, primarily handling manufactured products and parts, have been established in the United States and other parts of the world. Special advantages are granted to firms operating in such zones, including exemption from inventory and value-added taxes; exemption from various government regulations; reduced utility rates; and such assistance as shared computer and communications facilities.

In most countries the fullest range of such benefits goes to export firms or products. In the United States, however, such zones have done more to aid the flood of imports than to assist exports. And, to the best of my knowledge, no one has yet established a free-trade zone exclusively for the export of services. Insurance companies, banks, and other financial, informational, and entertainment service companies might find such a zone extremely interesting. Engineering, construction, telecommunications, transport, and other nonmanufacturing industries have entered the international market as never before and could also benefit from such a zone. Satellite communications are already being used for the international transmittal of financial and informational services, but no organized effort has been made to expand America's exports of such products. In fact, for several years American banks and insurance companies have been *importing* such services from places like the Bahamas, where low-cost, English-speaking data entry and word processing clerks handle work that used to be done by American workers in the back shops of those financial institutions. Partly as a result, the United States has lost its edge as a net exporter of services. In 1981, the United States had an impressive surplus of $41 billion in services. As recently as 1985, that surplus was $21 billion. By 1988, the trade balance in services had become a deficit, according to U.S. Commerce Department figures.

America does export billions of dollars' worth of such services as financial, informational, and entertainment products, but more, much more, can be done to encourage and expand such exports. The United States, despite its new status as the world's biggest debtor, continues to be the world's banker. America's basic wealth and political stability and the sophistication of its banking and communications systems make this possible. The dollar continues to be the only global currency, and most experts believe this will continue no matter how its value may fluctuate. Every foreign corporation wants to have its loans backed by American dollars. America's relatively high interest rates draw foreign investment like a magnet. Because currency fluctuations have become so important in international trade, the controller's office in multinational corporations has become a profit center, rather than just an accounting department, earning money by buying and selling various currencies. Currency translations can be as vital as sales volume for achieving profits. Making and quickly implementing the right decisions about when to pay bills, when to take on new loans, when to transfer currency from one country to another, can have a major impact on a company's profit-and-loss results. Information has become power, and the quick transmittal and analysis of information has become the key to financial success in many sectors of commerce and industry.

This concept of mine for a free-trade zone exclusively for the export of services has evolved through a series of speeches I have given. When I discussed it as guest speaker at a governor's business awards luncheon in Las Vegas in 1986, I included the idea of exporting entertainment services via satellite communications. At that meeting, sponsored by former governor Richard Bryan, who is now a United States senator from Nevada, I suggested that Las Vegas might create international gambling events, using high-tech satellite communications systems to hook up high rollers in Kuwait or Bahrain with casinos in Nevada. States like Nevada and New Jersey, which have legalized gambling laws, or any state with a lottery, could internationalize such events through satellite communications, raising revenues and also earmarking some of the income for further research into the export of high-tech services.

Entertainment is one of America's most successful exports. American music has incredible global impact, and each year the United States exports over $1.5 billion in film and videotapes. Satellite transmission from a free-trade zone could greatly enhance the profitability of such exports. Las Vegas, an entertainment and music mecca, is also an important center for professional boxing, transmitted nationally and even internationally by television. I suggested the possibility of establishing Las Vegas as a permanent center for the international transmission of sports and entertainment programming, packaged there and marketed around the world. New Jersey's Atlantic City could also profit from such a venture. But, as I suggested in my discussion of the importance of being first with technological innovations, being first in putting together an export-specific free-trade zone for services will be a big advantage.

Unlike the Industrial Revolution, which depended on proximity to cheap sources of power, the information revolution can be centered anywhere. Sophisticated financial and informational service export centers will, however, depend on a pool of skilled and educated experts in many disciplines. Industries located in the zone might well include a center for service export research and development, perhaps in cooperation with one or more universities. The development of new service export products, and research to help service exporters crack resistant foreign markets and to achieve more effective and cost-efficient means of transmission would be among the functions of such a service R&D center. In my view the development of a free-trade service export zone will require joint ventures involving a range of service industry firms and associations with a variety of government agencies. The Japan Camera Inspection and Service Institute, which I described earlier, is one example of a successful joint venture involving government and industry. In Japan there are many others. In the United States such cooperation is rare, but I believe that where there's a will there's a way.

I have several suggestions that I believe can help the United States achieve a more favorable balance of trade. Perhaps this book will help to get some of those ideas across. I hope so, because I'm convinced that if the United States does not expand its exports, America's growing international debt will lead to sharply reduced living standards for all Americans and an international trade crisis that will trigger a world depression. History tells us that America can expand its exports rapidly. During the 1950s, for example, the United States doubled its exports and closed out the decade with a very favorable balance of trade. It isn't likely that the United States will be able to expand exports by a comparable ratio during the 1990s, but it also isn't necessary. The trade statistics that concerned observers watch most closely give a misleading picture of what's actually going on in today's globalized economy.

But that's another chapter.

26

The Minds Behind Minolta

We met in absolute secrecy at a hotel on top of Mount Rokko outside Kobe. Key officials from around the world had been called to a product meeting that turned out to have a profound effect on the future of Minolta. No phone calls were allowed as we gathered in splendid isolation. The site was ideal not only for its privacy, but also for its echoes of Minolta's early years. From the mountaintop, there's a beautiful view of Kobe and its port, where KT had set sail for Europe on the 1927 trip that inspired him to create his own optical and camera company. Particularly at night, when the lights of the city below sparkle like stars, you can imagine that you are looking out over the history of Minolta. It's not far from the first Minolta plant built in 1928 on the banks of the Mukogawa River in what is now the city of Nishinomiya. The optical glass factory at Itami, built during the war at the request of the army, is even closer to Mount Rokko. After the war Minolta began manufacturing its Rokkor lenses, which were named for the mountain that looks down over the area, at the Itami plant. But, at that important product meeting on June 1, 1981, we not only caught reflections of the past but also our first glimpse of a new era.

241

We learned that Minolta's research and development engineers had been working in great secrecy on a single-lens reflex autofocus camera. If we decided to proceed with what promised to be a very expensive development program, it would be more fully computerized and easier to use than any 35-mm SLR autofocus camera then on the market. All the electronic wiring that was eventually supposed to be packed into a single microchip was then spread out and exposed, so that the prototype we studied was the size of a suitcase. We were used to looking at clumsy prototypes, but many of us had troubling questions about what our engineers were up to.

They said the new camera would require a new lens mount. We were proud that there had been no change in the bayonet lens mount we had first introduced with the Minolta SR-2 in 1958. This meant that all our interchangeable lenses could be used on any of our SLR camera bodies. Like most of the marketing people at the meeting, I opposed the idea of making such a change. I could foresee complaints from consumers who already had many of our lenses but would have to start all over again if they wanted the new autofocus camera. If the new camera proved successful, camera dealers might want to return all the interchangeable lenses they had in stock that would not work with the new lens mount.

A subdued but strong sense of excitement stirred beneath our misgivings, however. We realized that the first manufacturer to introduce a computerized, easy-to-use autofocus camera would have an enormous impact on the industry. Worldwide camera sales had reached a plateau and showed little prospect of more than marginal growth. Only a camera that could leapfrog over current technology had any chance of sparking a new sales boom. As far as we knew, none of our competitors were close to perfecting a computerized autofocus SLR. But someone was bound to come up with a winning technological breakthrough sooner or later. There was risk in proceeding, but there might be greater risk in standing pat, as we had for so long with our SR-T 101 camera and our EG 101 copier.

We had just introduced the X-700 SLR. In my opinion, it was the ultimate design for any camera using the technology then available. With the help of our "Only From the Mind of Minolta" campaign, it was selling extremely well. The X-700 had been the first Japanese camera to win the European Camera of the Year award; it also won the Grand Prix awards of Japan and Australia, giving Minolta the

opportunity to boast in its advertising, "We Own Three Continents."
It would have been tempting to concentrate on marketing the X-700
and forget about expensive new development projects that might not
succeed. But the X-700 also gave us the chance to gamble with the
new product. Even if it failed, we would still have the X-700 to keep
us going.

As our engineers described the new camera in more detail, I
realized that its many automatic features would be ideal for the American market, where the computer was already a factor in popular
consumer products ranging from hand-held calculators to luxury
automobiles. On the office automation side of our operations, the
research and development people were already working on a multifunctional computer, word processor, and electronic typewriter that
promised to be easy to learn and easy to operate, features that would
be particularly attractive in the American market. The new camera
our engineers were working on also used complex computer technology to simplify the task of the user. About the only thing it
wouldn't do for the consumer would be to put film in the camera.
Once that was done, the camera would automatically load the film
and advance it to the first frame, set the film speed and programmed
exposure, and focus each shot.

After lengthy and sometimes heated discussions about the new
product, we all looked to KT—and his son Hideo, who was being
groomed to take over the firm. I watched KT closely. Though he said
nothing, I knew him well enough to be sure that he favored going
ahead. Hideo, or Henry, as we called him since his three years in
America as Ken Nakamura's assistant, took the lead in formulating
our decision.

"This is a very risky product," he said, "but also very exciting.
Our research and development people tell us there's no way we can
step forward unless we commit ourselves to a new computerized
generation of autofocus cameras."

I was impressed as I listened to Henry. Like others at the meeting, I had not wanted to speak out with too loud a voice in front of
so many senior people. Because of my experience in America, Minolta's most important market, I knew that great weight would be
given to my opinion. I was afraid that if I spoke out too strongly, I
might wind up leading a conversation that Minolta's fate could hinge
on. That would be fine if my ideas proved correct, but not so fine if

the new camera turned out to be a failure. I looked around the room cautiously but said little. In short, I was a coward. Fortunately, Henry spoke up for all of us who favored the project.

"We have no choice but to go ahead," said Henry.

I was happy and very relieved. I watched Henry with great admiration. Thinking about that day years later, I remembered my young schoolmate in Korea who had spoken up so eloquently when another of our friends said it was our duty to take up arms against the Russians who were moving into Korea from the north. Henry was showing the courage and the leadership Minolta needed to lead us forward. I watched KT, and realized that he would soon pass the sword of leadership to his oldest son, and that Minolta was entering a new era, not only in terms of camera technology but also in terms of leadership.

Computerization was the key to the success of the new camera. It unlocked a whole new generation of SLR cameras. The first generation of mechanically controlled cameras had been bypassed nearly a decade before. The second generation, electronic autoexposure cameras, began when Canon introduced its AE-1 in 1976. The new camera being developed by Minolta opened a third generation of SLR cameras by introducing computerization of many functions, including autofocus.

We were three years away from seeing all those wires and parts packed into a single, marketable autofocus camera. Our research and development team applied for more than three hundred patents, and we kept our secret well. The introduction of the camera, marketed in the United States as the Maxxum 7000, took the industry by storm. My favorite demonstration of what makes the Maxxum so special is a simple one. If you look through the viewfinder at the subject you want to shoot, and then press the shutter release, you'll see a blurry image, even a rapidly moving image, come into sharp focus instantly. And you can hear the camera making its automatic shutter speed and f-stop adjustments. This simple demonstration results from an incredibly complex computerization of manual, mechanical, and electronic camera operations. The Maxxum, with integrated circuits that are the equivalent of 150,000 transistors, has indeed packed all those wires into a microchip.

But the proof is in the printing of the photos you can take with a Maxxum. Young children are notoriously difficult photo subjects. You can't get them to sit still. With the Maxxum, you don't have to. Once the image is in the viewfinder and the shutter release is pressed, the Maxxum's body integral motor brings the lens into focus in a fraction of a second and the camera snaps a perfect photo. It has to. Because the shutter won't work until the subject is in focus. In Japan, where the Maxxum sells under the name Alpha 7000, one Japanese camera magazine said you can divide family photo albums into two eras. In the pre–Alpha 7000 era, family snapshots, particularly of children, are often blurry and out of focus. But, the magazine said, you can tell the difference when the family moves into the post–Alpha 7000 era.

Because it focuses instantly and automatically, the Maxxum is also ideal for professionals—or amateurs—trying to capture sports events, dance performances, or other activities characterized by movement or changing light situations. In continuous drive mode, the Maxxum 7000 will keep clicking away almost like a movie camera at a rate of two frames per second. With the motor drive option available on the professional model, the Maxxum 9000, the camera can shoot up to five frames per second. Since film is cheap, this can be an excellent way to get the perfect shot. Print selection, cropping, and printing can then complete the creative process. Experienced photographers also can take advantage of manual overrides to maintain full creative control and achieve special effects.

I have a hunch that Minolta's professional-model Maxxum 9000 will eventually be adopted by most photojournalists, but some traditions die hard. Many professionals, heavily invested in their excellent Nikon systems, are reluctant to switch. But I believe that will change. Lens design has improved so much during the past few years that two or three lenses can now handle a range of tasks that once required a dozen. Professionals are also concerned about the durability of their cameras, which get heavy use, often under difficult working conditions. Professionals regard their Nikons as sturdier than most competing cameras, but I think that's mainly a matter of perception. Some modern synthetic materials are as tough as steel, and the body of the Maxxum 9000 is reinforced by steel.

We gave to the marketing of the new camera as much attention as we had to the technological development. From the early 1970s the Japanese yen had been falling sharply against most major currencies, particularly the American dollar. The strong dollar gave Americans the opportunity to buy Japanese imports at relatively low prices. In general, this was very good for Minolta Corporation, making our products less expensive in our biggest market, but it also created a flourishing "gray market." Minolta cameras sold in Hong Kong, and to a lesser extent in other Asian countries with weak currencies, could profitably be resold to American dealers for strong American dollars, then be shipped to the United States and sold to consumers for less than the cost of identical cameras bought from Japan. The strength of the American dollar as a medium of international exchange in those years made this possible.

There is nothing illegal in such transactions, but in the long run they do shortchange the consumer because the warranty for his camera is with a dealer in Hong Kong, not the United States. But consumers often are not aware of this until it's too late. The gray market also undermines authorized American dealers who buy from Minolta but face price competition from gray-market outlets that don't share in the cost of promoting the product and maintaining service operations.

The gray market can best be defined by contrasting it to the idea of a black market, which usually implies an illegal activity. In the case of consumer products, the black market generally describes goods that have been smuggled into a country or that are forgeries of established brand-name products. Goods sold on the gray market generally have entered the country legally and are actual products of established manufacturers. Gray-market goods, however, are made available through irregular channels, usually having been sold by the manufacturer to dealers who have taken advantage of foreign-currency fluctuations, different tariff levels, and other variable factors to resell the products in another country at a price lower than the same product could be bought directly from the manufacturer. It's a complicated business and, though it may offer the consumer apparent bargains, the products usualy have a warranty that is valid only in the country where they were originally sold.

The gray market thrives on products that are popular, heavily promoted, and that carry the name of a reliable manufacturer. One way to alert consumers to the fact that they are looking at a gray-market product without a local warranty is to promote the product under different names in different parts of the world. This was the strategy we adopted for our new autofocus camera. The first model, sold as the Maxxum 7000 in North America, was marketed as the Alpha 7000 in Japan and the 7000 AF (autofocus) in Europe.

Our photo advertising agency, William Esty, came up with the Maxxum name for the American market. The agency also came up

ABOVE: *Astronaut John H. Glenn, Jr., in 1963, meeting officials at Minolta's Sakai factory following his use of the Minolta Hi-Matic as the first camera to be taken on a manned space flight.* LEFT: *The Hi-Matic.*

ABOVE: *Glenn (center right in bow tie) with cast of the all-girl Takarazuka revue. Others, center: Sam Kusumoto; Glenn's teen-age children, Lynn and Dave; and his wife, Annie.* OPPOSITE TOP: *Sam Kusumoto cracking open a keg of* sake *in traditional* kagamiwari *ceremony at the May 1974 opening of Minolta's American headquarters in Ramsey, N.J., with Minolta founder Kazuo Tashima, left.* OPPOSITE BOTTOM: *Henry Tashima, left, president of Minolta Camera Company, Ltd., Osaka, and his father, the late Kazuo Tashima, founder of Minolta, visiting Times Square in March 1983.*

Sam Kusumoto being named to the Photo Marketing Association's Hall of Fame, February 1986, with former PMA president John Jackson.

The Minolta SR-T 101 camera, a big seller for fifteen years.

The Minolta X-700, the biggest technological breakthrough in cameras before the Maxxum.

TOP: Happi *coats festival at a July 1986 meeting of Minolta's American photo sales force in Osaka, celebrating the success of the Maxxum camera.* ABOVE: *The Minolta Maxxum 7000, the most advanced computerized, autofocus camera.* LEFT: *Mrs. Linda Haupt accepting the award honoring her father, Dr. W. Edwards Deming, the American who pioneered quality control methods in Japan, with Sam Kusumoto at the 1987 annual dinner of the Japanese Chamber of Commerce of New York.*

OPPOSITE: *Sam Kusumoto in 1987 with Minolta line of office and optical equipment, cameras, and lenses.*

Mrs. Jean MacArthur, widow of General Douglas Mac-Arthur; Kuniko Kusumoto; and publisher Malcolm Forbes aboard his yacht, Highlander V, during a February 1988 trip to the Galápagos Islands.

Eriko Kusumoto and Robert Gottner at the Plaza Hotel reception following their wedding at New York City's St. Patrick's Cathedral, May 29, 1988.

FROM LEFT: *Akio Miyabayashi, president of Minolta's European operations; Henry Tashima, president of Minolta Camera Company, and Sam Kusumoto at the October 1988 Photokina trade show in Cologne, West Germany.*

Sam Kusumoto with the Minolta Maxxum 7000.

with an eye-appealing design, spelling *Maxxum* with an interlocking double X. Unfortunately, the Exxon trademark uses the same device. Cameras and promotional materials were already in the pipeline when Exxon discovered Maxxum's interlocking double X. To defend the integrity of its logo, Exxon had no choice but to object. We were able to work out an agreement that was favorable to both companies—and that may one day prove a boon to camera collectors. Minolta agreed to change the Maxxum logo, and Exxon agreed to let us go ahead with cameras already produced. Those Maxxum 7000s with the interlocking double X will no doubt become a valuable collector's item.

The interlocking double-X problem had only a minor impact on the incredibly successful introduction of the Maxxum 7000. The camera's capabilities created a contagious excitement. We first told our photo sales representatives about the Maxxum at a January 19, 1985, meeting at the Hilton Hotel in Rye, New York. I have never seen such enthusiasm over a new product. Timing was important. Though we had enough product on hand to have introduced it in November, we wanted to wait till after the Christmas season. Inventories would be depleted, and not much else would be happening in the way of new consumer products being introduced. We next previewed the camera for a group of our dealers at a party at the Waldorf-Astoria on the evening of January 22, 1985. The next day we officially introduced the Maxxum 7000 at a New York City press conference. This was part of a well-coordinated, worldwide announcement. We had briefed key editors of photo magazines in various countries after getting them to sign secrecy agreements binding them not to reveal any details in advance of the official publication date. This gave magazine editors an opportunity to plan up-to-date coverage despite their longer lead time compared with that of daily media. Rumors about the Maxxum began circulating in the industry, but that only added to the media's interest. Our press conference was packed, and the media response was enthusiastic. In the evening, we showed the camera at a reception for a second group of dealers. That jam-packed press conference at the Plaza Hotel and the two dealer meetings were the first of a series we held across the country in Philadelphia, Chicago, Beverly Hills, San Francisco, Dallas, and, at the end of March, at the PMA convention in Las Vegas.

By the time we hit Las Vegas, it was clear that the Maxxum was a sensation. I couldn't help but think back to that first, lonely exhibit Bill Daly and I had manned at the MPDFA convention in Chicago in 1954. Now our huge booth was mobbed. Henry Tashima was there and, even though the camera had been on the market for three months, we were interviewed again and again by press people interested in the Maxxum. I have always been impressed by the fairness of American reporters. If you give them something truly newsworthy, even news about a product you're bringing to market, they can nearly always be counted on to give you the coverage your story deserves. This has certainly been the case with the Maxxum. Years after its original introduction, its continuing success and our development of new models generate good media coverage.

We backed our cross-country publicity effort with the biggest advertising campaign in Minolta's history. Sales soared around the world. Not just Minolta but the whole photo industry benefited from the introduction of the Maxxum. Our share of market grew, making Minolta number one in the United States, in Japan, and in the world, but the overall size of the SLR market also grew. Virtually all the manufacturers soon introduced and promoted computerized autofocus cameras, sparking competition that benefited the entire industry. The plateau soared to create a new peak as a market that many thought had matured started growing like a teen-ager.

Since 1985, the Maxxum 7000 has been my own primary camera of choice. When I travel, however, I still sometimes use the Minolta AFC, an excellent though rather expensive camera introduced in 1983. The technologically complex AFC has six F2.8 lens elements that give it an exceptional capability to correct for distortions. The AFC is so compact that it makes a handy traveling companion that takes very sharp pictures. I usually have two favorite cameras: a single-lens reflex unit like the Maxxum for serious photography and a compact camera like the AFC for snapshots. My compact camera becomes my personal memo pad, recording my travels and experiences in a visual shorthand. Before the Maxxum, the SR-T 101 and John Glenn's "space camera," the Minolta Hi-Matic, were my favorite models.

The ascent of the Maxxum wasn't the only important event for Minolta in 1985. That was also the year we introduced the breakthrough technology of the Minolta-Mitsubishi planetarium, Infinium, at the Tsukuba Science Fair. We also introduced our first color video camera, the world's first plain-paper reader-printer, the RP 503, and our first office automation product, the multifunctional PCW-1, continuing the diversification that KT had seen was necessary for our survival.

KT lived to see the success of the Maxxum and Infinium and the start of Minolta's move into office automation. But he did not live to see another of his dreams come true. KT had been born on November 20, 1899. He hoped to live at least until that date in the year 2000, so that his life would have spanned three centuries. But since 1982, it had been clear that KT was no longer as robust as he had been. He had been president of Minolta for fifty-four years, a record among companies listed on the Tokyo Stock Exchange. Many members of the board of directors felt the time had come for KT to turn the presidency over to his eldest son, Henry. KT agreed and in July 1982 took over the previously unfilled role of chairman of the board as Henry became president.

The changeover was announced and celebrated at a reception attended by two thousand people at the Royal Hotel in Osaka. Among the guests was the late Konosuke Matsushita, the founder of Panasonic and a famous man in Japan. Then in his nineties, he also founded the Matsushita Hospital in Osaka, where he maintained his own home until his death in 1989, assuring excellent medical care. Like KT, he was also from Wakayama prefecture and the two had been close friends for many years. It was always very moving to see them together, knowing each time might be the last. Though semiretired, KT remained an active chairman and was in the office almost every day. On all my trips I would always spend several hours talking with him in his office. But each time he seemed a little thinner, a little more pale.

Early in 1985 I had been told in great confidence what I had already guessed: KT's health was failing rapidly. On September 9—the date is etched in my memory—as we were talking in his office, KT unexpectedly asked me to join him at lunch. We went to Tsuruya, Osaka's most respected restaurant. The restaurant is housed in what looks like a modest, two-story, wood-frame building surrounded by downtown skyscrapers. But it's much bigger than it appears from the outside, with a lovely interior garden and surprising modern touches. For example, one wall folds away to reveal a stage, and the ceiling opens for stage lights. The restaurant has hosted heads of state ranging from Queen Elizabeth II to Marshal Tito. KT and I had entertained many of our foreign distributors there in the 1960s, those golden years when we were growing so rapidly and having so much fun doing it.

By this time, KT had reluctantly given up the Cadillacs he'd loved for so long. Though I continue to follow his early example and drive a Cadillac myself, KT had found that his repair bills in Japan were costing him the equivalent of $4,000 a year. Breakdowns had become frequent, and parts were expensive and hard to obtain. So on this day, his chauffeur, Mr. Ohtani, drove us to our elegant, two-hour lunch in a more reliable Mercedes. It was a sad ride. With my admiration for all things American, I missed the old Cadillac. I noticed that the robotic arm for paying tolls was also gone.

Our slow progress through the restaurant was also very sad. We had a long walk from the Tsuruya's front entrance to the private tatami room KT had reserved. KT had to stop and sit down several times. I honestly can't remember much of what we said during that lunch or what we ate. The restaurant people had noticed KT's condition and arranged for our car to be waiting for us at a rear entrance close to our room. I was later told that had been KT's last visit to a restaurant.

I was in Osaka again the following month. KT was in Kobe Hospital, and Henry managed to make special arrangements for me to visit him on October 15. I was allowed five minutes. KT, lying in his bed, could say only a few words. I told him of the great success of the Maxxum in America. He smiled and looked very happy. I never saw him alive again.

At five o'clock on the morning of November 19, my brother telephoned me at the hotel where I was staying in Osaka to tell me that KT had died during the night. It was the eve of his eighty-sixth birthday. I felt as though I had lost my own father, an ordeal I experienced the following year. KT's death was a great personal loss to me and to many others who knew and loved him. He had guided my life and shaped my beliefs since we first met in 1951. Without his support I would never have discovered the America I had been dreaming of since I was a child in Korea. KT had guided Minolta from nothing to the $2 billion corporation it became during the year of his death, when, for the first time, it also earned a place as a Fortune 500 international company. Yet, for all his achievements, KT remained the modest, unassuming man he had been when we first met in the fire-charred former high school building in Osaka where the company had its headquarters thirty-five years before.

Another of KT's few visitors during those last few days was Minolta's research and development director, Ichiro Yoshiyama. Ichiro, who had played a major role in the development of the Maxxum, had been in West Germany, receiving the European Camera of the Year award. He was informed that KT was near the end and rushed back to Japan so that KT could see the plaque before he died. The story of KT's last days is movingly told in a memoir written by his granddaughter, Naoko, who had accompanied her parents on the trip to America for KT's induction into the PMA Hall of Fame. She told how much that honor had meant to her grandfather and how moved he had been on seeing the plaque that Ichiro had brought to his bedside. By then KT could not speak at all, but Naoko felt she knew her grandfather so well that she could read his mind. She told Ichiro that she could see the joy in KT's eyes and knew that he was saying thank you. Her story was the best in a collection, *In Memory of KT*, that Minolta published. My own story told of KT's concern for Minolta's dealers and distributors throughout the world. I told of the personal steps he took, entertaining customers at lavish dinners even in his old age, to make sure that our overseas representatives never felt like foreigners but like part of our Minolta family. I was among the nearly one thousand Tashima family members and friends who attended a private service on November 21 at the family home. I was standing next to Ichiro Yoshiyama, outside the house waiting for the hearse, when Haruo Takada, the head of the labor union for Minolta workers, came up to us. The union leader touched Ichiro on the shoulder and said, "You gave the greatest gift to KT just before he died. Thank you." He was referring both to Ichiro's role in creating the Maxxum and to the plaque that Ichiro had rushed to KT's bedside. There were tears in Takada's eyes as he walked away.

On December 18, with over five thousand people I attended a memorial service at Midosuji Kai-Kan, a huge meeting hall in Osaka. *Asahi Shimbun*, one of Japan's leading daily newspapers, ran a special story that day saying that KT's entire life, almost to its final day, had been devoted to the camera industry. In the last year of his life he had introduced a camera that created a worldwide sensation. The newspaper described him as a man who loved his family, his company, his employees, and his customers. He lived modestly without the many luxuries he could afford such as the second villa that is a standard status symbol for men of his position. KT had few interests or pleasures apart from work. He was one of the last of the giants among the old-time entrepreneurs who devoted their lives to the business.

The story of the meeting on Mount Rokko at which Henry Tashima led us to our decision to go ahead with the Maxxum has become famous in Japan. The story has even been retold in a comic book that, fortunately, KT never saw. The drawings of him are very bad, almost like a caricature of an old gangster. Henry, on the other hand, looks very handsome. But what strikes me as most interesting about the comic book is its reflection of the extent to which success in business becomes part of Japan's popular culture. Though we have our fantasy comic books, too, the emergence of Henry Tashima as a comic-book hero says something about the values we instill, particularly in contrast to the United States, where popular culture, and especially television, depicts business leaders most often as villains. It's no wonder the American business community lacks popular support. In the years ahead American business firms will need all the popular and political support they can get in our increasingly competitive global economy.

New York's Plaza Hotel, where we held our first press conference officially introducing the Maxxum, was the scene of another important meeting that year, one that had a profound impact on Minolta—and the world. For several days during September the top finance officials of what was then called the "Group of Five" industrial nations met at the Plaza, formulating an agreement to undertake a coordinated effort to drive the value of the American dollar down in relation to other major currencies. That decision, designed to help reduce the United States' trade deficit, has had a debatable effect on America's trade balance. But there's no arguing about the negative effect it's had on Minolta's profitability. Though KT's emphasis on exports has proved successful, that success cost us dearly when the value of one U.S. dollar fell from 263.5 yen in early 1985 to a forty-year low of 120.25 yen in Asian trading on January 4, 1988. This means that, even with expanded sales, Minolta's export earnings from the United States were worth 54 percent less than they were in 1985 solely because of currency devaluation. Minolta is the most export-dependent of all the Japanese manufacturing companies listed on the

Tokyo Stock Exchange, and 40 percent of our production goes to the United States. When the American dollar sneezes, Minolta gets the flu.

Meanwhile, the attorneys general of thirty-six states were also developing a coordinated campaign, one that was soon to involve the Maxxum and the AF-Tele, another camera we introduced in 1985.

27

Why America Exports Japanese Cameras to Japan

Excellent products can cause exceptional problems. The Maxxum proved the point. When we were planning its introduction, the United States dollar was very strong in relation to other major international currencies. This was good for American consumers and tourists. It meant they could buy imported foreign goods at lower prices and, when they traveled to foreign countries, the favorable exchange rates made accommodations and shopping less expensive. On the other hand, the strong dollar put a burden on American exporters, making American products more expensive in foreign markets than competing products from countries with weaker currencies. The strong dollar was also good for Minolta Corporation. Like any other American consumer, we pay for the products we import from our parent company in American dollars. When the dollar is strong, our money goes further in buying cameras and business equipment from Japan. But for us there also were drawbacks.

We knew we would have a tough time protecting our dealers from gray-market competition. Using different model names in Japan, Europe, and the United States helped. But we feared that the combination of the strong dollar and the appeal of the Maxxum would be too powerful a magnet to keep gray-market substitutes from coming into the American market. A conversation I'd had with one of our dealers in 1982, when the Maxxum was still in the development stage, hit me hard. He said Minolta had been doing a marvelous job with its high-quality product line, its advertising, and promotional support. "So the good news is, you did a wonderful thing making our business big," he said. "But you did not bring us any profit."

I was aware of the growth of the big discount houses and of the gray market. But until that conversation, I hadn't been aware of how severe the impact had been, particularly on our dealers in the major cities. I discovered that many dealers weren't making any money at all on Minolta camera sales. In an effort to compete with the discounters, they were selling at cost or even below cost, using cameras as bait to develop customers for photo finishing and camera accessories, which for many had become their only source of profit. I was proud that Minolta had provided wonderful products at reasonable prices with strong marketing support. But I was left with an empty feeling as I discovered that our dealers weren't making money on our cameras. These were the people who had helped us build our business in America and now, at a time of great success, rapid growth and profitability for us, they were suffering.

Quality cameras are not a consumable commodity like bread or milk. The average consumer buys a new camera only once every five to ten years and needs good after-sales service to keep his camera working. We do have our own service centers, but they could never handle the needs of all our customers. For this we need a broad network of reliable dealers. Years ago camera stores in Europe were run like expensive jewelry stores, with thick carpets and salesmen wearing somber suits and white gloves. That may have been overdoing it, but buyers of expensive cameras do deserve consideration and service. If too many smaller dealers with reliable service departments are forced out of business by gray-market price competition, consumers will suffer and their anger will affect the reputation of the entire industry.

Anticipating the success of the Maxxum, I began to wonder if it would be possible to do something to restore a reasonable degree of profitability to our dealers. We reviewed regulatory policy on questions of price and concluded that the Reagan administration's reasonable approach to such questions gave us an opportunity to help our dealers. Manufacturers can list a suggested retail price. While it's perfectly legal to terminate dealers for a variety of reasons, it isn't legal to threaten to do so for selling below that suggested retail price. Our suggested retail was only 10 percent above dealer cost, which seemed to me quite modest. In fact, many department stores and dealers advertised the Maxxum at prices well above our suggested minimum and did quite well selling at that price level.

By this time two early recruits, Jim de Merlier and Bob Lathrop, had developed into a sophisticated and successful marketing and sales team. They came up with an integrated marketing strategy designed not only to make the Maxxum successful as a product but also to make it profitable for our dealers. In introducing the camera to our dealers, we pointed out that it represented brand-new technology with no competition likely to develop anytime soon. It would not be available in mass quantities and was being sold and promoted under different names in various parts of the world to limit gray-market competition. We set up programs to train dealer sales personnel to help them understand and sell the advantages of the Maxxum. We provided "loaner" cameras so sales personnel could become familiar with the Maxxum, counter cards with point-by-point details on operational benefits, demonstration videotapes, and other sales support material. For the first time in the industry, we also gave dealers the opportunity to buy low-cost service contracts from Minolta for profitable resale to customers. We told dealers that we did not expect that inexpensive off-brand lenses would be available, and that they should be in a position to sell the Maxxum and its accessories at the suggested list price and make a profit. We were correct in our assessments. For eighteen months there was no competition, and even today the original Maxxum and subsequent models and updates continue to dominate the SLR market.

What we didn't anticipate, however, was that state legal policies would not necessarily be the same as the reasonable policies of the federal government. The National Association of State Attorneys General decided to make price agreements a top priority for enforcement proceedings that year. Minolta was the first target picked. Maryland filed a suit against us, charging that consumers were being deprived of the benefits of open competition on prices for the Maxxum and another camera, the AF-Tele, that we introduced that year. Other states quickly followed with virtually identical suits.

I was shocked. Though the facts themselves did not support a case of price fixing, many newspaper headlines used that phrase, linked with the Minolta name. It has always been my policy to make sure that Minolta is an excellent corporate citizen in every way. I'm grateful for the freedom that the American democratic system allows and I'm determined to live up to my responsibilities under that system. I dropped the suggested price policy and Minolta met with the state attorneys general to negotiate a settlement. Under the terms of a 1987 settlement, we agreed to pay rebates of eight dollars to fifteen dollars to consumers who had bought the products affected.

I didn't think we had done anything wrong in our effort to protect both our dealers, whose profits had been deteriorating, and our customers, some of whom might wind up with no place to obtain service and spare parts for their cameras. But I was grateful to the state attorneys general for their corrective efforts to help us protect our customers in terms of price competition. I realize that America is a country of fifty united states, each with its own laws and officials who may have a different opinion than the regulatory officials in the federal government. I was gratified by the many letters we received from customers who wrote to us saying they felt they had paid a fair price for a good camera and didn't want a rebate. Minolta's good name suffered relatively little damage, and the extent to which the rebates and our legal costs cut into our profits was a small price to pay for an amicable settlement.

By the time the issue was settled, gray-market activity had pretty much stopped, primarily because of the decision made by the finance ministers of the United States, Japan, Great Britain, West Germany, and France to drive down the value of the dollar. In their September 22, 1985, meeting, the so-called Group of Five industrial nations agreed that an overvalued dollar had worked against efforts to improve the smooth flow of international trade. The strong dollar made American exports expensive on the world market and aided the flood of imports coming into the United States. Partly as a result of the strong dollar, America's trade deficit—the amount by which imports exceed exports—more than doubled between 1982 and 1983, nearly doubled again between 1983 and 1984, and climbed another $25 billion to a record—since surpassed—$132 billion for 1985. Through these years about one-third of America's international trade deficit resulted from its trade with just one country—Japan.

Despite the sharp fall in the value of the dollar in relation to the yen, the United States' trade deficit, particularly its trade deficit with Japan, continues to fuel tensions between the two countries. Needless to say, this saddens me. It's almost like seeing a married couple, both of whom you're fond of, having serious misunderstandings. What is particularly sad about the situation between Japan and the United States is that they are arguing about something that doesn't really exist.

Let me make a very bold statement. At present, the United States does not have a trade deficit with Japan. In fact, if we had a better measuring rod, we might discover that there's a trade surplus.

My professional career has been almost a capsule history of the evolution of Japan's economy. I started out with the Tashima Trading Company, involved at a low level in its efforts to export traditional Japanese products like silk and lacquer ware. But for the past quarter of a century I have been involved in the international marketing of photo and business equipment products based on the convergence of highly sophisticated optics and electronics technology. Of necessity, my study of international trade has not been casual. But I'm amazed that so many business leaders, economists, market analysts, and governmental policymakers often base their conclusions on a superficial reading of misleading data. I'm not a statistician, but I do know how to count. And I know we can't count on the most widely accepted statistics to give us an accurate picture of what's going on in international trade. Trade statistics that give a false picture of the real world are one of my pet peeves. They don't just make me mad. They make me want to do something about changing them. There are several reasons why trade statistics that show a continuing United States trade deficit with Japan are misleading.

First, they are measured in current U.S. dollars, and no adjustment is made for the fact that the value of the American dollar has fallen more than 50 percent in relation to the Japanese yen since 1985. The value of Japanese and most European goods imported into the United States would have had to fall by more than 50 percent since 1985 for the United States trade deficit as currently measured to show any reduction at all in dollar terms. If trade with Japan and Europe actually had fallen 50 percent, the resulting disruption of international trade patterns would have sparked a worldwide depression. Yet policymakers, using misleading statistical standards, continue to set U.S. deficit reduction goals that, if achieved, would cause an international disaster.

In 1984, the bilateral United States trade deficit with Japan, measured in dollars, was reported as $31.2 billion. In 1987, that deficit was measured as $52.09 billion, an *increase* of 67 percent. But Japanese don't live on dollars. They live on yen. I have used commonly accepted yen-dollar currency translations of 240 for the Japanese fiscal year that covers most of 1984, and 130 for 1987. Measured in yen, the 1984 United States trade deficit was 7488.0 billion. The 1987 deficit was 6771.7 billion yen, a *decrease* of 9 percent. While Americans see a soaring increase in the bilateral deficit with Japan, Japanese experience a slight decrease. However, because the dollar is the internationally accepted medium of exchange, Japan, like most nations, reports its own trade figures in dollars. As a result, even Japanese trade officials are defensive about the United States' apparently growing trade deficit with Japan.

Since my whole professional life has been built on international trade, I take these data distortions very personally. The dollar-based data used to measure international trade are additionally misleading because no adjustment is made for the price increases that Japanese companies have been forced to make to compensate for at least part of the losses they have suffered. Minolta, for example, has limited price increases on its business equipment products because of the overall competitive situation in that market. We have had more flexibility with our 35-mm cameras, but even in this area we have raised prices only about 40 percent, which is still less than the 54 percent increases we would need to break even because of the fall in the value of the dollar. But in measuring the trade balance by current standards, we account for neither the fall in the value of the dollar nor the increase in the cost of imports, nor for any corresponding decrease in the cost of American exports. My own guess is that such adjustments would cut the apparent American trade deficit at least in half.

Competition for market share forces Minolta to a level of restraint in our price increases that has cut severely into operating income. But some American industries don't show comparable restraint. Take autos, for example. The American auto industry had an excellent opportunity to win back market share from the Japanese manufacturers who were forced to increase prices. But the American firms, lured by the opportunity for short-term profits, took advantage of the rising prices on Japanese cars to raise their own prices. As a result, they did not regain market share and imports of Japanese and other foreign cars went right on increasing. The only effective restraint on American imports of Japanese autos has been the system of voluntary quotas adopted by Japanese manufacturers under pressure from the United States government.

Americans continue to be willing to pay heavy price premiums for Japanese cars. And the dollar volume of Japanese auto imports has gone up even more because the manufacturers have begun exporting more luxury cars to the United States. In addition, the Japanese auto manufacturers have expanded their production facilities in the United States, which helps them overcome the effects of both the weaker dollar and the quotas on the number of vehicles they can export to the United States. In the auto industry, at least, the overall effect of the weaker dollar has been to increase Japanese product penetration in the United States, exactly the opposite of the intended effect.

To a far greater extent than most people realize, American companies also have extensive production facilities overseas. Another of the major drawbacks in currently accepted trade statistics is that they measure only goods actually shipped from one country to another, but don't reflect overall product penetration that includes, for example, products manufactured or sold by American firms operating in Japan. In an important study based on 1984 data, Kenichi Ohmae showed that in terms of total product penetration, including exports and products produced overseas, Japan and the United States were just about equally balanced. Ohmae, in a 1987 article in *The McKinsey Quarterly,* showed that United States exports to Japan in 1984 totaled $25.6 billion, but the three hundred largest American firms operating in Japan, out of a total of three thousand, sold another $43.9 billion in American products in Japan for a total of $69.5 billion. Japan's exports to the United States that year totaled $56.8 billion, but Japanese firms operating in the United States added only $12.8 billion in Japanese product penetration in the United States for a total of $69.6 billion. If only exports and imports are measured, the United States trade deficit with Japan appears to be $31.2 billion. In terms of total product penetration, the deficit shrinks to only $100 million. Even that's only part of the picture, because American firms in one recent year earned $800 million in licensing fees from Japanese firms for the rights to manufacture another $60 billion in American brand-name goods. And there are another twenty-seven hundred American firms in Japan whose sales weren't included in this study.

Overall, it appears clear that, if trade data were adjusted for currency devaluation, price inflation, and product penetration, America would show a trade surplus with Japan. But it will take a major reeducation effort to convince most policymakers of that.

The success of American firms operating in Japan is one of the great untold stories of our time. I have some personal favorites of my own, including the story of Lyle Fox, who has become known as the "Bagel King" of Japan. In 1982 Fox and his Japanese wife cornered the entire bagel market in Japan with production of six hundred bagels a day. By 1985 he was selling over two thousand bagels a day, and Fox's Bagels had become so trendy in Tokyo that his customers included the elegant Hotel Okura. He no longer enjoys 100 percent market share because competitors have moved in. But, as more and more Japanese have developed a taste for bagels, the size of the market has grown. After years of patiently testing an old family recipe and adjusting for Japanese tastes, Fox has recently begun franchising bagel outlets.

Another product with a hole in the middle, the donut, was about as popular back in 1970 as the bagel was when Lyle Fox got started. But an American company, Mister Donut, was secretly testing its operations in Osaka. A full-size replica of a Mister Donut shop was built inside a warehouse owned by a linen supplier. Employees of the linen supplier became a marketing focus group. The Japanese complained that the counters were too high, the coffee cups were too heavy, and the donuts were too big. By the time the first Mister Donut franchise opened a year later, the American concept had been completely adapted to the Japanese market. Today, Mister Donut is third among American fast-food companies operating in Japan, with more than four hundred outlets. Only McDonald's and Kentucky Fried Chicken have more. The biggest American donut operator, Dunkin' Donuts, is not so successful in Japan. We have a Dunkin' Donuts near our office in New Jersey. It's pretty good. In Japan, Dunkin' Donuts started business a year before Mister Donut. Maybe that was a mistake. They rushed to market before they studied the market.

The Barbie doll is another classic story of successful adaptation for the Japanese market. Barbie dolls have been little girls' best friends since 1958. More than two hundred million have been sold worldwide. But for years they didn't catch on in Japan. The doll's full figure expresses a Western idea of glamor, but it was not appropriate for the Far East. Though American fashion models and storeroom mannequins are popular in Japan among Westernized shoppers, young girls see things differently. What they saw in the Barbie doll was too much bosom up front and too much curve behind. By Japanese standards, the shape of the doll seemed neither realistic nor ideal. After surveying the reactions of Japanese elementary schoolgirls, the doll's key target market, the American manufacturer, Mattel Toys, reached an agreement with its Japanese distributor, Takara, to market a revised model. They trimmed the bust line, changed the hairstyle, and made the eyes slightly different. Now, Barbie dolls are among Takara's top-selling toys.

In all these cases, patience paved the way to success. American companies successfully operating in Japan have learned that in our country patience is not just a virtue but a necessity. While many American businessmen complain about Japan's "closed" markets, others have learned that with patience and a willingness to adapt products to fit local conditions and cultural patterns, those supposedly closed markets can open up. And the American success stories in Japan aren't limited to Barbie dolls and donuts. The most successful American companies in Japan include major high-tech manufacturers such as IBM, Xerox, Texas Instruments, NCR, and Hewlett-Packard. Highly successful consumer-products firms include Coca-Cola, Johnson and Johnson, Johnson Wax, Ritz crackers, and Tupperware. One Japanese in ten owns a cancer insurance policy written up by the Japanese branch of American Life Assurance Company of Columbus, Georgia, one of several American companies that do more business in Japan than in America. Others include Max Factor, Caterpillar Tractor, and the licensing division of Walt Disney Productions.

The average Japanese spends twice as much on American brand-name products as the average American spends on buying Japanese products. Not all of this translates into an improved balance of trade for the United States. Recent import promotion programs in Japan have urged consumers to buy more American products. Japanese are puzzled by this. They are already buying lots of American brand-name products, not realizing that many may have been manufactured in Japan or in a third country like Taiwan or Korea. Such countries, rather than the United States, have been the major beneficiaries of the American-led campaign to drive down the value of the dollar. Many of the American-based multinationals manufacturing in Japan actually export to America, thus adding to America's trade deficit while adding to their own profits.

IBM, for example, has eighteen thousand employees in Japan and profits estimated at $1 billion on annual sales of $6 billion. It exports to more than seventy countries, including the United States. The $20 billion in crude oil from the Middle East that American companies sell to Japan has no effect at all on the nominal trade balance between the United States and Japan. Nor do products made by American companies in countries like Korea and Taiwan for sale to Japan. Matsushita, the parent company of Panasonic, in the fall of 1988 saw an opportunity to do something about the United States' pressure on Japan to open up its electronic chip market to a 20 percent penetration by American products. Matsushita placed a multi-million-dollar order with the American firm Motorola. Motorola made the economically intelligent decision to fill this order from its low-cost plant in Taiwan. But what was good for Motorola was no good at all for America's trade deficit with Japan, at least as it's currently measured.

Because of the inadequacy of the data used to measure international trade, the sales in America of products manufactured by IBM and other American firms with factories in Japan count as Japanese exports and add to the trade deficit with the United States. Under circumstances like these, discussing the trade deficit between the United States and Japan makes about as much sense as it would to discuss the trade deficit between New York and New Jersey.

Products made by companies in each of those states are sold in the other. But what difference does it make if New York sells more to New Jersey or vice versa? States do compete for jobs and tax dollars, but with economies as closely integrated as they are among the fifty states of the union, or between Japan and America, the idea of trade deficits and surpluses becomes irrelevant. The dollars New Yorkers spend on products made in New Jersey eventually find their way back to New York in the form of money that New Jerseyans spend on things like dinner, theater, and shopping in New York or on investments on the New York Stock Exchange or debt servicing on loans from New York banks. Those dollars have to find their way back to New York or New Yorkers won't be able to buy any more products from New Jersey. The same is true between the United States and Japan. In recent years the dollars Americans have spent on products from Japan have been coming back to the United States in the form of Japanese investment in U.S. Treasury bonds, which help the government to pay the interest on its budget deficit, and more recently in real estate, artworks, stock, and leveraged buyout funds.

When I was in college, I didn't study my economics texts very diligently. But necessity has made me an avid, late-life student. Though our dean told us we were the worst graduating class in the history of Keio University, I believe that by now I have earned my degree in the school of hard economic knocks. One thing I have learned is that international trade is too important to the world economy for us to continue to make decisions based on outdated statistical standards that don't take into account the globalization of production by the multinational companies that dominate the modern economy. A Chevy Spectrum, made in Japan by Isuzu for its joint venture partner, General Motors, has an American nameplate, but is it an American car? Is a Toyota Camry made in Kentucky by American auto workers a Japanese car? Toyota and Honda have actually begun to make a small contribution to decreasing America's nominal trade deficit by exporting to Japan cars made in their American plants. General Motors is doing the same with a small number of Chevrolet Berettas and Corsicas made in its Linden, New Jersey, plant.

Even Minolta has begun exporting from the United States to Japan, though not willingly. I mentioned that when the dollar fell from its 1985 levels to about 175 yen to the dollar in September 1986, the gray market in Minolta cameras stopped. But as the dollar continued to fall, a "reverse" gray market started. With the dollar below 150 to the yen and falling, it becomes profitable for dealers in the United States to resell the Maxxums they've imported from Japan to dealers in Hong Kong and even in Japan itself, where they can be resold for less than cameras bought directly from the Minolta factory. As the dollar continued its fall to 120 yen, the reverse gray market in the Maxxum became very profitable. It's almost like buying gold as a hedge against falling currency values. If the dollar continues to fall, the camera bought in America can be resold in Japan for a greater yen equivalent than its original cost. And so America has begun exporting Japanese cameras to Japan.

Inadvertently reexporting Maxxums was not Minolta's first experience in exporting from the United States to Japan. Several years ago we decided to make our own modest effort to balance trade by exporting American wine to Japan. We weren't very good at it and probably drank more of the wine ourselves than we ever managed to find buyers for in Japan. Toyota has begun a similar effort and in 1988 planned to export about $275,000 in California wines to Japan, not much compared to the $11.5 billion in cars and trucks Toyota sold in the United States the previous year. Other Japanese companies do better.

In fact, two of the top exporters of American products are Japanese companies. Boeing is usually America's number one exporter. Those two generals, General Motors and General Electric, are always near the top, along with Ford Motor Company and IBM. But the combined exports of Mitsui & Company (USA) and its grain affiliate generally place it in the top five among exporters of American products, and Mitsubishi International Corporation, based in New York, does almost as well. Mitsui, Mitsubishi, and eight other Japanese firms through their United States trading affiliates handle nearly 10 percent of all American exports. That group includes the trading company that helped Minolta get its start in the United States, Kanematsu-Gosho. It is generally accepted in international banking circles that less than five percent of the American companies that could be selling abroad actually do so. Congress tried to improve this situation by passing the Export Trading Company Act of 1982, allowing banks to invest in trading companies that could be part of an American equivalent of the Japanese "convoy" system linking banks, trading companies, and manufacturers. This is how Minolta and virtually every other Japanese company got its start in world trade. But after an initial surge of enthusiasm, the American banks began to lose interest. Timing was a factor. The American banks became active at a time when the dollar was strong, making American exports so expensive that they became less competitive in foreign markets. But at the exchange rates prevailing over the past two years there should be much more American export activity.

The current exchange rates act as both a strong form of American protectionism against imports from Japan and as an export subsidy. Economists continue to argue about the fair value of the dollar in relation to the yen. One rather complex approach is based on the theory of purchasing-power parity. Right now a Japanese tourist in America can get more for his money than an American tourist in

Japan. With purchasing-power parity, the currency of each tourist would have equal buying power in the other's country. And, in theory at least, international trade patterns would be better balanced.

I have my own simplified purchasing-power parity theory, which I call the Maxxum Maxim. It requires no statistical calculations and has the advantage of indicating not a specific and difficult-to-maintain exchange rate but rather a more flexible trading range. The Maxxum Maxim is that range of yen-to-dollar exchange rates at which there is no gray-market activity in the Maxxum in either direction. History has shown us that when the yen is above 200 to the dollar, there is a strong gray market in Japanese goods coming into the United States. The gray market appears to dry up when the yen is between 170 and 180 to the dollar. The reverse gray market starts when the dollar keeps falling below 170 yen.

According to the Maxxum Maxim, the American dollar should be worth 170 to 180 yen. That would give us a "level playing field" for trade between the United States and Japan—at least as far as currency rates are concerned. This is roughly the same conclusion reached by using another whimsical method of measuring purchasing-power parity—the Big Mac Index—which is based on the prices charged for McDonald's hamburgers in New York and Tokyo.

We need new ways of looking at trade and currency data if we're going to be able to make intelligent decisions about trade policy. The Maxxum Maxim and Big Mac Index may not be the answers, but I believe they may be more useful than many other closely watched trends.

The most closely watched trade statistic, and the one that triggered the October 1987 stock market collapse, is the monthly United States merchandise trade balance released by the U.S. Commerce Department. Economists know it is flawed in many respects, yet it has more impact on international markets and government policymakers than other figures that are at least marginally more reliable. For example, the Commerce Department merchandise trade-deficit figures do not include trade in services that play an increasingly important role in the economies of postindustrial societies like the United States and Japan. The so-called current-account figures, which include services and financial transactions, give a broader picture but come out later and attract less attention then the merchandise trade figures. The quarterly balance-of-payment figures are probably the most accurate and give a better picture of long-term trends, but they exclude military trade, another significant item for the United States, trade in nonmonetary gold, and freight and insurance costs as factors in the dollar volume of imports.

In addition, many experts believe the U.S. Commerce Department grossly underestimates service exports. A study of 1984 data by the Office of Technology Assessment of the United States Congress said that official data underestimated service exports by as much as $47 billion. Trade figures released by U.S. customs always differ from the Commerce Department's figures, adding to the confusion.

Clearly, we need better statistical tools to measure international trade. This is not merely an academic problem, because inaccurate data have contributed to the misunderstandings that exist between the United States and Japan. The Japan-bashing symbolically represented by American auto workers smashing Japanese cars on the dock and congressmen smashing Japanese electronic products on the steps of the Capitol frightens me. The public-opinion polls showing that respect for America is declining in Japan, especially among the young, also worry me. But I don't see any quick solutions until we begin to remove the many misconceptions Japan and the United States have about each other, including statistically based misconceptions about our trade relations.

Personally, I would like to see an international conference, under the auspices of the International Monetary Fund or some other multinational organization, that would examine current data measuring trade relations and recommend new international standards that reflect the globalization of the economy. The same conference should also seek to develop broader and more consistent ratios of fair currency exchange rates. I would volunteer to conduct a seminar on the Maxxum Maxim, and explain why America in 1988 was exporting Japanese cameras to Japan.

28

Don't Try Selling Yachts to China, but . . .

The United States has a strange passion for making major issues out of minor trade possibilities. Yachts are a good example. During 1987 and 1988 my wife and I were invited on unusual cruises on two magnificent yachts. The first, in 1987, on Trammell Crow's *Michaela Rose*, took us up the Yangtze River to a confrontation with history. The second, on Malcolm Forbes's *Highlander V*, moved us through the Panama Canal to the Galápagos Islands and an involvement with evolution. Both ships are oceangoing, luxury vessels, and I can understand the appeal of owning a private, oceangoing yacht.

I had met the younger Trammell Crow and his father several years back. In April 1987, the same month Minolta moved into Infomart in Dallas, Trammell Crow, Jr., invited Kuniko and me to join him on a cruise going up the Yangtze from Shanghai to Nanking. Kuniko and I flew to Shanghai, then boarded the *Michaela Rose* for our journey up the great river. The Yangtze flows nearly 4,000 miles across China from the mountains of Tibet to the East China sea. Much of the river isn't navigable at all, and swift rapids and deep, narrow gorges make other stretches extremely dangerous. Our journey to Nanking, with several stops along the way, took us only about 245 miles upriver from Shanghai. This peaceful stretch of the river carried us simultaneously through history and into the heart of modern China. Our traveling companions included Dwight Ryan, head of marketing for Xerox; John Foster of AT&T; Bill Patton of Basic Four; and Sam Weigand of Grid Company. All of our firms are involved to one degree or another in computers, office automation, and international trade, so there was lots of shop talk along with our fascination with life along the Yangtze. We were all traveling as couples, and we all got along very well. To me, however, the journey itself was a sad one.

The people of China have missed out on the economic advances enjoyed by their neighbors in Hong Kong, South Korea, Taiwan, and Japan. In fact, China today reminds me of Japan in the early 1950s, drab and gray and dull. For China, World War II was only one phase in warfare that began in the mid-1930s against Japan and continued through the late 1940s in the civil war between the Nationalists and Communists and into the 1950s with the Korean War. Though the United States supported China during World War II, postwar China did not benefit from being occupied and aided by the United States as Japan did. The advantages of America's generosity to Japan are particularly evident in contrast to today's China.

The photos I took in China are in color, but I feel I would have lost little by shooting in black-and-white. Though Shanghai is a vibrant, crowded city of over ten million, I kept looking for some signs of brightness, color, and gaiety. I looked in vain. The city seemed old, the people intense, jostling in the crowded marketplaces and furiously pedaling the bicycles that are the dominant form of transportation. Occasionally, I could catch a sense of Shanghai as it must have been in the years before the war when it was one of the world's most international cities, with its foreign "concessions" dating back to the mid-nineteenth century; these concession were, in effect, independent little countries for the British, American, and French communities. There was even a Japanese concession that became a center for cotton mills. The Shanghai skyline evokes images of Manhattan as I imagine it in the 1920s, and in the evenings you can see a few scattered art deco neon signs that are visual echoes of a lost era. But electric power is in short supply. When we visited museums, the guards would turn out the lights behind us as we left one room for another, and department stores were so poorly lit that we could barely see the limited range of goods.

As we started our journey upriver, it was a strange experience to be sailing aboard such a luxurious symbol of capitalism through the heartland of a Socialist country whose experiment with dialectical materialism has brought its people so little in the way of material benefits. The people looked healthy enough and food seemed plentiful, far more so than in postwar Japan. I must say the people were also friendly and curious about us and showed few signs of hostility or envy. Though people in the major cities we visited, like Shanghai and Nanking, are used to seeing foreigners, we visited several smaller cities along the river where we were a great curiosity. It wasn't unusual to stroll into one of the crowded public gardens and have people gather round to applaud us as a way of saying welcome.

Wherever we went, the children were fascinated by us and by the Polaroid camera that Trammell Crow, Jr.'s wife, Barbara, was using. She took hundreds of photos and gave away many to the children who hovered around us. I was impressed by the fun you can have with a Polaroid. The fact that you can see the photo you've just taken in a matter of seconds always amuses people. Though the novelty has begun to wear off in America, I'm convinced there's a market for Polaroids that is still largely untapped in many parts of the world.

In the case of China, however, interest doesn't necessarily translate into demand, particularly for imports. Over the years, Minolta has made a few rather substantial sales to China, sometimes closing orders for several thousand cameras at a time. However, years may go by between sales because China can only buy when it has surplus foreign-currency reserves. Since it exports relatively little, China can rarely afford to import, a lesson the United States should heed.

When American businessmen who are interested in exports look at China, they see a vast potential market. But as a market, China is vast only in terms of its area and population. China is still a poor country, and its Socialist economy, though liberalized somewhat in recent years, limits economic expansion. In addition, China is much less interested in imports than in developing its own industries, particularly when, in the process, it can obtain technologies it now lacks. Minolta, for example, reached a technical agreement with China in 1979 that allows China to produce cameras for its domestic market.

The Chinese passion for cameras rivals that of the Japanese. Though cameras are expensive, a surprising number of Chinese apparently make the sacrifice necessary to own one. Several times I recognized a Minolta made in China, though, of course, without the Minolta name. China is interested in importing technologies, machine tools, and other industrial equipment that will help it develop its own industries, but I suspect that for the foreseeable future China will be a limited market for consumer imports.

I must admit that I enjoyed my trips on the *Michaela Rose* and the *Highlander*. But I don't think Japan would be much better than China as a prospective market for American yachts. When I hear talk about Japan opening its markets for the import of more yachts, I realize that it reflects the American perception that Japanese are wealthy. As I've said before, we aren't. Nor do Japan's tough tax laws allow write-offs for luxury items like yachts used for business purposes. In addition, even men like KT who head multibillion-dollar corporations aren't likely to buy pleasure boats. Though there are some exceptions, most Japanese who can afford a yacht don't allow themselves the leisure to enjoy owning one. But the biggest problem in trying to sell big pleasure boats to Japan is that we don't have room for them. Japan is a nation of fish eaters and fishermen. According to tradition, fishing boats have priority for dock space. I don't know who gave fishing boats this right, but it has often been used to block efforts to establish marinas for pleasure boats. Even if Japan removed all barriers to the importation of yachts, the market would still be small and Taiwan would get most of the business because of its efficient shipbuilding industry and the advantage of a weak currency tied to the dollar.

Other minor markets that American trade negotiators have pursued with a passion include aluminum baseball bats, skis, beef, citrus fruits, and cigarettes. After years of bitter debate, Japan opened its markets to all of these products. But the debate fueled strong resentments on both sides of the Pacific. A good deal of silliness was involved. One Japanese trade official, for example, has been quoted as saying that American skis aren't suitable for import because we have a different type of snow in Japan. On the other hand, American trade negotiators, pressured by domestic manufacturing and agricultural interests, have taken tough positions demanding greater market access for products that, if all American demands were met, would reduce the trade imbalance by only a fraction. For example, updating figures from a study done by the American economist, Steve H. Hanke, I've estimated that if all Japanese restrictions on American agricultural products were removed, the United States trade balance with Japan would improve by not more than $1.5 billion, roughly 3 percent of the bilateral trade deficit.

If the United States wants to get serious about exporting more to Japan, it might reconsider restrictions imposed on American exports, not by Japan but by the United States itself. For example, United States government policy, based on laws supported by environmentalists and shipping interests, prevents Japan from importing unprocessed logs cut on federal lands in Alaska and Alaskan oil and natural gas. One small exception made by the Reagan administration allows oil exports from Alaska's Cook Inlet. If all restrictions on the export of Alaskan logs and oil to Japan were lifted, the bilateral trade deficit with Japan could be cut by about $15 billion, a significant 30 percent reduction. Private enterprise has shown the way by cashing in on an Alaskan resource that is much more difficult to exploit than oil and timber—melted glacier ice. Wetco, a small Alaskan firm, has begun exporting what it calls "Alaska's answer to Perrier" to Japan and other markets. In Japan, where Alaska has an image of being "pure," Wetco's pure bottled water has become a big seller. If private enterprise can turn icebergs into an asset, surely the government can release Alaskan oil and timber for export. Such a move would be applauded in Japan because, particularly in the case of oil, it would give Japan a chance to buy something it really needs from America.

Instead, as the new administration took over in Washington in January 1989, American trade officials seemed determined to make another major push to pressure Japan to open its tightly controlled rice market to American exports. Frankly, most Japanese would benefit by being able to buy imported American rice. As I've discovered during my years in America, California rice appeals to Japanese taste buds. It is also much less expensive than Japan's homegrown product. But there are other issues involved.

I will never forget the shock I experienced when I learned as a teen-ager that we were better off in Korea during the war years than our countrymen back in Japan. Rice was the most powerful indicator of our higher standard of living. Even the meager rice rations we carried with us as refugees from Korea made us better off than Japanese at home, who had no rice at all. Anyone who lived through that experience can easily be convinced that Japan must be self-sufficient in rice production no matter what the cost. And the cost is high.

Government subsidies to rice growers in 1988 reached $4.4 billion. Coupled with an almost total ban on rice imports, the subsidies push the price of rice in Japan to about eight times more than the world market price. But Japan has been a nation of rice growers since the sixth century, and rice cultivation is woven deeply into the cultural fabric of our nation. For example, the Japanese word for lunch translates literally as "midday rice" and the word for dinner means "evening rice." Shinto rites and local festivals mark the cycles of rice planting and harvests. Until his illness became serious in 1988, Emperor Hirohito tended his own small rice paddy on the grounds of the palace, making the royal family one of the 3.5 million Japanese households involved in rice cultivation. Just before he went into his final coma before his death in January 1989, the Emperor woke from sleep and asked, "How is the rice crop?" These may have been his last words.

The Emperor offered his rice harvest to the gods, but most of Japan's millions of rice planters offer their harvest to the farmers' cooperatives that sell it to the government at inflated prices for resale to wholesalers at lower, subsidized prices that are still way above world market levels. Only about 20 percent of Japan's rice farms are serious commercial operations. Most are tiny plots tended by part-time farmers. All benefit from government subsidies, and the cooperatives benefit most of all.

Recent surveys show that 70 percent of the people believe Japan must remain self-sufficient in rice. I count myself among that percentage, but there are those who believe this should not mean an absolute ban on imports. Yujiro Hayami, a university professor and author of the book *Japanese Agriculture Under Siege*, has not become popular by saying, "All this talk about rice self-sufficiency and national security is propaganda. Rice is a welfare program for the cooperatives. Nothing else."

A Japanese entrepreneur has challenged the rice monopoly by selling small bags of American rice, at airports, hotels, and tourist shops, under regulations that allow tourists to bring back foreign produce in limited amounts. The fall in the value of the dollar has brought a flood of Japanese tourists into the United States. About two million came in 1988, an increase of half a million from the year before. A loophole in the ban on imported rice allows each tourist to bring home 220 pounds of rice for personal use. But so far Kiyoshi Minagawa, through a company he operates in Los Angeles, each year sells only about sixty thousand red, white, and blue bags (at $2.50 apiece) containing two pounds of California rice. Even if he sold 220 pounds of California rice to all two million Japanese tourists, that would account for only about 2 percent of Japan's annual rice consumption. Minagawa has created more controversy than cash with his effort, but publicity surrounding his venture has made consumers more aware of what the import ban means to them. And who knows? If he has patience, he may in time influence consumer demand and begin to create a demand for American rice that the politicians won't be able to resist.

Japan's ruling Liberal party depends heavily on support from voters in rural areas, whose voting power, based on election districts drawn long ago when rural population was much higher, far outweighs that of urban voters. One vote in the countryside counts as much as six votes in the city in terms of electing representatives to Japan's parliament. But there isn't much protest about rice prices from urban consumers. Japan is a nation of consensus. We don't tackle problems with the adversarial traditions that come naturally to Americans. Japan's consumer advocacy groups have close ties to the agricultural cooperatives and support rice subsidies and import restrictions in the name of Japan's cultural heritage, the demands of self-sufficiency, and even national security. It is a game that all nations play.

There were strong reactions, on national security grounds, when Fujitsu in 1986 offered to buy Fairchild Semiconductor. Political opposition in the United States cited the dangers of foreign ownership of a firm involved in such a sensitive industry. Somehow it didn't seem to trouble the politicians that the American-based company was already owned by a foreign firm, the French oil giant Schulmberger. Fujitsu withdrew its offer.

Norway and France are among the NATO allies who have agreed to restrict the export of military sensitive equipment to the Soviet bloc. However, the congressmen who were photographed sledgehammering a Toshiba radio on the steps of the Capitol in Washington did not seem equally disturbed when Toshiba's Norwegian partner, Kongsberg Vaapenfabrikk, sold precision milling equipment to the Soviet Union. The fact that a now bankrupt French firm, Rattier-

Forest, had previously sold restricted machine tools to the same Leningrad shipyard caused barely a ripple of protest. Germany has replaced the United States as the world's biggest exporting country and enjoys a huge surplus in its trade with America. But I haven't seen any congressmen smashing the products of the German firms accused of helping Libya develop a chemical warfare capacity.

Exporting chemical warfare materials should be stopped, but I do question the wisdom of the export restrictions on some supposedly "sensitive" equipment, whether the target nations are left-wing, like the People's Republic of China and the Soviet Union; right-wing, like South Africa; or anti-American like Libya, Iran, and various Third World countries. Getting such countries involved in the global economic order that makes the United States the prosperous envy of the world is the best way I know of defusing tensions and avoiding hostilities.

I hope there is no racism involved in finding these activities objectionable in a Japanese firm but okay when the company involved is European. I can understand the widespread, if shortsighted, feeling that local industries must be protected from foreign "invasions." Given such national tendencies, coupled with the special role of rice in Japanese culture, this may be another of those areas where American efforts to open a Japanese market are poorly aimed. The American effort comes at a time when rice consumption in Japan is decreasing as Westernization turns Japanese taste buds toward McDonald's hamburgers, bread and jam, and Häagen-Dazs ice cream. According to Japanese government estimates, per capita rice consumption was six bowls a day in 1955 but declined to only two bowls, or 220 pounds a year, by 1986. In addition, even though Japan's rice-producing farms are inefficient, bumper crops in recent years have created huge government surpluses. In an effort to reduce the surpluses, the government has cut both the price it pays to the cooperatives and grocery-store prices. But the surpluses are still high. I question the wisdom of trying to sell rice to a country that has a surplus.

Construction has been another area in which the United States seems to have misdirected its pressure on Japan. Since 1986 American trade negotiators have argued that Japan should allow American firms to bid on public projects such as the controversial expansion of Kansai airport near Minolta's hometown of Osaka. Bowing to American pressure despite strong objections from its domestic construction industry, in March 1988 Japan signed an agreement on Kansai and other public works construction bidding, but by then there were indications that there was only limited interest in the project on the part of American construction companies. One embarrassing mix-up typified the confused approach.

The Japanese goverment arranged a seminar on the Kansai project for a visiting United States presidential commission of construction industry and government officials. The seminar opened, but the American guests never showed up. Given the scope of the project, it may be years before we know how it finally works out. After all the bitterness stirred up by the prolonged negotiations, it remains to be seen how many American firms will get, or even bid on, any of the work. My own guess is that the amount of work going to American firms will not justify the resentments stirred up on both sides of the Pacific.

Prolonged and bitter talks on various agricultural products finally led in 1988 to agreements covering several areas, including beef and citrus fruit, that had been major issues for the Americans. Japan also agreed to American demands to ease restrictions on cigarette imports. The potential increase in American exports to Japan that may result from the agreements is likely to be less than 1 percent of the current trade deficit. Japan is already the world's biggest market for American beef and citrus fruit. How much more can we buy? Japan is also America's number one market for commercial aircraft and parts, data processing equipment, inorganic chemicals, pharmaceuticals, broadcasting equipment and, of course, movies. Japan is also one of the top markets for American cotton, tobacco, corn, sorghum, food grains, coal, and timber. Japan can do more, much more, to improve trade relations with America, but we need some help from Americans, particularly on issues like Alaskan oil and logs.

The Japan External Trade Organization—as its name implies—promotes Japan's international trade relations. JETRO realizes international trade can't all flow one way and, in addition to supporting Japan's export efforts, it works hard to assist American firms in exporting to Japan. In March 1985 JETRO sponsored a "Made in U. S. A." trade fair in Nagoya. The fair was open to all products but recommended categories included medical equipment and supplies, computer-assisted design and manufacturing, biotechnology, analytic instruments, sporting goods, recreational equipment, and health products. Though the fair was only a limited success, mainly because of limited American participation, it did point the way toward the development of markets in Japan for American products that Japanese want to buy.

I have no quarrel with the American manufacturers of aluminum baseball bats. They have a product they want to sell and, unlike many American firms, they show a real interest in exports. That's great. But I'm not sure it's in America's interest to burn up its reserves of goodwill with trading partners like Japan by fighting over products that have limited market potential. Democratic governments tend to respond to the demands of lobbies that make the most noise, whether they are the rice cooperatives of Japan or the baseball-bat makers of America. But the United States lacks an organization like JETRO that can take a broader view of trade issues and formulate approaches that are in the national interest, rather than in the interests of a particular industry or company.

If America wants to export more to Japan, more attention must be paid to what the Japanese want to buy. The list of products sought by JETRO for its "Made in U.S.A." trade fair was one good indicator. Another form of market research is simply to watch what Japanese tourists buy when they're in America. I have noticed that bathroom furnishings and fixtures are always a big item for homeward-bound Japanese tourists. Larger, American-style homes have become popular in Japan, which opens up possibilities for the increased export of coffee tables and other small items of American furniture, as well as home furnishings and appliances—*if* they are adapted for the Japanese market.

The American media and at least some American politicians create the impression that Japan bars American products while the American market is totally open. The truth is more complex. Even before easing restrictions in 1988, Japan was already importing a total of 30 percent of its beef. By contrast, American beef imports are limited by law to 8 percent. And forty-four American states have laws that ban Japanese mandarin oranges. Among other items protected by heavy American tariffs, quotas, and other import restrictions are steel, automobiles, candy, radios, handbags, rubber boots, blue jeans, men's sweaters, and women's dress gloves. Such barriers added an estimated $65 billion to the cost paid by American consumers for all items protected by special trade regulations in 1985.

Clearly, I have some misgivings about American trade policy, but not about Americans. Virtually every American I have talked to about international trade has shown an ability to understand the realities of the situation, including some like Richard Gephardt, the congressman from Saint Louis, who have reputations as diehard protectionists. When Representative Gephardt sought the Democratic party presidential nomination, his campaign stressed America's trade problems. He and I participated in a panel on world trade at an International Leadership Seminar sponsored by the Hugh O'Brien Youth Foundation at Washington University in Saint Louis in July 1988. I found him to be well informed on the subtleties of international trade and on Japan's efforts to improve the trade imbalance between our countries. Some of the protectionist measures he favors might prove harmful, particularly if they sparked retaliation by America's trading partners, but his approach is not as hard-line as the media and his political opponents have indicated. He is open to a reasoned discussion of the trade issue, as are most Americans I have talked to.

The Americans who were with us on our cruise up the Yangtze were all involved with industries that have felt the threat of Japanese competition. But they also recognized America's dependence on Japanese imports and investment. Though Kuniko and I were the only Japanese in our group, we felt comfortable traveling in China with our American companions, even when the controversial topic of trade relations came up. But I did have disquieting moments when we took a bus tour to the memorial for those killed in the fall of Nanking to the Japanese army in 1937.

History books in many parts of the world use the phrase "The Rape of Nanking" to describe what in Japan we call "the Nanking Incident." I can imagine the troubled emotional reactions Americans who lived through World War II must have when they visit the memorials in Hiroshima and Nagasaki. As a young boy I had accepted the propaganda of our military government, and I remembered the patriotic fervor I felt during the celebrations among the Japanese community in Seoul when Nanking fell in December 1937. These memories crowded through my mind, bumping against the words of our tour guide, who told us that 200,000 innocent people had been slaughtered in just one week by Japanese troops during the fall of the city, which was then the capital of China.

If our guide recognized the fact that Kuniko and I were Japanese, he did nothing to show it. His manner was calm and matter-of-fact as he recounted rapes and other atrocities. I have seen even higher estimates of the death toll, up to 400,000 residents. I felt a great sense of shame that Japan had been responsible for such crimes, but my mind resisted, not the fact that civilians had been brutally raped and murdered but the numbers. Perhaps because I'm a businessman, I tend to take a skeptical approach to casually compiled statistics. I couldn't help, for example, comparing in my mind the reported death tolls in Nanking in 1937 with the combined death-toll estimates of 200,000 in Hiroshima and Nagasaki in 1945. It doesn't seem humanly—or inhumanly—possible for soldiers armed not with atomic bombs but with rifles, grenades, and machine guns, to have killed so many people in Nanking in such a relatively short time. The Japanese forces would have had to be very efficiently organized for the sole purpose of killing as many civilians as possible, and there is no evidence to indicate that this was the case. Rather, it seems that the Japanese soldiers were out of control. The population of Nanking was then about one million, and the slaughter took place in just one week. The wildly divergent estimates of the death toll also make me wonder about the reliability of the numbers.

Even if the death toll at Nanking had been one-tenth of the 200,000 estimate, the atrocities, the rapes, and the killing of so many civilians should make all Japanese feel a great sense of shame. But that is not the case. Perhaps because we find it difficult to face up to the shame, most Japanese tend to ignore what happened at Nanking and other stories of Japanese atrocities from the Philippines to Burma. It may never be possible to have an accurate estimate of the needless deaths that Japanese troops were responsible for at Nanking. But it should be possible for Japan to acknowledge that its military was responsible for some terrible things during the war years and to educate the younger generation about the war. For example, in a footnote to a brief discussion of Japan's invasion of China, one high school textbook, *New Detailed Japanese History*, says: "At the time, the Japanese military killed many Chinese people, including civilians, and it became a big issue after the end of the war at the Tokyo Tribunal." That's all.

We all have reason to shudder at the horrors of war and at the capacity of so many to forget or ignore those horrors. Japan's Asian neighbors take offense at these tendencies. Two cabinet officials in Japan have been dismissed in recent years because China and South Korea so strongly protested their public remarks that played down Japan's faults during the Sino-Japanese War and during the long occupation of Korea. I didn't speak of my troubled feelings that day in Nanking, but I can't shake loose the conflicting thoughts and emotions I experienced.

The year before, during an incentive trip to Hawaii for our business equipment dealers, I made my first visit to the Pearl Harbor memorial. I had been in Hawaii many times before but had always managed to avoid a visit, without doubt because of the pangs of a guilty conscience. Pearl Harbor was another great shame for Japan, and there is no denying that our envoys in Washington were conducting peace talks as our fleet sailed toward Hawaii. Seeing the Pearl Harbor memorial, and especially the battleship *Arizona*, in the company of so many American friends, was not an easy experience. I seemed, I suppose, the usual inscrutable Oriental, but, though I said little, I was rocked by strong emotions. The *Arizona*, disabled that day and later restored, is still the tomb of some of the sailors entangled in the wreckage. It was hard for me to imagine the remains of those young men still entombed as part of history so far from their homes in the continental United States.

We have an expression in Japanese that means "Let it go in the stream." The English equivalent might be "That's water under the bridge." But in Japan the sentiment is very much part of our national character. Most Japanese would prefer to forget not only the war years, but also the period of the occupation.

The Japanese capacity to forget the past, including the immediate past when it is unpleasant, can have its positive aspect. One reason the American occupation went so smoothly was the fact that Japanese could let such horrors as Hiroshima and Nagasaki and the firebombing of Tokyo, Osaka, and other cities "go in the stream." But when Japanese forget the American generosity that helped us rebuild our cities and re-create our economy, we put ourselves in danger of letting our current success delude us into the arrogance that paved the way for so many past mistakes.

In this age of new affluence and a strong yen, many Japanese can now afford to travel abroad. Hawaii is a popular tourist destination. A fair number of younger Japanese visit the Pearl Harbor memorial but few of my generation ever go there. I don't blame them. It's a disturbing experience for anyone who lived through the war years. But I wish every Japanese had the opportunity to visit Pearl Harbor and Nanking, just as I wish every American could visit Hiroshima. Such eye-opening experiences might save us all from arrogance—and future mistakes.

In November 1987, my long effort to arrange an award for Dr. Deming at the annual dinner of the Japanese Chamber of Commerce of New York took an unexpected turn. In an earlier chapter I described the Cosmos Club dinner at which I asked Dr. Deming if he would accept the chamber's annual award for the contributions he had made to Japan's industrial recovery in the years since World War II. He was more than pleased at the honor being accorded him, but I left our dinner meeting aware that we faced major problems. The first was Dr. Deming's crowded schedule. The second was his insistence on speaking for at least thirty minutes. Chamber protocol called for the major speaker to be an invited guest from Japan. The award winner, generally an American, was expected to make only brief acceptance remarks. In negotiations conducted by phone over the weeks that followed, we managed to work out the scheduling difficulty, but the length of Dr. Deming's remarks continued to pose a problem. Dr. Deming remained adamant while my Chamber of Commerce colleagues pressed me to get him to agree to a shorter speech.

Eiji Toyoda, chairman of Toyota Motor Corporation, had agreed to be the keynote speaker. His remarks would be delivered in Japanese and then read paragraph by paragraph by an interpreter, which meant we had to set aside about an hour for our main speaker. With the other ceremonies scheduled for the evening, a second lengthy speech could have carried our program past midnight. I was worried about that. On the other hand, we arranged what turned out to be a well-attended press conference for Mr. Toyoda on the afternoon of the November 9 dinner, and *The Wall Street Journal* agreed to run an article under my byline on its editorial page that morning, referring to the dinner and Dr. Deming.

But as the night of the dinner drew near, I still didn't know what to do about Dr. Deming's speech. I suggested that his message might be more effectively conveyed if we distributed copies of the full text to the media and each of the dinner guests while he delivered only a summary. No luck. Dr. Deming let us know that he prefers to speak from notes rather than preparing a formal text. Then, two weeks before the dinner, Dr. Deming's secretary, Cecelia Kilian, called to tell us Dr. Deming had been hobbled by a foot infection. He had canceled several appointments and trips but, if his doctors allowed it, he still hoped to be on hand for the chamber dinner and his acceptance speech. Dr. Deming asked that, if he couldn't make it, arrangements could be made for his daughter, Mrs. Linda Haupt, to attend the dinner and accept the award on his behalf. Personally, I still hoped that Dr. Deming would somehow get to New York and deliver his speech, but I think it's fair to say that some of my colleagues at the chamber were relieved at the possibility that Mr. Toyoda might be our only major speaker.

My *Wall Street Journal* article played an important role in the genesis of this book. The original title, "The Secret of Japan's Success: Made in the U.S.A.," was also the first title I thought of for the book, and many of the themes touched on in the book first appeared in print in that article. *The Wall Street Journal* reaches the audience of top American managers that Dr. Deming wants to motivate with his message about the need for continuous quality control. So I'm glad my article appeared on the day of the chamber's dinner and that it covered at least part of the message Dr. Deming would have wanted to deliver that evening.

But Dr. Deming's foot problem finally did keep him from joining us that night. His daughter's gracious remarks in accepting the award on his behalf were well received but no substitute for the speech her father had hoped to deliver. The Toyota Motor Corporation had won the Deming Prize in 1965, and in his own speech that night, Eiji Toyoda praised Dr. Deming for his many contributions to Japan's industrial recovery and high product standards. The chamber's dinner filled the Grand Ballroom of the New York Hilton with fifteen hundred guests, the biggest crowd that could be packed into any comparable auditorium in New York City. The eighty blue-ribbon special guests on the dais made up a virtual "Who's Who" of the business community in the United States. The dinner's success, after many difficulties and some nervous moments, crowned my activities with an organization that has played an important role in my life and in strengthening the ties that link the American and Japanese business communities.

I was still nervous, but very proud, on the night of the dinner itself. My wife tells me that my delivery of the speech I gave was the worst I have ever made. "You kept your head buried in your papers and talked so fast no one could understand a word you said."

I had practiced so often that I almost knew the speech by heart, but it didn't help.

I was pleased that New York's mayor, Ed Koch, managed to get to our cocktail reception and say a few words. I had first met Koch several years before at Japan Air Lines' Sakura lounge at Tokyo airport. Tokyo and New York are sister cities, and Koch was returning to New York after some important meetings with Japanese officials. We had a pleasant talk in the lounge as I told him about my great love for his city, and I looked forward to a longer talk with him on our flight back to the States. One thought I had in mind as I settled into the comfort of my first-class seat was to let the mayor know what I felt about the deterioration of city services. I must admit that I wondered about the city sending its mayor off on a trip to Tokyo while it couldn't afford to spend money on hospitals, subways, schools, and city streets. I planned to give the mayor a piece of my mind.

But once we were in the air and I looked around my first-class cabin, I saw that Mayor Koch was nowhere to be found. I checked with a flight attendant and discovered that the cost-cutting mayor was flying tourist class. I felt a bit shamefaced, remembering my own first trip across the Pacific in third-class accommodations aboard the SS *President Wilson*. It was a crowded flight, and I had no chance to break the class barriers and go back into the tourist section to talk with the mayor. But I was impressed that the mayor, who is fairly tall, was saving the city money even at the cost of squeezing into a cramped tourist seat for a fourteen-hour flight.

I greeted him warmly when I saw him again at the reception. His friendship for Japan is very real, as is his appreciation of Japan's role in the economy of the city. I was saddened in August 1987 when Mayor Koch suffered a mild stroke on his way to a cherry-blossom tree-planting ceremony in Riverside Park. I was representing the Japanese Chamber of Commerce, and the mayor and I were scheduled to plant the first tree together. In his absence, I handled the shovel myself and was happy to hear on the television news later that evening that he was recovering. Dr. Deming also recovered from his foot infection and the last time I spoke to him, in January 1989, he was about to take off on a lecture tour in Australia.

The annual award dinner is the chamber's main source of funds for its extensive charitable work with a variety of American public service organizations. This is something relatively new for Japanese corporations. In Japan, charitable donations are not tax deductible for either individuals or firms. Fortunately, Minolta gives me a free hand in the charitable work we do in the United States, though I know that some people in our home office think I'm crazy for giving away Minolta's money. And, I must confess, with the squeeze on income we've suffered as a result of the falling value of the dollar, we haven't had much of a margin for generosity in the past couple of years. But I'm grateful to the chamber for leading the way in an organized effort by the Japanese business community to reach out with a helping hand to our American neighbors.

That night at the Chamber of Commerce dinner, like the evening of February 1986 when I was named to the Hall of Fame of the Photo Marketing Association, ranks among the proudest occasions of my life. When I look back on what I have managed to achieve since I first arrived in America with two suitcases of cameras in 1954, I can't help feeling a real sense of accomplishment. With KT, Kinji Moriyama, and Takeshi Mitarai of Canon, I am only the fourth Japanese ever named to PMA's Hall of Fame. It is a great honor, but one that I know I must accept in the context of all the help Minolta has had from the many Americans who have taught us how to work in their markets, who have distributed our products through their dealerships and retail outlets, and who have been our loyal customers and employees. Millions of Americans have been involved in the Minolta success story, and I can never forget all that America has meant not just to me personally, but also to my company, Minolta, and to Japan, my country.

29

Evolution Is a Capitalist Tool

Our journey up the Yangtze in 1987 had taken me back in time to the years when Japan waged war in China. Our voyage the following year aboard the *Highlander V*, with Malcolm Forbes and Mrs. Douglas MacArthur, took me back to the postwar American occupation of Japan—and even further back to the dawn of evolution. There was considerable irony in the fact that these two cruises took place under such luxurious circumstances. I know I have been blessed by good fortune. So has Japan. When I think back on the poverty and destruction that covered Japan at the end of World War II, I'm convinced that if our country could recover so strongly, there's hope for other nations that confront poverty today and bleak prospects for the future. But only if not just the United States but also Japan and the other developed nations are willing to help.

As I have learned to enjoy life, I have also learned to wonder what I can do to help others. The trip that Kuniko and I took on *Highlander V* in 1988 moved my understanding forward another notch. Malcolm Forbes has fascinated me ever since we met more than a decade ago. His zest for life typifies the American entrepreneur who enjoys all the trappings of success. He is almost the exact opposite of KT, my mentor and role model from the earliest years of my business career. Except for his chauffeur-driven Cadillacs and entertaining American camera distributors at hostess bars, KT lived an austere life. He concentrated his energies on the business, dressed conservatively, and was nearly always very serious. Malcolm, by contrast, once told me the only difference between a man and a boy is the price he can pay for his toys. With his yacht, helicopter, private plane, his multimillion-dollar collection of diamond-studded Fabergé eggs, his motorcycles and hot air balloons, his castles in Morocco and France, and his Pacific island, Malcolm has all the toys any man might dream of. And he finds the time to enjoy them despite the long hours and hard work that go into running his highly successful publishing empire. He also likes to share his fun and good fortune with others.

For me, Malcolm is more a fantasy figure than a role model. Though we have been friends for many years, he still has trouble understanding that I'm not nearly as rich as he is. His *Highlander V* includes a helicopter berth. He told me that from now on when I was invited for a cruise, I needn't battle traffic to get to the West Twenty-third Street dock in Manhattan, where he berths the *Highlander*. He said he would just send the helicopter to pick me up, assuming that I live on an estate like his where there would be plenty of room to land a helicopter. I'm lucky to have room enough for my car in the crowded parking lot of my apartment building.

A few years ago Keizo Saji, president and chairman of the giant Japanese distillery and brewing company Suntory, had a much more troublesome experience with American misperceptions of how Japanese live. Suntory has been very successful at distributing Budweiser beer in Japan. To show its appreciation, Anheuser-Busch sent Mr. Saji two of the beautiful Clydesdale horses that are a symbol of the brewery. Again, the assumption was that Mr. Saji must live on a huge estate where the mammoth Clydesdales would have plenty of room to roam and graze. Again, not so. Mr. Saji's rather modest-sized home has neither sprawling acres nor well-appointed stables. Though he appreciated the gift, he was forced to donate the horses to a public zoo.

Like another successful American publisher, Hugh Hefner, Malcolm Forbes has developed a life-style that is the envy of many men. I suspect that most men of my generation are more drawn to Malcolm's version of the good life than to the *Playboy* world, though that, too, has its definite appeal. But if I were a rich American, rather than a Japanese salaried man, I would like to live the way Malcolm does.

We have had many good times aboard Malcolm's yachts, including one day in 1986 when Malcolm caught me using a Polaroid. This was just a short "cruise to nowhere" up the Hudson River. Malcolm had provided his guests with cameras, and we were having a great time taking instantly developed snapshots of each other. I was taking a shot of a group that included Roger Smith, chairman of General Motors; John S. Reed of Citicorp; and I. M. Booth, chairman of Polaroid. Nobuo Ishizaka, president of Toshiba's American affiliate, took a Polaroid shot of me using a competitor's camera. Malcolm later ran the photo in *Forbes*, his flagship magazine. The Polaroid is one of the few cameras still made in America, and since I have been known to chide photographers for using any camera other than a Minolta, the joke had a double edge. Even I had to laugh.

But the best time I ever had with Malcolm was on the cruise he took us on through the Panama Canal to the Galápagos Islands in February 1988. In addition to Douglas MacArthur's widow, Jean, and her escort, Robert Devine, a retired *Reader's Digest* vice-president, among the guests were Gerry Grinberg, president of the Swiss Watch Company of North America, and his wife, Sonia, as well as Malcolm and his son, Tim. Kuniko and I flew from New York to Panama on Malcolm's plane, a Boeing 727 that takes its name—*Capitalist Tool*—from the motto of *Forbes* magazine. We were a compatible group, but I must admit that for me the highlight of the trip was getting to spend an extended period of time with Mrs. MacArthur.

I had first met Mrs. MacArthur at a dinner party arranged by the Wine and Food Society. Each of several courses was prepared by the chef of a head of state. One of Emperor Hirohito's chefs, for example, prepared several of the appetizers, and President Reagan's chef was responsible for the entrée. The dinner was held at New York's Waldorf-Astoria Hotel, where Mrs. MacArthur makes her home. When I heard she was among the guests, I had my wife come with me as I rather boldly sought her out. Mrs. MacArthur was very gracious as I told her of my long interest in her husband's role in Japan. The next day I sent her some newspaper interviews and excerpts from my speeches in which I talked about Japan's debt to the general.

Malcolm, aware of my interest in General MacArthur, thought

it would be a good idea for me to have a chance to spend more time with Mrs. MacArthur, who has been a friend of his for many years. In December 1987, a few months before our trip, he invited me to Mrs. MacArthur's eighty-ninth birthday party at his offices on lower Fifth Avenue in Manhattan. I made a little speech about Japan's great debt to General MacArthur and America, which was covered in the *New York Post*'s "Suzy" column. This was the only time in my life that I have ever been mentioned in a society column. After that meeting, Malcolm was sure that Mrs. MacArthur and I would have a lot to talk about. He was right. So it was no coincidence that we were shipmates on the *Highlander*.

Mrs. MacArthur is one of the most delightful women I have ever known. Malcolm and the rest of us were up until midnight almost every evening during our seven-day cruise and up again early the next morning. Mrs. MacArthur was there with the rest of us morning till night, bright, alert, elegant, charming, and intelligent. I was full of questions about her husband and his role in Japan. I even asked her about the famous photo showing her husband without a tie towering over the formally dressed Emperor. Mrs. MacArthur said her husband had been dressed that way only because they had had almost no notice that the Emperor was coming to visit. MacArthur returned to his residence at the American embassy for lunch nearly every day. One day he arrived earlier than usual and told Jean he had been informed that the Emperor would pay a visit before the noon hour. MacArthur did not intentionally appear tieless, but neither did he go out of his way to dress more formally. In fact, said Mrs. MacArthur, he paid no attention at all to his own appearance and going tieless was standard for him on a normal working day. His greatest concern was what to do about the Japanese domestic servants and their reaction to being in the presence of a man still considered to be God. When Jean asked if they should serve tea, MacArthur said an emphatic "no." He ordered all the servants to stay in the kitchen until the Emperor left.

Mrs. MacArthur said that from that first meeting a warm friendship evolved between her husband and the Emperor. MacArthur later told Jean it was a shame the Japanese people didn't know that their emperor was a wonderful man of good character. When MacArthur first encouraged him to travel among the people, the Emperor appeared stiff. But he soon became more natural, and the people loved it.

On the *Highlander*, I brought along three chapters of this book to get Malcolm's opinion. He was very enthusiastic and volunteered to read to Jean and his other guests the pages on General MacArthur's role in helping the Japanese camera and watch industries. "I thought I knew just about everything my husband did," Jean said after the reading. "But that's one story I hadn't heard." It was an amazing experience for me to be sitting with the widow of a man I had known only from books but had admired so much. One of my ambitions is to one day write a book on General MacArthur, in English but from the Japanese point of view. Many such books have been written in Japanese, but to the best of my knowledge, none have been written in English that tell how much MacArthur meant to Japan and to Japanese of my generation. The translation of such a book into Japanese might help younger people understand their history a bit better. I told Jean that even in Japan the memory of General MacArthur has begun to fade. Today many Japanese believe that Japan's postwar recovery is something accomplished entirely by the Japanese themselves. There is an understandable tendency to take pride in our achievements, but also a troubling capacity to forget all that we owe to Americans like Douglas MacArthur and Dr. Deming. My conversations with Mrs. MacArthur on the *Highlander* reminded me that my generation has an obligation to do all that we can to keep alive the past, to remind us how fully interdependent our two nations are.

Malcolm, his son, Tim, and my wife are all avid bridge players. Malcolm and Kuniko had often played together on other occasions, and Malcolm had always assumed that I was also a bridge player. He was greatly disappointed to discover that I am not. He canvassed the other guests and the crew of fourteen but could find no one to make a fourth for their bridge table. I felt sorry for the bridge players who couldn't play bridge, but I had Mrs. MacArthur to talk to and a chance to enjoy myself in the ways I usually do when traveling: reading, thinking, and enjoying the scenery.

Our party was aboard only for the Panama-Galápagos leg, but the *Highlander* went on to circle the Pacific on a thirty-thousand-mile voyage designed to underline the close economic ties linking twelve very different countries such as Australia, the Pacific island nations, Singapore, Thailand, Malaysia, Indonesia, China, Korea, Japan, Mexico, and the United States, as well as Hong Kong. Our slow journey through the canal fascinated me. The Canal Zone still plays an important role in international trade, both as a link between the Atlantic and Pacific and as a free-trade zone. Both roles are in danger, however, as Panama's economy grinds to a halt under the rule of General Manuel Noriega, who is under indictment in the United States for drug dealing. These are tense times in Panama, and we avoided going ashore.

The trip was eventful enough. We sailed through a series of locks in which the water level was raised or lowered, carrying the *Highlander V* through the various elevations that prevail across the isthmus. One lock jammed, forcing us to use an alternate channel, and, near the Pacific side, we were delayed by a landslide that had washed millions of tons of earth into the waterway. The experience had special meaning for me, bringing back memories of my schoolboy days during the war, when our teachers had me convinced that America could never match Japan's naval power because warships big enough to challenge our own battleships could never get through the Panama Canal to reach the Pacific.

I have always been fascinated by canals, bridges, and tunnels, links that transcend barriers to bring people together through both travel and trade. My apartment in Fort Lee, New Jersey, overlooks the George Washington Bridge, one of the links that ties Manhattan Island to the mainland of the United States. I often contemplate that graceful bridge, both for its inherent beauty and as a symbol of our effort to bring together the separate islands we inhabit. As we moved slowly through the canal, from one elevation to the other, my thoughts also turned to the bridge I had been building for more than thirty years, my bridge across the Pacific that links Japan and America, and to the book I had begun to work on with my American friend Ed Murray. I wanted our book not only to tell the story of my life but also to help in the task of bridge building between two nations so closely connected in such areas as defense, the economy, and a shared commitment to the ideals of democracy. Sadly, Japan and the United States have been drifting apart as tensions develop over so many issues. Our journey to the Galápagos Islands provided me with new ideas and the leisure to explore them, both in my own mind and in conversations with my traveling companions.

The Panama Canal brought us from the Atlantic, which has long dominated America's thinking because of America's historic and economic ties with Europe, to the Pacific, which may hold the key to America's future. Japan and the United States have a history of conflict during World War II against an earlier background of indifference and common traditions of isolationism. In the years since Douglas MacArthur ruled Japan, we have become increasingly interdependent, yet too often we ignore the realities of each other's history, culture, and current economic and political situation.

Malcolm Forbes and I have often discussed America's relations with Japan. He realizes the importance of world trade and appreciates the efforts Japan has made to expand the orderly flow of trade, a position he underlined when he sent the *Highlander V* on its Pacific tour. In announcing the voyage, he said: "The countries rimming the Pacific are increasingly where it's at these days for the businesses of America and for every multinational corporation." He added that the aim of the voyage "was to strengthen the friendship and understanding that is more and more vital to the economic well-being of us all."

With the bridge tables idle, most of the evenings during our leg of the trip were given to watching movies on the shipboard VCR. Since I'm a great movie fan, this was fine with me. It was a relief to be spared for a while the daily details of running an $800 million company. My mind was free for a more reflective consideration of our world. Our destination provided a framework for some of my thinking.

It was primarily the time that Charles Darwin spent on the Galápagos more than a century ago that led to the speculations that developed into his great work on evolution, *On the Origin of Species*. The Galápagos make up an archipelago that stretches along the equator but is cooled by the Humboldt Current. Seals and penguins manage to co-exist with tropical iguanas and parrots as the archipelago's hot, equatorial sun competes with cold ocean breezes. The islands' unusual climate and isolation have created an incubator for breeding an incredible variety of plants and animals, many of which exist nowhere else in the world. Darwin described the islands as "a living laboratory of evolution." I can see why. We walked across a strange landscape of lava rock and sand dunes with dense, green rain forests at higher altitudes. The unusual creatures that have over time adapted for survival include the blue-footed booby, the bump-head, the bearded titmouse, the short-eared owl, and thirteen varieties of finches that Darwin concluded had evolved from a single common ancestor. The giant tortoises that gave the islands their Spanish name, like many of the other creatures we saw, are so used to people poking around that they pay little attention. Jean MacArthur discovered that the tortoises, some of which weigh as much as five hundred pounds, like to be scratched under the neck. Animals were everywhere, and we took many photographs of the strange and intriguing creatures we saw.

While we were anchored off the Galápagos, I was amazed by the sudden appearance of a tanker that had come to refuel the *Highlander*. Once we cleared the Panama Canal, the yacht had raced through the Pacific at full speed, no doubt burning up fuel at a rapid rate. But that is how Malcolm lives. I had been told that it costs $100,000 just to fill the tanks of Trammell Crow's yacht, the *Michaela Rose*. I suppose the normal cost of refueling the *Highlander* is about the same, but it boggles my mind to think what it must have cost to have a tanker make a special trip to the Galápagos to get the job done.

When the time came for us to return to New York, our departure was undertaken in typical Malcolm Forbes style. The yacht's helicopter took us to the airport on Santa Cruz Island. From there, the *Capitalist Tool* flew us in Boeing 727 luxury to Ecuador and then on to Newark airport. Malcolm flew back to New York with us. He and Elizabeth Taylor later flew to Singapore, where they joined the *Highlander* on its journey to Bangkok. When the *Highlander* stopped in Japan, guests at a shipboard party included Minolta's president, Henry Tashima; Ned Moro, our director of corporate communications; and their wives. But since I wasn't on that leg of the journey, I missed out on the opportunity to meet the glamorous Liz Taylor.

As we took off from Santa Cruz, Charles Darwin and the Galápagos were much on my mind. That isolated Pacific archipelago, like Japan, has bred an incredible variety of survivors. Many species and varieties perished, but the fittest survived, adapting to the strange environment. I thought of those thirteen varieties of finches that Darwin thought had evolved from a common ancestor and of the people of Japan, homogeneous but varied, adapting to a changing economic world and surviving. I thought of the ways Minolta has evolved from a narrowly focused camera company to a corporation involved in a wide range of complex imaging technologies for the office and laboratory and a world leader in innovative photo technology. I thought of the giant multinational companies that have evolved into entities so complex and flexible that traditional statistical methods can no longer tell us what the world economy is doing. To survive we have adapted, and as our plane soared toward home I thought of the lessons of the Galápagos.

With a glance toward Malcolm, I concluded that evolution is a capitalist tool, weeding out the weak and the inflexible and leaving us with a robust world economy. I remembered the days when there were forty Japanese camera companies and that fewer than ten really matter today. I thought of all the German camera firms that have faded away because they did not adapt to changing international market conditions. I thought of the American camera companies that have ceased production and of Kodak, big enough and flexible enough to survive primarily on its film business and then, in 1988, returning to the manufacture of 35-mm cameras ranging from a "disposable" at a price of $8.35 to a dual-lens automatic costing $230. I thought of the converging technologies, particularly in the business equipment industry, that are creating new species of office automation systems.

I also thought of the evolutionary changes going on within Japan. We are moving from a predominantly industrial society to an economy in which high-tech services play an increasing role. Chains and discount stores, to appeal to a new "consumer generation," now operate parallel to the small, independent dealers and stores that typify Japan's traditional distribution system. We are changing, with evolutionary slowness, from a nation of workaholics to a new breed of consumers who respond to the appeals of leisure, and from an economy driven by exports to an economy that looks more to its domestic markets for future growth.

No economist has yet come forth to do for the corporation the job Charles Darwin did in developing a theory for the evolution of the species. But corporations—and economies—do evolve. Adaptation plays a major role. And only the fittest survive. Survival today means understanding and adapting to the world's postindustrial, multinational economy. So far, Japan seems to be doing fairly well in making this adjustment. The giant, American-based multinational corporations are also doing well for themselves, although their operations contribute heavily to America's apparent trade deficit. Economic evolution has brought back the dinosaur. The colossal conglomerates that stride across the globe adapt well to shifting currency values, varying interest rates, and changing trade currents. They are as complex as some of the species we encountered that are unique to the Galápagos Islands. Understanding their impact on the world economy will require studies and statistical tools more sophisticated than those that now dominate our media and influence political opinion. I came back from our voyage on the *Highlander* with a renewed sense of the importance of adaptation. The Japanese have always been good at adapting—not copying, but adapting to changing technologies and markets. Through most of its history, Minolta has been a manufacturing and marketing innovator. We will need to evolve that tradition to a higher plane to meet the challenges of today's rapidly changing world.

30

Death and Reflection

Death speaks with a very loud voice. Four deaths since 1985 have knocked on my door, signaling the end of an era and reminding me of my own responsibilities to continuity and change. KT's death was the first. My father died the following year. Kinji Moriyama's death occurred in 1987, and Emperor Hirohito succumbed in January 1989.

Representative Moriyama was a relatively young man when a heart attack suddenly ended his life. My father, KT, and the Emperor had been born around the turn of the century and were in their late eighties when they died. All three had clung to life tenaciously, and all three affected my life profoundly. In their later years, KT and my father were keenly aware of each other, even though they saw each other rarely. Whenever I visited one, he always inquired about the health of the other.

"How is Mr. Tashima?" my father would say.

"How is your father?" KT would ask.

They were always checking each other out, and at times I felt like the thermometer they used to take each other's temperature. With some hesitation, in early 1985 I let my father know that KT's health was failing. My father was in good health at the time, but he was clearly upset to hear about KT. It is difficult enough to confront the failing health of people we are close to when they are a generation older. When our contemporaries begin to fade, we can hear our own mortality knocking.

My father said nothing when I broke the news to him of KT's death. He looked away. I knew he was shocked, however, and from that point his own health went downhill. Over the course of the next year, each time I visited him it was clear that he was failing. His dying followed a pattern similar to the long, final illness of the Emperor. Each had a serious intestinal operation from which he never fully recovered, but each lived on for another year after surgery.

Kuniko and I returned again to Osaka in April 1986 after hearing from my mother that the end was near for my father. My father, like KT before him and Emperor Hirohito two years later, did not go easily. Each waged a long battle against death. I visited my father in the hospital every day. I remembered my own weeks in that strange world between life and death as a young man in Tanabe. My father had bathed my feverish head with ice and I fell through a sinking dream and was saved by hands that grabbed me and pulled me back from death. I sat by my father's side but I could not pull him back.

During that period, my thoughts often turned back to those years when "The Henry Ford of Korea" expanded the business my grandfather had created. I remembered our sad exodus as refugees after the war and how, like Japan itself, my father had struggled to find his way in those postwar years, living off the limited resources of the tree-covered hills our family owned outside Tanabe. First through politics and then through his return to the auto industry with Prince and Nissan, my father had recovered and prospered again. The years of his retirement in Osaka had been comfortable and, as the end of his time drew near, I could mourn his passing and yet take pride in his passage through life.

I know I had disappointed my father by never owning a Ford even after all my years in America. I think I may also have disappointed him by not making a pilgrimage to Detroit to seek out those shrines of the auto industry that he so much admired. In fact, it wasn't until the mid-1970s that I made my first visit to Detroit to visit with local photo dealers. And, though I did visit a Ford showroom, I never made it to a factory. Perhaps in a small way I made it up to my father years later when I visited an antique auto museum in Reno. There I found a miniature 1937 Lincoln—a Ford product—that I bought for my father. I suspect he must have liked it almost as much as I had treasured the little electric car with its directional signals and tire skirts that my grandfather had bought for me when I was a child in Korea. Whenever I visited my parents, that antique model Lincoln was always out on the table for everyone to see. But it was sad to see it, still sitting on the table in his home, when he was in the hospital.

Two weeks passed, and my father's condition seemed to stabilize. With misgivings, I returned to my responsibilities in the United States. In August, Kuniko flew to Osaka to be with my family. Kuniko and I are glad that she at least was able to be with my family through most of that period. About ten days after Kuniko herself finally returned to America, my mother, Fumie, called us, on September 22, 1986, to tell us that my father had died. Koji happened to be in New York on business at the time, and we flew back to Japan with Kuniko the next day.

As the elder son, it was my responsibility to handle all the arrangements that a death in the family demands. I must admit the details of those days blur in my mind. I functioned but I was numbed by loss. I remember my mother telling Koji and me her fears during the war years that Koji and I might both be taken into the military. It often happened in those days that sons would be away at war and unable to attend the funeral when a close relative died. Fumie said she had feared that as the war went on and both Koji and I became old enough for the draft, that might happen in our family.

"But I never dreamed," she said, "that in peacetime, my two sons would be out of the country when their father died." In that moment, I knew she might be wondering where her sons would be when her own time comes. Despite her eighty-two years, she is in good health and excellent spirits. She may survive us all. During the war, it had been a matter of pride to have sons serving overseas, and this pride showed through at funerals when absent sons could not attend. In her old-fashioned way, my mother, despite her protests, took pride in the fact that her sons were working so hard, contributing to their country and their company, almost as though we really had been soldiers away at the front.

"Your father was pleased," she told us. "He was proud of his sons."

The funeral itself reminded me how full my father's life had been. The crowds of mourners, the flowers, the cables told me how many people his life had touched and how strong his impact had been. Relatives, friends, people from Minolta all came in large numbers. But I was especially impressed by how many people from Nissan attended, even though my father had retired more than a decade before. Though many were younger, some must have been close to my father's own age, perhaps measuring themselves by him as he had with KT.

The death of Emperor Hirohito carried great symbolic weight for Japanese like me who had lived through nearly all of his sixty-two-year reign, which spanned the years of war, the postwar desolation, and the economic rebirth of Japan. His death drove home the fact that a new Japan has evolved, a Japan quite different not only from the way the world sees us, but also from the self-image we have clung to despite great changes. With the death of Hirohito, we realize that a generation has passed. For many of us, our fathers, our mentors, now are gone. And so is our Emperor. His death brought with it many memories: his thin voice coming to us over our family's radio in Korea to tell us that the war was over and to prepare "to suffer the insufferable"; that photo of him with the tall, tieless American general; his transformation from a divine, remote monarch to a friendly man of the people; and his role as an enduring, unifying symbol through decades of drastic change. As a new sun rises in the east, I realize that it dawns on a world very different from what we have known before.

In Japan, the Emperor's death, so long expected, touched off a wave of soul-searching among Japanese who still have difficulty coming to terms with his role—and their own—in history. For many still living, he was a divine being, not quite in the Western sense of God, but clearly beyond the norm of ordinary man. During the war years, we had been told that he was the supreme being who embodied Japan's military destiny. Photographs and newsreels showed him in military uniform astride his white horse, reviewing the troops under his command. After the war, we were told that he had been a powerless figurehead who reigned in an era when industrial and military leaders conspired to rule. And we were told by the divine being himself that he was not divine.

I remembered his thin voice as it had been heard by his subjects for the first time on August 15, 1945, when he told us the "new and most cruel bomb" dropped by the Americans on Hiroshima meant the war must end. I remembered our train ride five weeks later through the remains of that ghostly city. I remembered how I felt when I visited the war memorials at Nanking and Pearl Harbor. I thought of Kuniko's father, one of the few who had survived that fatal day in Hiroshima. How terrible that war had been.

As long as this planet lasts, historians may argue about Hirohito's responsibility for World War II. In my own mind, no matter what his guilt or innocence, I can absolve the man but not the forces that pushed Japan into that war. I know I will earn enemies by saying what I have to say, but with the perspective of time I applaud the late Emperor and those who supported him for stepping forth to end the war when they did. And I understand why the president of the United States, Harry Truman, had to make his terrible decision to drop the atomic bomb on Hiroshima.

He saved the lives of millions of Japanese.

Even on the day of the Emperor's historic broadcast, diehard fanatics in the military stormed the radio station in an effort to seize the recording he had made before it could be broadcast. While military leaders loyal to the Emperor were alerted, workers at the station, with a combination of heroism and deception, claimed that no one knew where the recording was. The rebellion was put down and the broadcast aired as scheduled. Many others in the military, however, were determined that Japan must fight on till none were left to face dishonor. The military were being trained to fight with bamboo staves even when the last bullet was gone. If the atomic bomb had not shocked Japan into surrender, an inevitable invasion would have cost the lives of millions of Japanese and hundreds of thousands of Americans.

The military had made plans to take the Emperor to an underground palace in Nagano in the mountainous region known as Japan's Alps. Had that happened, a central command could have held out for months in that inaccessible region. It is frightening to imagine the loss of life that would have resulted from prolonged resistance to an invasion. Horrible as it is to contemplate the loss of life that took place on a single day in Hiroshima, it is even more horrible to contemplate the death toll that would have resulted had the war continued for several murderous months.

At a press conference with foreign correspondents in 1980, the Emperor was asked what he felt about the use of that first atomic bomb. He answered that it was regrettable—but "unavoidable." For a man whose language was seldom direct, that was a fairly direct statement. In their hearts, many Japanese feel as I do, that the nuclear bombing of Hiroshima was a terrible necessity, but few dare say so openly. I know I may be attacked for saying so, but it needs saying. There is so much that we need to acknowledge about ourselves—Japanese and Americans alike—and about the events of those years.

In my own soul-searching that followed the death of the Emperor, I saw a chain of linked events that stretched from Nanking to Hiroshima and beyond to Nagasaki. Though a secret, romantic part of my soul still harbors dreams of being a fighter pilot, I recognize the horror of war. I remember the wounded Japanese soldiers I saw recuperating at Shirahama in 1939, and I remember the war memorial at Nanking. There are no excuses for what happened at Nanking, even though the scope of that tragedy may be exaggerated by some historians and propagandists. There is some justification for what happened at Hiroshima, but none for what happened at Nagasaki. Japan had already begun surrender negotiations in the Soviet Union when that second new and most cruel bomb killed tens of thousands of defenseless people in the atomic rape of Nagasaki. Without the shock of Hiroshima, I do not think Japan would have surrendered. Nagasaki was needless slaughter.

The death of the Emperor who reigned through the war and the postwar economic recovery of Japan also touched off speculation about Japan's future. Like postwar Germany, postwar Japan has achieved a miracle of economic recovery. Where it will take us is a subject for debate as intense as the debates over what we have done.

31

Henry, the Future, and Me

On April 15, 1988, my daughters hosted a surprise sixtieth birthday party for me. The party observed traditions that are typically Japanese. It was held at a fairly new but traditional-looking Japanese restaurant called Mount Fuji that sits on a mountaintop in Mahwah, New Jersey.

The view in one direction looks out on the rolling green foothills of the Ramapo Mountains and in the other on an industrial area dominated by a towering new hotel, the Sheraton International Crossroads, and by the American headquarters and distribution center operated by Sharp Electronics, one of Minolta's Japanese competitors, on the site of a former Ford assembly plant. Minolta's own North American corporate headquarters is not far away in Ramsey, and within a few miles you can find the American headquarters of several multinational companies, including Sony, BMW, and Mercedes-Benz.

Most of the more than sixty guests that day were Americans but the setting was Japanese, including the huge, multicolored kites representing giant carps that crackled in the breeze under brilliant blue skies. In Japan, the sixtieth birthday is supposed to represent the beginning of the second half of your life—a very optimistic idea for a people whose average life expectancy for men is only seventy-five years. Since you are starting a new life, your sixtieth birthday also represents a return to childhood, and you put on a bright red cap and jacket considered typical of what a child would wear. It makes for a festive occasion, but it is also a time for reflection. I later looked back on my life and realized that, though I am very Japanese, by the time of my sixtieth birthday I had lived only twenty years of my life in Japan. For my first seventeen years, I grew up in Korea. I then lived nine years in Japan, completing my higher education and beginning my business career. After my first four years in America, I lived another eleven years in Japan. For the past two decades, America has again been my home. Since 1984, I have been an executive director of our Osaka-based parent company. That's in addition to my position as a member of the board of directors, which I have held since 1974. My responsibilities as an executive director may one day draw me back to a permanent assignment in Osaka, but I believe Minolta still needs me in America.

Most photographs of that birthday party show me grinning broadly under my red cap. But as I study those photos, seeing so many American friends in that beautifully decorated Japanese restaurant, my mind is drawn back over the years of my American experience. I remember looking out the windows of Mount Fuji, thinking how much that area had grown since I first saw it and realizing how much of that change has occurred not because of an "invasion" of foreign companies, but because of the complex appeal of life in America.

America is a magnet that inevitably draws the attention of the world. America's freedom, stability, and economic opportunity attract more immigrants, investment, and imports than any other country in the world. Criticisms of the United States, including my own occasional criticism, must be judged in this light. Many Americans don't appreciate how well off they are. Even the poor in America are better off than the comparably poor in any country I know of. Minority groups and women, who justifiably believe they are discriminated against, suffer far less repression in the United States than they would in any other country.

Per capita income in Japan may exceed per capita income in America—but only if measured by the currently undervalued American dollar. And health and other public welfare services in Scandinavia may be better than in America. But overall, Americans enjoy a far higher standard of living than people in any other country in the world. What makes all this happen, I believe, is partly the magnetic pull of the vast American market. When I criticize American firms for not adapting their products to other markets, I have to remind myself that there are no other markets as big as America's. Naturally, the rest of us want to adapt our products for America. America, on the other hand, could afford to say for many years, "Why should we bother adapting for the Japanese market? It isn't big enough to bother about."

That was true once, but no longer. Not only does America need to export more today, but Japan and other once limited markets in Europe and Asia now have a strong effective demand, not because they have gotten bigger but because they have grown richer. Countries like Japan will never have the economic pull that America exerts on the rest of the world. Japan has only half the population of the United States, plus higher taxes, a bigger government deficit when measured as a percentage of gross national product, and a tradition of saving rather than spending. Japan just isn't a great consumer market. But the pull of America goes beyond economics.

It is also a question of freedom and of opportunity. There are far more foreign students and scientific researchers in America than there are Americans who study or conduct research abroad. Political, ethnic, and religious refugees in great numbers from all over the world seek asylum in America. Hardly any Americans seek exile abroad.

As I looked back from the perspective of my sixtieth birthday, wearing my child's costume of red cap and jacket in that mountaintop restaurant, my past seemed more like a child's dream than a man's reality. With the turning point of my sixtieth birthday behind me, I know that during this "second half" of my life my own priorities will have to change. Japan's priorities have already changed. We are no longer as export-oriented as we were a few years ago. Minolta will have to shift gears with the rest of the Japanese economy to increase our share in the domestic market. The Maxxum—or the Alpha as it's called in Japan—opened up some possibilities as Minolta again became *ichi ban*, number one, in Japan's 35-mm SLR market. In the pre-Alpha fiscal year that ended March 31, 1985, overseas markets accounted for 83 percent of our worldwide sales. By fiscal year 1987, the peak year for Alpha sales in Japan, overseas markets accounted for only 73 percent of sales.

Marketing also played a role in Minolta's domestic sales expansion. In 1986 Minolta invested heavily in a domestic advertising campaign using the tag line, "Yes, We Can," which stressed the company's commitment to products other than cameras and copiers. The campaign won the prestigious Asahi Advertising Prize. For a while, it looked as though Minolta were marching in lockstep with the rest of Japan, with growth fueled by an expansion of our domestic markets rather than by exports.

But by the end of 1988, I began to wonder about the relative strength of our domestic growth. After declining since early 1987, Japan's trade surplus began to grow, hitting a new record in December 1988, as exports surged again, outpacing an impressive 11.3 percent growth in imports. And for Minolta, with Alpha sales leveling off, our proportion of overseas sales has expanded again to just under 80 percent, still the highest of any industrial company listed on the Tokyo Stock Exchange. Meanwhile, sales of our nonphoto products— copiers, office automation systems, and planetariums—which had fallen to roughly 45 percent of total sales in 1986 and 1987, have again moved up to account for more than half our revenues.

Like Japan's new emperor, Akihito, Minolta Camera Company's new president, Henry Tashima, will preside over an empire very different from the one his father ruled for so long. Each man was groomed as his father's successor for many years. Both are now in their fifties and, if the example of their fathers is any guide, should be with us well into the twenty-first century. By then Japan will probably be more important as a financial power than as an industrial nation. Minolta's income will probably be less dependent on exports and cameras than it has been through most of its first sixty years.

During the 1980s Japan became the world's biggest creditor, foreign investor, and foreign-aid donor, replacing the United States in all three categories. The world wonders what Japan will do with its newfound financial power. So does Japan. No consensus has developed. Criticism of the power Japan has already achieved has created confusion, caution, and, in some cases, anger among my countrymen. There is a strange tendency in international circles to blame Japan for achieving what other nations have pressured us into doing. For example, in the nineteenth century it was international pressure, primarily from the United States and Great Britain, that forced Japan to open its markets and play a greater role on the world stage. It has been said that the gods punish us most cruelly by answering our prayers. The Western powers prayed for Japan to end its isolationism and open up to international influences. Japan did so, but with a success that continues to dismay the West.

In 1946, after the crushing defeat of Japan's militaristic ambitions in World War II, Japan accepted as its own a constitution written by Americans in which the country renounced militarism and pledged to maintain only minimal, purely defensive armed forces. In Article 9 of the constitution, titled "Renunciation of War," Japan renounces war "forever" as an instrument of policy and agrees not to maintain "land, sea and air forces, as well as other war potential." Japan has lived by its American-made constitution, and again, the results have dismayed our mentors. The United States now criticizes Japan for not bearing its fair share of free-world security costs, forgetting that we are forbidden to do so by the constitution America gave us. There is no denying that Japan benefits greatly and much appreciates its security arrangements with the United States, but it is not the "free ride" that some American critics depict it as. Japan, for example, now contributes $45,000 per year toward the costs of maintaining each of the American military personnel based on its soil. Japan's total "host-nation" support to the cost of maintaining America's military presence runs to about $1.5 billion per year. Hardly a "free" ride. In fact, Japan pays a higher rate for maintaining United States service personnel than any other host nation with American military bases. And Japan increased its host-nation support payments in its fiscal 1989 budget.

Constitutionally limited by what it can channel to its own military, Japan instead has concentrated its resources on savings and investments, fueling an industrial economy that continues to dismay our trading partners and free-world allies. Despite its dependence on exports, Japan agreed in 1985 to participate in the efforts of its European and American trading partners to drive down the value of the dollar, a move designed to reduce the flow of Japanese exports, particularly to the United States. Japan also agreed to its trading partners' pressures to stimulate its domestic economy and to play a greater role in international finance. The dollar fell sharply. Japan's domestic economy surged. And Japan has become a major international investor, particularly in the United States. As a result, Japan is being criticized, particularly in the United States, for "taking over" American industries and real estate and posing a threat to American sovereignty and security.

I shudder to think what would happen if Japan found a way to change its constitution, which is very difficult to amend, and built up its military forces as the United States and the European nations in NATO have urged. In fact, I wonder if the United States really wants Japan to play a bigger military role in the Pacific. I hope not. After all, I remember the militarism that infected our school and so many other aspects of life when I was a boy in Korea. I remember those Japanese soldiers we met who had been wounded in China in the late 1930s. I remember Nanking, and I haven't forgotten Hiroshima. And, above all, I remember Pearl Harbor.

Surely if Japan bent to pressures to build up our military, within a few years the allies who now advocate this would begin criticizing the resurgence of Japanese militarism. Caution may be Japan's best course. My own view is that Japan did well in accepting the aid and advice offered by the Americans, like my heroes Dr. Deming and General MacArthur, who advised us in the postwar years. But our national tendency to seek approval should not propel us into accepting bad and inconsistent advice.

Minolta's example may be a good one to follow. Minolta has so far been more conservative than some of our competitors, and firms in other industries such as automobiles, in establishing production and assembly facilities in the United States. In early 1989 we did expand our corporate headquarters in New Jersey and opened a relatively small and highly automated plant to produce toner for our copiers in Goshen, New York. The toner plant may turn out to be a pilot project, possibly paving the way for a business equipment assembly plant. The United States continues to be our biggest market. Producing in America makes sense, particularly if the dollar keeps falling in value and if we gain some useful experience from operating our toner plant. Minolta has already established business equipment plants in Malaysia and West Germany. The United States may be next, but I doubt that it will be anytime soon. I think there is even less prospect of our ever manufacturing cameras in the United States. There are limits to how fully camera production can be automated, and young Oriental women are unique in the skills and patience they bring to the task. We have begun assembling cameras in Malaysia and plan to begin parts production there. But I don't think we could duplicate that work force in America or Europe, our major markets. In addition, cameras are cheaper than business equipment to ship and insure, which keeps export costs down.

During this second half of my life, my expertise in exports may be of more use to my second country, the United States, which needs to export more, than it will be to Japan and Minolta, both of which need to become less export dependent. There are many people in Japan who are expert at restricting imports—too expert. But I am not one of them. I know more about expanding exports. Whenever I'm invited to speak on this topic, my audience, including the journalists who cover the speech, always listen politely and then ask the same, invariable question: "Mr. Kusumoto, when is Minolta going to build a plant in our community?"

I also try to be polite, but sometimes I'm afraid my answers mislead people. In my speeches I never tell my listeners that Minolta plans to build a plant in their town or their state. However, after my speech, when that inevitable question comes up, I may in all honesty say something like, "This area offers some very strong advantages. If Minolta were to build a plant in the United States, this is an area we would consider very favorably."

Usually, the full news story reports my remarks quite accurately, but sometimes we end up with headlines saying something like:

MINOLTA PRESIDENT SAYS YES
TO LOCAL PLANT PROPOSAL

This can get me in trouble, especially back in Osaka. One of my colleagues once chided me by saying, "Kusumoto-san, the publicity is wonderful, but please stop building so many plants in America."

Henry Tashima, whom I have known well for many years, will be a strong leader as he guides Minolta into the next century. His early years working as an assistant to Ken Nakamura in New York have given him a firm recognition of the importance of the American market.

In recent years, Minolta has been the original equipment manufacturer for copiers and office automation products sold by foreign firms under their own name. Such agreements have included copiers sold by IBM in the United States, document-imaging reader-printers for Rhône-Poulenc Systèmes in France, the engines for Kodak's computer-assisted document image retrievers, and our SP 50B multi-functional scanner, intelligent copier, and printer, which has been marketed in the United States by various companies.

I anticipate that under Henry, business equipment will become increasingly important both in our product mix and in our corporate culture. Minolta Camera Company, Ltd., as our name reflects, is still predominantly a camera company in its corporate thinking, even though our product line has branched out into nonphoto areas. There has been some discussion of changing the name of the company, possibly to Minolta Incorporated, and that is one change I think we may see in the future.

A *New York Times* article written by Zbigniew Brzezinski in April 1987 caught my attention and led to an interesting meeting. Brzezinski had been President Carter's national security advisor from 1977 to 1981. He has more recently been affiliated with the Foreign Policy Research Institute and Columbia and Georgetown universities. The article advocated closer private-sector cooperation between Japan and the United States, including cross-fertilization of Americans and Japanese on the boards of each other's corporations. Brzezinski is much admired in Japan because of his work as the first director of the Trilateral Commission, which seeks to improve ties among the United States, Western Europe, and Japan. I arranged to meet with Brzezinski and discuss some of his ideas over lunch at what was then his favorite Washington restaurant, the now defunct Mel Krupin's on Connecticut Avenue.

We met at Brzezinski's nearby office on K Street, then headed for the restaurant. We were greeted by Krupin himself, the large, jovial owner. He glanced at our party, took the cigar from his mouth, and yelled, "Hide the pickles. Here comes Brzezinski." Brzezinski has a passion for dill pickles that matches mine for linguine and clam sauce. Our waiter placed a huge dish on the table Krupin had directed us to. Between bites of pickle, Brzezinski explained the seating protocol. We had been assigned one of two booths that face the flight of stairs that leads down into the restaurant from its street-level entrance. The other had been reserved for Lynn Nofziger, a former assistant to President Nixon.

"These are the top power tables," said Brzezinski. "If Mel puts you here, it means he thinks your star is riding high. There are other good tables and then there are some in the back that are like being sent to Siberia. People have been known to leave town in shame after finding themselves seated back there. Today, Mel must think I'm with a pretty important Japanese political leader or businessman. Or I wouldn't rate such a good table. And maybe no pickles."

The opposite was the case, of course. We were at the table near the stairs because I was with a man who is one of Washington's top power brokers and also one of America's leading geopolitical intellectuals. We lunched on club sandwiches—and pickles—and I told Brzezinski of my admiration for the ideas outlined in his article, particularly the idea that the private sector can play a more important role in improving trade relations and easing tensions between Japan and the United States. His ideas parallel some of my thinking on the need for a joint industry/government agency to cope with America's trade problems. I believe it's vital for me to do everything I can to further understanding between my two favorite countries and between the very different cultures of government and business.

This "culture gap" is greater in the United States than it is in Japan, which makes it even more difficult for most Japanese to understand the hostility expressed toward Japan's business practices by some American political leaders. America lacks a tradition of joint government/business ventures like the Japan External Trade Organization and the role the government played in cooperating with the photo industry to get the Japan Camera Information and Service Center started in New York in 1955. There has been some United States government involvement in specific joint ventures with industry in areas such as satellite communications and the more recent Pentagon involvement in Sematech, the research consortium funded equally by the semiconductor industry and the Defense Department. But the United States has never had an organization quite like JETRO, which promotes all aspects of international trade. JETRO is a branch of the Ministry of International Trade and Industry, the organization that for many American commentators embodies "Japan, Inc." Frankly, as I told Brzezinski, I don't think America has much to gain by trying to imitate MITI and creating a so-called industrial policy. Both the power and the success of MITI have been greatly exaggerated by American observers, but America could profit by creating an organization similar to JETRO.

I'm not speaking about an agency that becomes a funnel for export subsidies. In fact, like most businessmen, I do not believe in government subsidies. But government, in cooperation with the private sector, can provide important indirect assistance to exporters.

Information, not regulation or subsidies, would be the method by which the organization I envision would change America's approach to international trade. One function of this agency would be to serve as an accessible and aggressive conveyor of information on export possibilities and procedures. Many small to middle-size firms, often with specialty products that might be of interest in foreign markets, miss out on their export potential simply because they don't know how to explore the possibilities and lack experience in dealing with the complexities of the regulatory process, financing, shipping, insurance, et cetera. A one-stop agency with specialists trained to show potential exporters how to do it could make a major contribution to expanding American exports.

Another function would be to educate the people of America and their leaders on the intricacies and importance of international trade, and particularly on the need to expand exports. JETRO, for example, provides secondary and even elementary schools with educational materials on the importance of exports. By the time they graduate from high school, all Japanese students are aware of Japan's dependence on exports. By contrast, most Americans have virtually no idea of the importance of international trade. Surveys show that when Japanese were asked to name the nation's biggest economic problem, more than half cited trade frictions. When researchers asked Americans a similar question, only 12 percent mentioned trade.

At present, American trade policies emerge out of a loud but confusing clash of federal, state, regional, and even municipal agencies, industry organizations, and individual companies all competing for special attention and special projects. For example, at last count thirty-three state governments and four port authorities had offices in Tokyo competing for Japanese investment and business opportunities in the United States. To the Japanese, this is confusing. Though I believe in competition, the intensity of competition by all these state and regional government branches seems to me wasteful and counterproductive.

In addition, the federal government handicaps many American overseas business ventures with inconsistencies in trade programs. Export decisions about agricultural and manufacturing products are made by separate agencies, and there is no clear-cut authority for making decisions about the export of services. Often agencies with a stake in export practices are not consulted when new policies are adopted on the recommendation of other, competing agencies. Linking export policies to political policies, as in the export of computers, machine tools, and other "strategic" items, has also hurt American competitiveness in overseas markets.

During the Reagan administration, efforts to create a cabinet-level agency dealing with trade, which might have solved some of these difficulties, met with opposition in Congress and among some cabinet officers. What I am proposing is something more modest— an agency that might influence, but not create or administer, a national trade policy that would again make the United States the financial and industrial linchpin for world trade and the international economic system. The United States needs to speak with one voice on trade issues. The joint business/government organization that I propose could provide the research, the rationale, and the business-oriented point of view that would be helpful in creating a unified national policy for international trade. Perhaps its most important function would be to focus public attention on trade issues that really matter.

The agency I envision should include a research center designed to explore new ways of expanding American exports and recommend new product developments and consortiums to explore the future. Japan tends to be way ahead of the United States in such developments. The American consortium, Sematech, for example, will be playing catch-up in the semiconductor field, and so will the various late-starting joint ventures to develop practical applications for superconductor metals and high-definition television, which will be among the most important products of the next decade.

Making the public and its political leaders more aware of the export potential of such natural resources as Alaskan oil and timber and, most important of all, of such service industries as finance, insurance, real estate, entertainment, foreign exchange and commodity trading, large-scale building maintenance, information, transportation and construction design, and engineering could be another important function of the agency. Mobilizing public support could help the United States to win concessions from Japan and its other trading partners in the vast and vital service area, an area that rarely generates much media attention or public awareness. The agency might also make an effort to coordinate the often counterproductive efforts of the states and regional authorities that compete for business investment from Japan.

There is nothing wrong with importing factories and other forms of investment from Japan. Such efforts can help to reduce the flow of manufacturing imports from Japan and provide financing for America's twin deficits in trade and the federal budget. Nor do I believe that such investments are in any real way a "threat" to America's security or independence. Investment, no less than manufacturing, has become internationalized. The central banks of the United States, Japan, Canada, Great Britain, France, West Germany, and Italy don't intervene in currency markets in pursuit of narrow national interests. They follow a coordinated policy of trying to stabilize exchange rates. And the investment decisions of an American-based multinational are no more—or less—patriotic than those of a multinational based in Great Britain, Germany, or Japan. However, I do believe the United States should be investing more in its own future, not on national-security grounds but rather to ensure that the American economy will expand at a rate that will not only protect current living standards but also make it possible for those Americans now locked in poverty and welfare to participate more fully in their country's prosperous economy. Reviewing federal tax policies that discourage savings and investment, while providing incentives for some forms of credit that fuel consumption, might not be a bad idea. From what I've seen, however, more initiative seems to be developing on the local level.

During a 1985 trip to the Boston area, I learned of an ambitious development program involving the state government, universities, and the private sector. High-tech firms in the state already provide jobs for nearly a quarter of a million workers, 40 percent of the manufacturing work force. The research triangle in North Carolina is an area where dwindling textile employment is being replaced by high-tech research and development. Pittsburgh has overcome the decline of its steel industry and emerged as a prosperous center of finance and medical research. The Thomas Edison Program in Ohio, the Ben Franklin Partnership in Pennsylvania, and the academic and industrial research programs coordinated by New Jersey's Commission on Science and Technology are other examples of what can be done on the local level.

In his final year as America's ambassador to Japan, Mike Mansfield revived his proposal for a free-trade zone between the United States and Japan. The United States now has such agreements with Canada and Israel, and I can see great merit to Mansfield's idea. However, Japan and the United States might benefit even more from beginning with a bilateral free-trade zone and then taking a leadership role in expanding that zone to the entire Pacific Rim. Though I was only on board for the first leg of the journey, the elliptical route followed by Malcolm Forbes's yacht, *Highlander V*, on its 1988 Pacific Rim voyage focused my thinking on the extent to which the economies of the countries of the Pacific have already become interdependent. As the European Economic Community (EEC) moves closer to the full economic integration projected for 1992, the United States may find itself with less access to the traditional markets it has enjoyed with its Atlantic alliance partners. A Pacific Rim free-trade zone could be a useful counterbalance for trade negotiations with an integrated EEC. Studies are already under way in Japan and the United States to determine the possibility of a bilateral free-trade zone. It's my guess that we may be into the twenty-first century before a carefully phased-in, bilateral program can be achieved, and extending this to the entire Pacific Rim will be an even more time-consuming process. But the future has a habit of catching up to us rather quickly.

I recognize the continuing importance of working within the multilateral framework of the General Agreement on Tariffs and Trade (GATT) and the current "Uruguay Round" of talks that began in 1986 and are scheduled to continue until 1990. GATT works by consensus, and its slow-moving methods often frustrate American trade negotiators. GATT has been particularly ineffective in dealing with agricultural subsidies, which have become a major issue in international trade. Yet, the best hope for eventually resolving the dispute over Japan's ban on rice imports probably lies with GATT rather than in a bilateral political agreement. No Japanese administration could sign such an agreement and hope to survive. But a multilateral agreement reached through the mechanism of GATT and involving the agricultural subsidies of several countries could ease the domestic political burden for the Japanese government. Chances for acceptance could be further improved by giving the Japanese agricultural cooperatives a role—and a profit—in the distribution of imported rice.

Clearly, there is a role for the multilateral GATT approach. But bilateral and regional agreements, like the developing EEC free-trade zone or a Pacific Rim free-trade zone don't necessarily undermine GATT. Many of the ninety-six GATT signatories have shown that bilateral or regional agreements can be worked out in harmony with the multilateral GATT approach.

The bilateral free-trade-zone studies now going on in Japan are being conducted by the Ministry of Finance and by MITI, which includes JETRO and has close ties with industry. In the United States, the concept of a free-trade zone with Japan is being researched by the International Trade Commission, a federal agency. Personally, I would like to see more direct involvement by American industry in these studies. This could be another priority for the joint industry/government agency that I believe should be created to further America's interests in international trade.

JETRO and another Japanese organization, the Manufactured Imports Promotion Organization, both help American businessmen export to Japan. Both have active offices in the United States. But there is a need for an *American* organization with offices throughout the United States and abroad to assist the American business community in expanding its involvement in international trade and in strengthening its export capabilities. When I imagine the future of such an American organization, I think of that "power table" Zbigniew Brzezinski introduced me to at Mel Krupin's restaurant in Washington. You can't miss it as you enter the dining room, and you can't miss its message about whose star is riding high. The American export agency I would like to see created would be like that power table. It should be positioned in a way that everyone will see that in the United States exports are on the ascendancy, given top priority by business and government.

Japan must export to survive, not only because its domestic market is relatively small but, more important, because it must export to earn the foreign exchange needed to pay for the fuel and food it has to import. The United States is not so dependent on imports as Japan is. But the American consumer, though generally not aware of it, enjoys a higher standard of living because of imports. Competition from foreign manufacturers helps to keep quality up and prices down for the wide choice of goods available to the American consumer. So far, the United States has had no problem in paying for its imports. Because the dollar is the universally accepted medium of foreign exchange, the United States doesn't need foreign reserves to pay for its huge volume of imports. Unlike the rest of the world, it can pay in its own currency, a unique advantage that greatly benefits the American consumer.

What keeps the process going is the fact that many of the dollars earned by foreign companies are reinvested in the United States. In effect, the rest of the world subsidizes America's trade deficit. As a result, however, in the past decade the United States has changed from the world's biggest creditor nation into the world's biggest debtor. The combination of high American interest rates and a weak American dollar makes the United States a bargain basement for foreign investors. By West German, Dutch, French, British, and Japanese standards, American real estate, financial instruments, and companies are very inexpensive. Instead of selling more automobiles to foreign countries, the United States is selling more Treasury bonds, hotels, factories, and advertising agencies. To my way of thinking, this transfusion of foreign money is a good thing for the United States right now. But, as the cost of paying off its foreign debts increases, America's buying power will be reduced drastically unless export earnings increase. Imports continue to help the American consumer enjoy the world's highest standard of living. But that standard of living can slip badly if America tries to reduce its trade deficit by cutting back on imports rather than by expanding exports.

In Japan, meanwhile, individual standards of living have finally begun to catch-up with the prosperity Japan enjoys as a nation. Increased imports, driven primarily by the increase in the value of the yen, have been a major factor. The government has taken several other steps to stimulate the domestic economy, which grew at an annual rate of about 4.5 percent during 1987 and 1988. By American standards, the average Japanese consumer still does not live well, but things are changing. The spread of discount houses and chain stores has helped to lower prices. Japanese, particularly younger Japanese women, have begun to travel abroad in greater numbers. Again, the stronger yen is a factor. But there is another reason. There are now many young Japanese girls in the work force who still live with their parents. Since they don't have the expense of maintaining homes of their own, their disposable income is relatively high, allowing for such unaccustomed luxuries as shopping and travel abroad. I have noticed that New York stores like Bloomingdale's and especially Tiffany's have become major tourist attractions for groups of young Japanese women. They may not be able to buy much at Tiffany's, but they enjoy window-shopping and picture-taking. What they see in America, even more than what they buy, will influence the way they live back in Japan. The average Japanese working woman may not yet have become that *"Cosmopolitan* girl" that fashion-industry marketing directors love, but she is beginning to get the idea.

Not every effort that the Japanese government has made to stimulate the domestic economy has worked out quite as planned. Abolishing tax-exempt savings accounts didn't encourage people to save less and spend more, as anticipated. Instead, Japan's habitual savers have started to become enthusiastic investors, driving the Tokyo stock market up to new heights. Efforts to create a shorter work week, in the hope that people with more leisure will spend more, have so far met with mixed results. As a nation of workaholics, we don't yet have much experience at enjoying leisure. Maybe we need some enterprising Americans to set up "self-fulfillment" seminars to teach us how to enjoy ourselves, spend more money, and replace our savings accounts with credit cards.

Given the Japanese penchant for technology, it's surprising how little automation has affected daily life. Relatively few Japanese offices are computerized, for example. I expect this to change, opening new opportunities in information technology for firms like Minolta. I'm also convinced that we are on the verge of a revolution in video-based marketing and distribution in both the United States and Japan. By the time the twenty-first century gets here, people may be doing much of their shopping, and that includes business-to-business shopping, by computer, video screen, and modem. Federal Express has shown us how efficiently—if expensively—home and office deliveries can be handled. People are not only shopping but also dating and partying over telephone networks. We could be on the brink of moving into a global village dominated by the "big brother" image of the video display terminal. In such a world we could see the virtual disappearance not only of offices but, according to some futurists, even of stores. God forbid. I must confess, I find that prospect depressing. Being a salesman won't be as much fun. I'm a very social animal, and I hope the social instincts we all share will keep us from locking ourselves up in a world of automated communication systems. I already look back with a sad nostalgia on those golden years when entertaining clients at the hostess bars of Tokyo and Osaka was an integral part of doing business. The business world will never be as much fun with computer terminals replacing pretty girls.

As president of Minolta Corporation in the United States, my own day-to-day responsibility remains doing my best to expand Minolta's major overseas market and to increase its profit ratio. But as an executive director of our parent company's board of directors, I also have a responsibility to do all that I can to help Minolta Camera Company adjust to the changing realities of the world economy. Both responsibilities present tough challenges.

Minolta announced rather disappointing profit results for the half-year ending September 30, 1988. The basic reason for this was the fall in the value of the dollar, which made it more difficult for all Japanese companies to be price competitive in most foreign markets, and particularly difficult in the United States. As the most export-dependent of all major Japanese companies, Minolta was hurt very badly by this development. At the time, however, we were criticized by analysts for failing to maintain the momentum we had created in 1985. To a degree, they did have a point. Minolta's first significant technological breakthroughs since 1985—when we introduced the Maxxum, Infinium, and our first office automation system, the PCW-1—was the Maxxum 7000i, which we introduced in the spring of 1988. The Maxxum 7000i brought something entirely new to creative photography with the world's first creative expansion card system. Ten cards, which can be slipped into a camera in the same way a software disk can be slipped into a computer, give the photographer new dimensions of creative control.

The various cards can let you bracket up to seven consecutive light exposures; control highlights and shadows; shift the speed at which the subject in an action photo appears to be moving; create soft-focus fantasy effects; imprint technical data on each frame you shoot; provide the ideal exposure setting for portrait photography; control depth of field for maximum sharpness; select the necessary shutter speed to freeze sports or other fast-action shots; and determine ideal shutter speed and aperture for close-up photography. The Maxxum 7000i's computerized autofocus system determines the speed of a moving subject, predicts its distance when the shutter opens, then adjusts focus during the shutter-release sequence—another first. Such technological advances have helped Minolta sales to grow, but the sharp fall in the value of the dollar continues to have a negative effect on revenues and profitability.

Under Henry Tashima's leadership, however, Minolta has instituted several moves that assure a bright future. Research will be the key to expanding our product line and opening doors to market expansion. I expect that business equipment will take on a larger role in Minolta's product mix, particularly in the domestic Japanese market. As Japan becomes more of a service-oriented society, the demand for office automation and communications equipment will expand. Minolta is already well positioned to grow in this area. Minolta will also be open to joint venture possibilities as it seeks to strengthen its position in Japan's domestic market. Converging technologies in business equipment are moving us toward the era of the compact, multifunctional unit that will fit at an ordinary secretarial work station and combine the tasks of a computer, word processor, typewriter, printer, reader-scanner, facsimile, telephone, and electronic filing and mail systems. Single-function equipment will survive, of course, but the multifunctional unit will play an increasing role. The convergence is taking place from three different angles: the keyboard, the reader-printer, and the facsimile system. Minolta is well positioned in all areas. This book, for example, was written on a Minolta PCW-3 word processor with an attached laser printer. Minolta microfilm and microfiche equipment in place in the New York Public Library system has been helpful in much of our research, and my co-author and I sometimes shuttle information back and forth using a Minolta facsimile system. Someday all of these will be one piece of equipment, and Minolta will be a major factor in the integrated office networks of the future.

Our research capabilities assure Minolta a strong place in the photo equipment market and an increasing role in such areas as industrial meters and optical-electronic medical equipment. Our state-of-the-art planetarium, Infinium, will soon be marketed worldwide, and within a decade our production and assembly facilities will also be more conspicuously multinational. For Japan, for Minolta, and for me, the future looks bright. And the more I reflect on that bright future, the more I realize how much we owe to America.

As of May 29, 1988, my personal debt to America went up still another notch. That day, thanks to my daughter Eriko, in an impressive ceremony at St. Patrick's Cathedral, I gained an American son.

32

The Bridge Complete

In one of the conversations we had had during our cruise on *Highlander V*, Mrs. MacArthur told me she had never eaten Japanese food. It wasn't from lack of interest, however. General MacArthur was acutely sensitive about the shortages of basic Japanese food staples, particularly in the cities, during the postwar years. Since the occupation forces had access to the military post exchange commissaries, which were well stocked with American goods, MacArthur insisted that American personnel refrain from eating up scarce Japanese produce. MacArthur wasn't the type to make exceptions for himself or his family.

When I heard this story and sensed Mrs. MacArthur's regret, I invited her and her escort, Robert Devine, to join Kuniko and me for dinner at my favorite Japanese restaurant, the Nippon on Fifty-second Street. I have known the owner, Nabuyoshi Kuraoka, for many years. He treated us royally. Mrs. MacArthur tried everything, and she thoroughly enjoyed her first Japanese meal. She not only congratulated Kuraoka, but accompanied him to the kitchen so she could shake hands with the chef. During the course of the dinner,

Kuniko told Jean about our daughter's upcoming wedding and invited her to attend. Jean said she would be there.

Bob Gottner and my daughter Eriko had met when both were first-year students at Stanford University. Each lived in that co-ed dorm that caused Kuniko and me so much worry. They had gone together through college, graduate school, and Bob's long medical-school grind at Columbia University College of Physicians and Surgeons in New York City, where Eriko was working as foreign editions manager of *Omni* magazine. I can't say that Kuniko and I were surprised when Eriko finally told us that she and Bob planned to get married. By then they had been going together for seven years, but I must be honest about my reaction. Though attitudes are changing, marriage to a foreigner is still not easily accepted among Japanese. I remembered the gentle persuasion I was subjected to when I returned from my first four years in America, my head still floating in dreams about Western women. Meeting Kuniko quickly put an end to that problem.

Even in 1988, had my father been alive, I'm sure he would have been shocked by the thought of his granddaughter marrying a foreigner. My mother, on the other hand, is much more open-minded and readily accepted the marriage. My own misgivings were not because Bob is not Japanese, but because of the high divorce rates and many broken families that prevail among Americans. Nearly half of all marriages in the United States now end in divorce. In Japan, though the divorce rate is growing, it's still under 10 percent. My concern for Eriko's happiness made me wonder about the wisdom of marrying into a society where marriage has only a fifty-fifty chance of success. But I realized that Eriko wasn't marrying an American statistic. She was marrying Bob, a wonderful young man whose affection for Eriko is solid and sincere. Eriko and Bob are both level-headed people. A relationship that has already lasted seven years is clearly serious and clearly has a better than fifty-fifty chance of lasting.

I gave them my blessing. As the father of the bride, I feared the worst in the great American tradition of awesome wedding arrangements. But Bob and Eriko handled just about everything themselves, much to my relief. Bob's family is Catholic, and we all agreed to a Catholic wedding at St. Patrick's. I had admired the church since my early days in America when the Easter parade of fashions passed St. Patrick's along Fifth Avenue. Father James McIlhone, pastor of the family's parish church in Arlington Heights, Illinois, came to New York with Bob's parents, Mr. and Mrs. Robert Gottner, Sr., to conduct the ceremony. Father McIlhone was, I think, as thrilled as I was to be participating in a wedding in that famous cathedral. The wedding was very formal and colorful. The groom and I both wore cutaways, but Eriko, as it should be, was the center of attention in her long white gown with its beautifully embroidered train. With the bridesmaids, including our younger daughter, Mariko, several of Eriko's friends, and my secretary, Diane Allen, in dusky rose, we made a colorful assembly as we gathered on the steps of the church to greet our guests as they arrived in a parade of limousines and even a few horse-drawn carriages. I was very moved when Kuniko and I welcomed Jean MacArthur. Fuji Television covered the wedding, and I learned later that the scene with Mrs. MacArthur was part of the footage shown in Japan, though the narrator apparently did not know who she was. My mother still can't get over the fact that she saw her granddaughter's wedding on television news from America. I wonder how my father would have felt.

It was a bright, sunny Sunday afternoon, and, as we started our procession down the long aisle, shafts of sunlight cut through the cathedral's stained-glass windows, lighting the altar in a rainbow of color. Escorting Eriko, with the music of the cathedral's great organ accompanying us, and the smiling faces of so many friends turned toward us, I remembered my own very different wedding ceremony. The two families had sat facing each other: Kuniko with her family; I with mine. After I spoke the vows of our marriage, I took Kuniko to sit with my family, symbolizing the bride's departure from her own family to become part of her husband's. Even in America, the father's role is described as "giving away the bride." But, when Eriko and I reached the altar, I didn't feel that I was losing a daughter. As I watched Eriko and Bob join hands, I felt that I was gaining a son. It would not have been the same in Japan.

At the end of the ceremony, when Bob and Eriko turned from the altar to walk up the aisle together, I felt that my bridge to America was complete. The Gottners had made me part of an American family and given me a wonderful American son.

In America, women cry at weddings. Men grin. I'm sure that as I followed my daughter and son up the aisle, I was grinning broadly. In Japan, I would have been expected to look very solemn.

On our way to the reception at the Plaza Hotel, the two families made a detour to Central Park for our official wedding photograph. For the reception, Eriko changed to a traditional Japanese kimono. Memories of Kuniko, as the shy young bride of our wedding day, flooded over me. So much has changed and so many unexpected things have happened in our lives, but perhaps our history had already been written that day. Though Kuniko was a young girl from the countryside, she was already intrigued by America. And I had already been seduced by my first four years in America and was sure that one day I would return. When we did come to the United States together in 1969, we didn't expect that we would live in America continuously for more than twenty years. With our daughters in American schools for all of their education, it perhaps became inevitable that America would become their home. Mariko, like her older sister, enjoys her life as a young career woman in America. Her work for Japan Air Lines in New York takes Mariko back to Japan occasionally, but I'm fairly sure that America will be her permanent home.

Eriko and Mariko have taught me something about America. Though they would have lived a life of relative privilege in Japan, they made a choice made by millions before them. They chose America. What they have decided to do with their lives pays a tribute to America far more profound than any words I can say.

I got a little bit drunk at the reception that day, but I felt that I deserved the good time I had. I danced with my daughter in her kimono, feeling for that moment at least very Japanese. The reception was held in the Plaza's Terrace Room, which also brought back many memories, for Minolta has held many events there, including the press conference at which we introduced the Maxxum. But my strongest cue to memory was prompted by my long-time friend Dick Ohtomo. We first met back in 1955 when he was the Canon representative in New York. Among his many other accomplishments, Dick has a wonderful singing voice. Accompanied on the piano by my friend Bob Materna, a Peat Marwick Main partner, Dick made a big hit at the reception when he sang "I Left My Heart in San Francisco." He dedicated the song to Eriko and Bob, who had met at a school not far from San Francisco. His wife, the television star Mari Yoshimura, was with him in New York for the wedding. I must say they form one of the most attractive couples I have ever known and being with them brought back pleasant memories of times past in New York and later in Japan.

That day at the Plaza, with Dick singing while Bob and Eriko danced, I felt as happy as I have ever in my life. Even in the glow of that day, I realized that the company, Minolta, and the countries, America and Japan, that have meant so much to me face difficulties. So do Bob and Eriko, starting out married life while he is still a resident surgeon at Northwestern University Memorial Hospital in downtown Chicago. But Eriko has a new job with *Longevity* magazine in Chicago. Their future is bright, and I know that with all I have learned through these first sixty years of my life, I still have a contribution to make back and forth across my bridge from Japan to America.

As I looked around at the guests that day, I realized that many of them made up a gallery of portraits from my life. Along with friends of Eriko's and Bob's friends and relatives, there was my brother, Koji, and his wife; Kuniko's uncle, George Aratani, and his wife; Kuniko's brother, Norio, who is now the treasurer for Minolta in Great Britain; key dealers for our photo and business equipment line; friends from the advertising and public relations agencies who have worked so hard to make the Minolta name famous in the United States; key managers from all the Minolta divisions; our bankers; our accountants; and, of course, our lawyers, who are very important in America. As I studied all those faces, I realized how many people there are whom I am grateful to. It was Bob and Eriko's day, but I'm grateful to them for letting me share it.

Soon after their wedding day, Bob and Eriko left on their honeymoon trip to Japan. My mother was their host in Osaka. They returned, glowing with excitement. They agreed that Japan is a wonderful place to visit, but America is home.

So much has been packed into my life since that surprise sixtieth birthday party Eriko and Mariko gave me in April 1988. Though I have been extraordinarily busy, it has also been a time for contemplation and reflection. The strongest realization, perhaps, has been that there's so much still to do. I look forward to the years ahead with the same sense of excitement I felt when I boarded the SS *President Wilson* for my first trip to America in 1954. There's a new world out there, waiting to be discovered.

Epilogue

My Debt to America

I tried to sum up my complex feelings of gratitude to America in a short speech I made during a trip to Japan with our award-winning business equipment dealers just a few months after my induction into the PMA Hall of Fame.

That evening, as we crowded into a gaily decorated room at the Tokyo Imperial Hotel, I was happy to welcome our guests to Japan. I told them how important their contributions to Minolta had been.

"You gave us the skill and the knowledge we lacked to sell our products in each of the individual, local markets that make up the great and vast country that is the United States. We owe you a debt of gratitude for that."

My wife tells me that I spoke slowly enough to be understood that evening. I said that I recognized my debt to Minolta's hundreds of American employees and to the thousands of Americans who make up our network of independent dealers.

"Without you," I said, "we are nothing."

I told them about Japan's debt to Americans like Dr. Deming and Douglas MacArthur. "In the United States," I said, "Dr. Deming is virtually unknown. In Japan, he is a hero of industrial development.

In the United States, Douglas MacArthur got in trouble because of what was viewed as a challenge to the constitutional authority of his president and commander in chief, Harry Truman. But in Japan, Douglas MacArthur is a hero of constitutional democracy." As usual, in my pronunciation, the word came out sounding like "demo-krassie."

"Forty years ago," I told them, "American generosity and know-how helped us to rebuild our war-shattered economy.

"We owe you for that. In these postwar decades, America's liberal trade policies and openness to new ideas and new products have given Japan its biggest and most valued market.

"My native country, Japan, is also in your debt for the alliance with the United States that has given us a strategic shield that enhances our national security in a troubled world."

I reminded our guests that the following year, 1987, marked the two hundredth anniversary of the Constitution of the United States, and I let them know that 1987 would also be the fortieth anniversary of the Japanese constitution. I told them that on May 3, 1947, "soon after the end of World War II, the generous people of America gave the people of Japan the greatest gift we have ever known.

"On that day, forty years ago, Japan adopted the constitution drafted by young lawyers attached to the United States army, a democratic constitution that still governs our nation today. The liberty, the democratic form of government, and even the prosperity that Japan enjoys today, can all be traced to the influence and generosity of the United States.

"Our constitution, thanks to General MacArthur and those bright young army lawyers on his staff, bears the label 'Made in the USA.' With that constitution," I told my American audience, "you gave us the gift of democracy. I value that gift. Someday, I may even learn how to pronounce the word.

"God bless you all," I said, "and God bless America."

Index

GI camera sales and, 68–69
girls and, 30, 33–34, 43–44
given name of, 3, 91
Glenn and, 166–73
as head of export division, 154–65
on the *Highlander V*, 268, 271, 285–94
in Hong Kong, 174–81
as houseboy, 56–59
illness of, 41–42, 296
instruction manuals and, 108–109
Japanese friends of, 106–108, 110
at Keio University, 52–59
marriage of, 147–53
marriage of daughter, 318–23
Maxxum Maxim of, 266
on the *Michael Rose*, 268–71
as "midnight president," 140–46, 152
Minoltaflex of, 9–10, 28
movies and, 8–9, 57, 58–59, 86, 109
patience and, 131, 154, 174, 175
as photographer, 9–10, 28, 57, 60, 61, 109, 126
"pitcher-catcher" system and, 154–58, 162–63, 206
on postindustrial economies, 235–40
posting to New York, 75–82
as president of Minolta U.S.A., 316–317
reeducation as a Japanese, 123–31, 147–53
as refugee in Japan, 33–42
repairing cameras, 92–94
reports sent to Japan, 85, 87–90
returns to Japan, 115–58
returns to the U.S., 181–325
rival of, 71–72, 115–16, 127, 129, 154–55
in sales planning department, 118–22, 138, 143, 154
at Seoul Middle School, 13–21
sixtieth birthday party of, 301–302
at Tashima Shoten, 62–64

on trade statistics, 258–67
treatment of, in America, 80–81
U.S. occupation of Korea and, 24–30
"wet side and dry side" of business and, 130, 132, 140–46
during World War II, 10–23
Kusumoto, Seichi (uncle), 10
Kusumoto, Yasuko (sister-in-law), 179
Kusumoto, Yuki (grandmother), 4, 151

Ladies' underwear, 99–100
Las Vegas, 239
Lathrop, Bob, 199, 256
Leica cameras, 64, 66–67, 84, 97, 159–60
joint products with Minolta, 164–165
Leon, Ken, 199
Levi Strauss, 222
Levin, Al, 85
Libya, 275
Life, 84–85, 104, 120, 203
Lindsay, John, 203
Lipton, Norman, 84
Lovell, James A., 170

MacArthur, General Douglas, 41–56, 134, 177, 231, 319
importance of, to Japan, 41, 43–51, 54, 56, 66–68, 116, 222, 287–89, 324–25
Truman and, 70, 325
MacArthur, Jean, 285, 287–89, 291, 319–20, 321
McCann-Erickson-Hakuhodo, 222
McIlhone, Father James, 320–21
McKinsey Quarterly, The, 260
Macy's, 186
Mamiya cameras, 104
Manchester, William, 47
Mansfield, Mike, 231–32, 312
Manufactured Imports Promotion Organization, 314
Marcus, Stanley, 226–33

Tupperware, 262
Tweed, Shannon, 220

Umeda, Kaz, 225
Union of Japanese Scientists and Engineers (JUSE), 134, 135
United States, 302–303, 309–16, 324–
  25
  adapting products for export, 124–
    25, 160–61, 277
  breaking into the Japanese market,
    124–25, 129–31
  competition in, 215–16
  currency fluctuations, 235, 238,
    245–46, 252–67, 273, 305, 314–17
  education in, 189–93
  exporting services, 237–40
  free-trade policies of, 98, 140, 211,
    215–16, 218
  help given to Japanese economy,
    98
  joint business/government organiza-
    tion in, 309–11, 314
  lack of interest in exports, 178,
    234–40
  litigation in, 186–87, 221, 256–57
  management style of, 199–201
  marketing failures of, 195–98
  merchandise trade balance, 266–67
  military expenditures in Japan, 70–
    71
  military heroes in, 80
  minor markets pursued by, 271–278
  occupation of Japan, 33–51, 55–59
  occupation of Korea, 24, 25–30
  restrictions on exports, 272, 274–75
  smell of, 7, 58, 79
  space program of, 166–73
  standard of living in, 302–303, 312,
    314–16
  technology of, 160–61, 194–98
  tensions between Japan and, 230,
    234–40, 257–67, 271–78, 308–16
  trade deficit of, 257–67, 271–78,
    312–16
  as training ground for Japanese
    business leaders, 101–102, 158

  World War II and, *see* World War
    II
U.S. Camera, 90
United States Space Camp, 170, 171
Universal cameras, 98
Ushiyama, Zensei, 105

Varian Corporation, 206
Vietnam War, 19, 71, 203
Visual Communication Congress
  Award, 180
Voigtlander cameras, 197

Wall Street Journal, 186, 197–98,
  281, 282
Walt Disney Productions, 262
Walton, Mary, 134, 135
Washington, D.C., 205
Weigard, Sam, 269
Wesco distributors, 186
Wetco, 272
Whitehead, Graham, 231
Wilkes, Jesse, 95, 96, 104, 105, 107,
  108, 116, 203, 226
William Esty advertising agency, 219,
  224–25, 246–47
Wine and Food Society, 287
Winston Churchill Foundation, 231
Wolfman, Gus, 91
World War I, 54
World War II, 10–26, 80, 120, 127
  air power and, 15–17
  atomic bomb and, 22–23, 24, 278–
    81, 298–300
  concentration camps for Japanese
    during, 188
  effects of, in Japan, 37–38, 116
  end of, 23
  Japanese atrocities during, 278–80,
    300
  Korea and, 20
  Midway Island, 17, 19–20
  Minolta and, 65–66
  oil and, 18–21
  origin of, from Japanese point of
    view, 10
  Pearl Harbor, 14, 15, 16, 280